Englisch

Lernen Sie Englischsprechen wie ein Einheimischer in nur einem Kurs
für vielbeschäftigte Leute

Fluent English Publishing

Xiao, Ken

Englisch: Lernen Sie Englischsprechen wie ein Einheimischer in nur einem Kurs für vielbeschäftigte Leute

Copyright © 2018 durch Ken Xiao

ISBN: 978-1987737745

Alle Rechte vorbehalten.

Es dürfen keine Teile dieser Publikation reproduziert, übertragen, verkauft oder in jeglicher Art und Weise verwendet werden, elektronisch oder mechanisch, inklusive fotokopieren, aufnehmen oder speichern auf Datenträgern oder Wiederherstellungssystemen, ohne die schriftliche Genehmigung des Autors.

Contents

ÜBER DEN AUTOR..v
Kapitel 1: Sie können wie ein Einheimischer sprechen. Ja, Sie können es!..1
Kapitel 2: Sie beherrschen bereits 68%, Ja, das tun Sie!...................4
Kapitel 3: Fließend in einem Kurs, ein Kinderspiel..........................8
Kapitel 4: Drei Elemente um Englisch wie ein Einheimischer zu sprechen..9
Kapitel 5: Das Ein-Wort-Geheimnis zum Erfolg............................14
Kapitel 6: Hol sie Dir, Tiger!..19
The English World...23
Kapitel 7: 1 – 10, My First Day Of School In New York...............26
Kapitel 8: 11 – 20, My First Year In America................................35
Kapitel 9: 21 – 30, My First Job in Arizona...................................44
Kapitel 10: 31 – 40, The World..53
Kapitel 11: 41 – 50, English-Speaking Countries...........................61
Kapitel 12: 51 – 60, Types of English...68
Kapitel 13: 61 – 70, American English...75
Kapitel 14: 71 – 80, North America Climates................................84
Kapitel 15: 81 – 90, 10 Largest Cities in America..........................93
Kapitel 16: 91 – 100, U.S. and Canada Culture............................102
In the supermarket...110
Kapitel 17: 101 – 110, The Produce Department..........................113
Kapitel 18: 111 – 120, The Floral Department.............................123
Kapitel 19: 121 – 130, The Dairy Department.............................133
Kapitel 20: 131 – 140, The Beverage Department.......................144
Kapitel 21: 141 – 150, The General Supplies Department...........156
Kapitel 22: 151 – 160, The Pharmacy Department.......................169
Kapitel 23: 161 – 170, The Health & Beauty Department............180
Kapitel 24: 171 – 180, The Meat & Seafood Department............193
Kapitel 25: 181 – 190, The Deli Department................................204
Kapitel 26: 191 – 200, The Bakery Department...........................217
School, Work, Society...228
Kapitel 27: 201 – 210, In High School...231
Kapitel 28: 211 – 220, More High school!...................................241
Kapitel 29: 221 – 230, College..251
Kapitel 30: 231 – 240, More College..261

Kapitel 31: 241 – 250, In the Society..272
Kapitel 32: 251 – 260, More in the Society!..282
Kapitel 33: 261 – 270, a Job or a Career...292
Kapitel 34: 271 – 280, More a Job or a Career....................................300
Kapitel 35: 281 – 290, Making Friends...310
Kapitel 36: 291 – 300, More Making Friends......................................319
Was auf Englisch zu sagen ist..329
Kapitel 37: 301 – 310 What to Say in English.....................................332
Kapitel 38: 311 – 320, What to Say in English....................................340
Kapitel 39: 321 – 330, What to Say in English....................................348
Kapitel 40: 331 – 340, What to Say in English....................................357
Kapitel 41: 341 – 350, What to Say in English....................................366
Kapitel 42: 351 – 360, What to Say in English....................................374
Kapitel 43: 361 – 370, What to Say in English....................................382
Kapitel 44: 371 – 380, What to Say in English....................................390
Kapitel 45: 381 – 390, What to Say in English....................................398
Kapitel 46: 391 – 400, What to Say in English....................................406
Specialized Knowledge..414
Kapitel 47: 401 – 410 Specialized knowledge.....................................417
Kapitel 48: 411 – 420, Specialized knowledge....................................426
Kapitel 49: 421 – 430, Specialized knowledge....................................434
Kapitel 50: 431 – 440, Specialized knowledge....................................442
Kapitel 51: 441 – 450, Specialized knowledge....................................450
Kapitel 52: 451 – 460, Specialized knowledge....................................458
Kapitel 53: 461 – 470, Specialized knowledge....................................468
Kapitel 54: 471 – 480, Specialized knowledge....................................477
Kapitel 55: 481 – 490, Specialized knowledge....................................486
Kapitel 56: 491 – 500, Specialized knowledge....................................496
Ja! Wir haben es geschafft!..504

ÜBER DEN AUTOR

KEN XIAO ist ein Englischlehrer der sich auch schon in Ihrer Lage befand. Als er mit 17 Jahren in die Vereinigten Staaten kam sprach er kein Englisch. Nach drei Jahren des Nichtbeherrschens der englischen Sprache über gebrochenes Englisch hinweg, hat Ken den Schlüssel zum Sprechen von fließendem Englisch gesucht und das Geheimnis des Erfolgs gefunden. Er verwendete dieses Geheimnis um in nur sechs Monaten zu lernen, Englisch wie ein Einheimischer zu sprechen.

Ken war als Übersetzer für das amerikanische Verteidigungsministerium tätig. Er besitzt einen Bachelor Abschluss in Informationstechnologie und einen Master Abschluss in Weltraumforschung.

Ken ist jetzt Englischlehrer, Schulleiter und Autor.

Zu lernen, wie ein Einheimischer Englisch zu sprechen, schien mir unmöglich, aber ich habe es geschafft. Und Sie können dies auch!

Ken Xiao

Kapitel 1: Sie können wie ein Einheimischer sprechen. Ja, Sie können es!

Sie möchten lernen, Englisch zu sprechen, aber Sie denken, es ist viel zu anstrengend, Sie denken, es ist zu viel zu lernen und Sie denken, es braucht viel zu lange.

Dazu kommt noch, Sie können schon ein bisschen Englisch, aber dennoch sprechen Sie nicht gut Englisch. Sie haben schon vieles ausprobiert und noch immer machen Sie viele grammatikalische Fehler, noch immer sprechen Sie nicht flüssig und noch immer können Sie englische Wörter nicht korrekt betonen. Sie können Englisch lesen, Sie sind aber zu nervös oder schüchtern, um Englisch zu sprechen.

Hinzukommt, wenn Sie bereits Englisch sprechen und Sie denken, dass Sie es richtig sprechen, vertrauen Sie mir – Sie sprechen nicht richtig. Auch ich war zuvor in Ihrer Position und ich weiß, dass Sie nicht korrekt Englisch sprechen.

Die guten Nachrichten sind, dass dies ganz normal ist. Sie haben noch keine effektive Methode angewandt um zu lernen, wie man Englisch spricht.

Mein Name ist Ken Xiao. Auch ich war zuvor in Ihrer Situation, aber jetzt spreche ich Englisch wie ein Einheimischer und dies habe ich in sechs Monaten erlernt. In diesem Kurs werde ich Ihnen beibringen, wie Sie Englisch wie ein Einheimischer sprechen werden.

Wenn Sie Englisch auf der Schulbank gelernt haben, fragen Sie sich, „warum spreche ich nicht fließend Englisch wie ein Einheimischer?"

Dies kommt daher, dass Klassenräume dafür gedacht sind, damit Sie Englisch lesen und schreiben lernen, nicht aber sprechen.

In diesem Kurs zeige ich Ihnen in Schritt-für-Schritt Anleitungen, wie Sie Ihren Akzent komplett verlieren und Englisch wie ein Einheimischer sprechen werden, sogar wenn Sie einen straffen Zeitplan haben.

Schenken wir einer Nachricht eines Schulabgängers Gehör.

In einem armen Bauerndorf wurde ein Kind geboren. In seiner Kindheit war der kleine Junge sehr hungrig. So hungrig, dass er sich sogar nach über 30 Jahren noch lebhaft an das Hungergefühl erinnern kann. Es gab kein fließendes Wasser, daher musste er in zwei Eimern das Wasser von einem weit entfernten Brunnen nach Hause tragen. Er war sieben Jahre alt. Die Eimer waren so schwer, dass es sich wie Berge an seinen Armen anfühlte. Im Alter von sieben Jahren begann er auf den Feldern zu arbeiten, zu pflanzen, zu kultivieren und zu ernten. Im Alter von sieben Jahren begann er Brennholz zum Kochen und Backen zu sammeln. Im Alter von sieben Jahren begann er auf dem offenen Feuer für seine ganze Familie zu kochen. Es gab keinen elektrischen Herd und er konnte sich glücklich schätzen, wenn er einmal wöchentlich Strom für Licht hatte. Er wurde mit acht Jahren in die Grundschule eingeschult und ging mit 13 Jahren von der weiterführenden Schule ab.

Im Alter von 17 Jahren wanderte er in die Vereinigten Staaten von Amerika aus und sprach kein Englisch. Er begann Englisch in Kursen für *Englisch als zweite Sprache* zu lernen und nach drei Jahren war er in der Lage, gebrochenes Englisch zu sprechen. Dann begann er, sich nach dem Schlüssel zu fließendem Englisch umzusehen und entdeckte das Geheimnis. Er wand dieses Geheimnis für sechs Monate an und begann endlich, Englisch wie ein Einheimischer zu sprechen.

Er beendete die Hochschule, schloss die Fachoberschule ab und machte einen Abschluss an der Universität. Später war er Übersetzer für das Verteidigungsministerium der Vereinigten Staaten.

Und hier ist der beste Teil: Dieser Junge vom Land, ein Schulabgänger, der erst im Alter von 20 Jahren anfing Englisch wie ein Einheimischer zu sprechen, brauchte dafür nur sechs Monate und hatte dafür keine spezielle Gabe! Er ist nur ein durchschnittlicher Junge, den Du und Ich auf dem Land antreffen würden. Er ist nur ein durchschnittlicher Mann, den Du und Ich auf der Straße treffen würden. Alles was er tat, war einem Geheimnis auf die Spur zu gehen, einem Geheimnis, das nun hier in diesem Buch ist.

Dieser Schulabgänger sprach direkt vor Ihnen. Dieser Schulabgänger bin ich.

Nun sagen Sie sich: Ich kann wie ein Einheimischer Englisch sprechen! JA, ich kann es!

                                            Ken Xiao

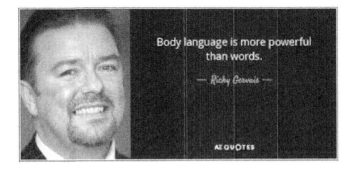

Ricky Gervais Zitat, http://www.azquotes.com/quote/1065499. Vom 10/18/2017.

Kapitel 2: Sie beherrschen bereits 68%, Ja, das tun Sie!

Falls Ihnen die englische Sprache komplett neu ist, dann Herzlichen Glückwunsch – Sie kennen bereits 68% der englischen Sprache.

Nun lassen Sie mich dies wiederholen.

Falls Ihnen die englische Sprache komplett neu ist, dann Herzlichen Glückwunsch – Sie kennen bereits 68% der englischen Sprache.

Schwer zu glauben? Es ist wahr.

Wie viele englische Wörter müssen Sie kennen um 68% Englisch verstehen zu können?

Die Antwort ist Null.

Ja! Sie müssen kein einziges englisches Wort verstehen können um 68% der englischen Sprache verstehen zu können.

Und hier ist der Grund dafür:

Achtundsechzig Prozent der Kommunikation erfolgt durch Körpersprache, nicht durch Wörter.
Lassen Sie uns dieses Bild betrachten.

Sie haben nichts gesagt, und doch haben sie uns folgendes mitgeteilt: Wir sind ein Paar. Dieser romantische Moment gehört uns. Bitte nicht stören.

Nun sehen Sie sich dieses Foto an.

Er hat nichts gesagt und doch sagte er Ihnen: Bleiben Sie fort von mir.

Lassen Sie uns die fünf folgenden Beispiele betrachten:
1. Normal: Ich sagte Dir, die Vögel werden den Fisch fressen.
2. Wütend: Ich sagte Dir, die Vögel werden den Fisch fressen.
3. Frage: Ich sagte Dir, die Vögel werden den Fisch fressen?
4. Traurig: Ich sagte Dir, die Vögel werden den Fisch fressen.
5. Glücklich: Ha, ha, ha, ha, ich sagte Dir, die Vögel werden den Fisch fressen!

Jetzt verstehen Sie die viel größere Bedeutung der Stimmlage als die Bedeutung der Wörter. Sie können die Bedeutung der Körperbewegungen weitaus besser verstehen als die Bedeutung der Wörter.

Lassen Sie uns den Blick auf einige Beispiele werfen:
1. Sie anlächeln – bedeutet meistens, dass sie freundlich sind.
2. Vor Ihnen davonlaufen – bedeutet meistens, sie vermeiden die Kommunikation.
3. Ihnen zuwinken – sie möchten Ihnen Hallo oder Auf Wiedersehen sagen.

Sich selbst auszudrücken ist genau das Gleiche. Sie müssen kein einziges englisches Wort beherrschen um 68% dessen auszudrücken, was Sie zu sagen versuchen. Sie können dies allein mit Ihrer Körpersprache tun.

Lassen Sie uns einer Geschichte lauschen.

Eine meiner Freunde reiste als Austauschschülerin nach China. Sie sprach Englisch und ein wenig Mandarin. Ihre Zimmergenossin war aus Korea und sprach ausschließlich Koreanisch.

Am ersten Tag, als sie sich trafen, versuchten sie, zu kommunizieren. Sie verwendeten ihre Körpersprache. Bald schon nahmen sie einen Stift und ein Blatt Papier und begannen zu zeichnen.

Meine Freundin sagte, sie verstanden einander zu 90%.

Ohne Stift und Papier kannst Du schätzungsweise 68% jeder Sprache verstehen.

Also sagen Sie sich selbst: Ja! Ich verstehe Englisch zu 68%. Ja, das tue ich!

Der Wille zu gewinnen, das Bedürfnis erfolgreich zu sein, der Drang Ihr volles Potential zu erreichen... dies sind die Schlüssel, die die Tür zu Ihrer persönlichen Exzellent öffnen werden.
       Konfuzius

Kapitel 3: Fließend in einem Kurs, ein Kinderspiel

Die englische Sprache ist eine Sprache, die sehr offen gegenüber anderen Sprachen ist. Als Resultat wächst das Vokabular stetig. Heute hat das englische Vokabular bereits über eine halbe Million Wörter. Eine halbe Million bedeutet 500,000.

Können Sie sich 500,000 Wörter beibringen? In **1** Lektion?

Die gute Nachricht ist, Sie müssen nicht 500,000 Wörter lernen um gesprochenes Englisch verstehen zu können. Die meisten der englischen Wörter werden nicht in alltäglichen Konversationen verwendet.

Ich habe noch mehr gute Nachrichten für Sie: Aus diesen 500,000 Wörtern werden 100 Wörter in 50% tagtäglicher Unterhaltungen verwendet.

Dies bedeutet, wenn Sie nur diese 100 Wörter erlernen, würden Sie 50% der alltäglichen Unterhaltungen führen können.

Und ich habe noch viel mehr gute Neuigkeiten für Sie: Aus diesen 500,000 Wörtern werden nur 300 Wörter in 65% tagtäglicher Unterhaltungen verwendet.

Die guten Nachrichten gehen weiter: Aus diesen 500,000 Wörtern werden nur 500 Wörter in 80% tagtäglicher Unterhaltungen verwendet.
In diesem Kurs bringe ich Ihnen diese 500 Wörter bei um

Ihnen dabei zu helfen, 80% der alltäglichen Englischen Sprache wie ein Einheimischer zu sprechen.

Kapitel 4: Drei Elemente um Englisch wie ein Einheimischer zu sprechen

Es gibt drei Dinge, die ich mit Ihnen teilen möchte um Ihnen dabei zu helfen, Englisch wie ein Einheimischer zu sprechen.

1. Betonung (wie ein Wort klingt)
2. Intonation (die Erhöhung und Senkung oder das Hoch und Tief einer Stimme)
3. Liaison (Wortverbindungen)

1. Betonung:
Kriegen Sie Ihre Betonung richtig hin, üben Sie viele Male.

Wie oft sollten Sie üben? Lassen Sie uns hören, was Bruce Lee sagte.

"Ich fürchte mich nicht vor dem Mann, der 10,000 Tritte einmal geübt hat, aber ich fürchte mich vor dem Mann, der einen Tritt 10,000 Male geübt hat."

Wie oft sollte ich üben? Zehntausend Mal?

Ich selber habe hunderte von Malen in sechs Monaten geübt. Sie sollten so oft üben, wie es nötig ist, bis Ihre Betonung korrekt ist. Und dann verankern Sie dies in Ihrem Unterbewusstsein indem Sie noch weiter üben.

In der Audioversion dieses Buches hören Sie, wie die Geschwindigkeit der Betonung langsam beginnt und im Verlauf nach und nach schneller wird.

In der Audioversion dieses Buches werden Sie Betonungen

von "sommmmmma" hören anstelle von "some." Ebenso werden Sie "strongggggga" hören anstelle von "strong." Dies ist vollkommen normal beim natürlichen sprechen. Jedoch ist der Schlusslaut sehr zart. Es ist anders als extra Silben hinzuzufügen. Es ist nur ein Hauch eines Geräuschs am Ende.

Einige Wörter wie „semicolon", „researcher" und „either" können auf zwei Arten betont werden. Sie könne auf die eine oder auf die andere Art betont werden. Wenn Sie in der Audioversion beide Arten hören, entspannen Sie sich! Ich zeige Ihnen beide Arten auf, diese Wörter zu betonen. Sie können Sie die Version aussuchen, die Ihnen zusagt oder beide Arten verwenden.

Einige Endlaute wie das T oder das D gehen beim natürlichen Sprechen verloren. Das ist ganz normal. Anstelle eines absichtlichen „sunri**Z**e" mit dem /z/ Laut könnten Sie ein „sunri**S**e" mit einem /s/ Laut hören.

Manchmal hören Sie vielleicht /**TH**at/ anstelle von /**TH**at/. Auch dies ist normal. Wenn schnell gesprochen wird, hört es sich natürlicher an, /**TH**at/ zu sagen anstelle eines absichtlichen /**TH**at/.

Andere Male hören Sie eventuell „an" anstatt „and". Dies ist ebenso ganz normal. Wenn schnell gesprochen wird, hört es sich natürlicher an, „an" zu sagen anstatt „an**D**" zu sagen.

Folgen Sie den Instruktionen in dem Buch, un**D** Sie werden es richtig hinbekommen!

2. Intonation:
Wenn man Englisch spricht, verändert man regelmäßig die Stimme. Wir erhöhen sie bei einigen Worten, bei anderen senken wir sie.

Betrachten wir diese beiden Sätze.

1. It's <u>Emily</u>'s book.
2. It's Emily's <u>book</u>.

Im ersten Satz ist Emily das unterstrichene Wort. „Emily" ist das wichtigste Wort in diesem Satz. Es sagt Ihren Zuhörern, dass es hier um die Person geht, der das Buch gehört. Es gehört Emily. Daher ist „Emily" hervorgehoben.

Versuchen Sie den ersten Satz mit Betonung auf dem Wort „Emily" zu sagen. Erhöhen Sie ihre Stimme bei dem Wort „Emily" um die Deutlichkeit hervorzuheben.

Versuchen Sie jetzt den zweiten Satz zu sagen. Das unterstrichene Wort ist „book". In diesem Satz ist nicht „Emily" das wichtigste Wort. Es ist „book". Es sagt Ihren Zuhörern, dass es um Emily's Sache geht. Um Emily's Buch. Daher ist „book" das hervorgehobene Wort.

Dies ist Intonation. Das was Sie betonen ist das, was Sie Ihren Zuhörern vermitteln möchten.

Einige Wörter werden in verschiedenen Situationen anders betont. Werfen wir einen Blick auf die folgenden Wörter. Erhöhen Sie Ihre Stimme bei den unterstrichenen Teilen der Wörter.

- Those apple trees pro**duce** 2000 pounds of **pro**duce each year.
    Pro**duce**, **Pro**duce

- The in**crease** of the air in the balloons **in**creases the pressure of the balloons.
    In**crease**, **In**creases

- The children pre**sent** their father a birthday **pre**sent.

Pre**sent**, **Pre**sent

- Per**fect** your intonation to make your English **per**fect.
  Per**fect**, **Per**fect.

Obwohl die Wörter die gleichen sind, verändern wir die Betonung um die Bedeutung der Wörter zu verändern.

3. Liaison:
In ganzen Sätzen werden die Wörter nicht einzeln betont. Sie werden verbunden betont. Sehen Sie sich die folgenden Wörter an.

Bes**t t**ime
Jus**t t**alk
To**p p**erformance

Lassen Sie uns einen Schritt weiter gehen. Bei den folgenden Wörtern können die unterstrichenen Buchstaben perfekt mit den Anfangsbuchstaben des nächsten Wortes verbunden werden.

Li**ke it**
Hol**d o**n
Pu**t u**p
Stro**ng e**nough

Wenn sie sich verbinden bilden Sie einen neuen Klang. Folgende Sätze sind mit den Vokalen a, e, i, o, u am Ende des Wortes und direkt am Anfang des folgenden Wortes.

I a**lso i**nvited th**e o**ther team.
I unzipped th**e ai**rbag.
G**o o**n to Aven**ue A**.

Wenn wir a, e, i sagen, fügen wir automatisch einen "y"

Klang hinzu um eine Verbindung zum folgenden Wort herzustellen. Wenn wir o oder u sagen, fügen wir ganz natürlich einen "w" Klang hinzu um eine Verbindung zum folgenden Wort herzustellen.

Hier noch einige Beispiele.

> Wha**t y**ou need is practice.
> Ac**t y**our part.
> I go**t y**ou.
>
> Di**d y**ou see that?
> Woul**d y**ou like one?
> How di**d y**esterday go?
>
> That sound**s yummy**.
> Si**x y**ears.
> Deliciou**s y**ams
>
> Sei**ze y**our sword.
> Reali**ze y**our potential.
> Murphy'**s y**ams.
> U**su**al way.

Verwenden Sie diese drei und Ihr Englisch wird genauso natürlich und flüssig werden wie das eines einheimischen Sprechers.

Eine Unze Übung ist mehr wert als eine Tonne zu predigen.
                    Mahatma Gandhi

Kapitel 5: Das Ein-Wort-Geheimnis zum Erfolg

Wie werden Sie Englisch wie ein Einheimischer sprechen?

Übung!

Das ist das Ein-Wort-Geheimnis zum Erfolg.

Wieso nenne ich dies ein Geheimnis? Eigentlich ist es gar kein Geheimnis. Es wird immer und immer wieder in Büchern und im Internet aufgegriffen, aber nur sehr wenige Menschen wissen davon oder haben es verstanden und so bleibt es praktisch ein Geheimnis.

Das haben einige große Menschen unserer Zeit gesagt.

Mahatma Gandhi sagte: "Eine Unze Übung ist mehr wert als eine Tonne zu predigen."

Zig Ziglar sagte: "Wiederholung ist die Mutter des Lernens und der Vater der Tat, was sie zur Architektin des Erfolgs macht."

John F. Kennedy sagte: "Jeder Erfolg beginnt mit der Entscheidung es zu versuchen."

Nochmals, Bruce Lee sagte: "Ich fürchte mich nicht vor dem Mann, der 10,000 Tritte einmal geübt hat, aber ich fürchte mich vor dem Mann, der einen Tritt 10,000 Male geübt hat."

Wenn wir in etwas gut sein möchten, müssen wir es üben.

Wie üben wir es?

Wiederholen Sie was Sie hören immer und immer wieder.

Das ist, was Sie von den anderen Schülern unterscheiden wird. Wie oft wiederholen Sie in Kursen was Ihr Lehrer vorsagt? Zwei Mal? Drei Mal?

Dies ist bei weitem nicht genug!

Im Englischen sagen wir "practice makes perfect." Sie müssen immer und immer und immer und immer wieder wiederholen bis Sie wie ein Einheimischer sprechen und dan wiederholen Sie es immer und immer und immer und immer wieder.

Es geht noch weiter:

"Routine hat nichts mit Wiederholung zu tun. Um in etwas richtig gut zu werden müssen Sie es üben und wiederholen, üben und wiederholen."
  Paulo Coelho

"Um es zusammenzufassen, es geht nur um die Wiederholung."
  David Jackson

"Erfolg erfordert die Wiederholung der richtigen Taten."
  Jeffrey Benjamin

"Erfolg ist die Summe von kleinen Einsätzen die tagtäglich wiederholt werden."
  Robert Collier

Ich möchte Ihnen eine Geschichte erzählen.

Im Jahr 2000 fand ich einen guten Grund um mich aus dem Bett zu reißen und zu lernen, wie man klassisch tanzt. Dies war für mich komplettes Neuland, ich wusste nichts darüber. Ich begann in der Tanzschule Stepping Out Studios in New York City Tanzstunden zu nehmen.

Ich übte was ich vor der Tanzstunde gelernt habe, ich übte was ich nach der Tanzstunde gelernt habe und ich übte was ich während der Tanzstunde gelernt habe. Ich übte zu Hause, im Studio, in den U-Bahn-Stationen und in den Zügen selbst.

Genau wie die Worte, die ich von den Berühmtheiten zitiert habe, übte ich, immer und immer wieder, jeden Tag und immer, wenn ich einen Moment Zeit hatte. Ich übte wenn ich eine Stunde Zeit hatte, 20 Minuten, fünf Minuten oder 60 Sekunden.

Sechs Monate später dann tanzte ich schon besser als die meisten Tanzschüler, die bereits seit zehn Jahren tanzten. Bei einer Schüleraufführung stellte mich der Besitzer des Tanzstudios als „einen seiner BESTEN Schüler" vor.

Weitere sechs Monate später nahm ich an den internationalen Rumba und Cha-Cha Wettkämpfen teil und gewann die Goldmedaille.

Es ist genau das Gleich mit dem Erlernen der englischen Sprache. Üben Sie Ihr Englisch wann immer Sie Zeit haben. Üben Sie, was Sie gelernt haben immer und immer wieder. Üben Sie jeden Tag. Üben Sie, wenn Sie eine Stunde Zeit haben, 20 Minuten, fünf Minuten oder 60 Sekunden.

Haben Sie einen gut gefüllten Terminplan? Sehen Sie sich dies an:

Zig Ziglar, ein erfolgreicher Motivationstrainer, sagte "wenn Sie nur in Ihrem Auto etwas zuhören würden, wenn Sie wohin fahren, würden Sie mehr lernen als auf einer Universität."

Benutzen Sie öffentliche Transportmittel? Dies ist eine großartige Gelegenheit! Fahren Sie selbst? Dies ist eine großartige Gelegenheit! Laufen Sie? Treiben Sie Sport? Kaufen Sie ein? Kochen Sie? All dies sind großartige Gelegenheiten! Arbeiten Sie? Ermöglicht Ihr Job es Ihnen, zu üben?

Greifen Sie jede Gelegenheit beim Schopf und üben Sie Ihr Englisch. Tun Sie dies für sechs Monate und Sie werden erstaunt sein, wie gut Sie Englisch sprechen.

Lauschen Sie den Worten und wiederholen Sie sie immer und immer wieder. Lauschen Sie den Sätzen und wiederholen Sie sie immer und immer wieder. Lauschen Sie der gesamten Lektion und wiederholen Sie sie immer und immer wieder. Machen Sie dies indem Sie den Schritt-für-Schritt-Anweisungen in diesem Buch folgen.

Lassen Sie mich nun ein Zitat von Earl Nightingale über den Erfolg verwenden. „Wenn Sie sich entschieden haben, was Sie wollen und Sie arbeiten stetig darauf hin, ist es so gut wie sicher, dass Sie es erreichen werden. Es führt kein Weg daran vorbei."

Sind Sie in der Lage, 300 Pfund zu heben? Wahrscheinlich nicht. Dies ist für die meisten von uns zu schwer. Sind Sie in der Lage, drei Pfund zu heben? Ja, das können Sie. Lassen Sie uns klein anfangen indem wir heute drei Pfund heben, vier Pfund am folgenden Tag und so weiter. Indem Sie dies tun, werden Ihre Muskeln von Tag zu Tag wachsen und Sie werden sich nach und nach aufbauen, Tag für Tag. Bevor Sie es merken haben Sie bereits genügend Muskelmasse aufgebaut um problemlos 300 Pfund heben zu können!

Das Gleiche gilt für die fließende Aussprache. Fangen Sie klein an und bauen Sie nach und nach darauf auf, Schritt für Schritt, Tag für Tag. Bevor Sie es merken haben Sie genug aufgebaut um ohne Anstrengung so fließend Englisch zu sprechen, was vorher undenkbar schien.

Bleiben Sie am Ball, üben Sie tagtäglich Ihr Englisch und Sie werden erstaunt sein, wie viel Sie in wenigen Wochen erreichen können. Sie werden erstaunt sein, wenn Sie realisieren, dass Sie Englisch wie ein Einheimischer sprechen!

Englisch: Lernen Sie Englischsprechen wie ein Einheimischer in nur einem Kurs

**Handeln ist der fundamentale Schlüssel zu allem Erfolg.
Pablo Picasso**

Kapitel 6: Hol sie Dir, Tiger!

Katzen Spiegelung,
https://www.amazon.es/Demiawaking-Reflexin-Diamante-Diamantes-50_x_50_cm/dp/B06XGB462S?psc=1&SubscriptionId=AKIAJD4AUHJTR44IQJHQ&tag=echollo-21&linkCode=xm2&camp=2025&creative=165953&creativeASIN=B06XGB462S. Accessed 10/17/2017.

Wussten Sie, dass Sie einen schlafenden Riesen in sich haben?

Nun lassen Sie mich dies nochmals sagen. Wissen Sie, dass Sie einen schlafenden Riesen in sich tragen?

Es ist wahr und ein Großteil der Menschen wissen dies nicht.

Wenn Sie die Tatsache akzeptieren, dass Sie eine Katze sind, können Sie all die Dinge tun, die eine Katze tun würde.

Wenn Sie die Tatsache akzeptieren, dass Sie ein vollzeitbeschäftigter Angestellter sind, werden Sie all die Arbeit erledigen, die ein vollzeitbeschäftigter Angestellter tun würde.

Wenn Sie jedoch die Tatsache akzeptieren, dass Sie ein Tiger sind, werden Sie all die Dinge tun, die ein Tiger tun würde.

Wenn Sie die Tatsache akzeptieren, dass Sie Englisch wie ein Einheimischer sprechen können, werden Sie Englisch wie ein Einheimischer.

Nehmen Sie mich als Beispiel. Ich, Ken Xiao, der Autor dieses Buches, ein Landjunge und Schulabgänger, ich glaube, dass ich Englisch wie ein Einheimischer sprechen kann und ich spreche Englisch wie ein Einheimischer.

Sind Sie besser als ein Junge vom Land? Sind Sie besser als ein Schulabgänger?

Sogar wenn Sie nicht besser sind, als ein Landjunge, sogar wenn Sie nicht besser sind, als ein Schulabgänger, wenn Sie aber daran **glauben**, dass Sie Englisch wie ein Einheimischer sprechen können, handeln Sie und Sie **werden** Englisch wie ein Einheimischer sprechen.

Lassen Sie uns den schlafenden Riesen in Ihnen wecken. Folgen Sie meinen Schritt-für-Schritt Anleitungen um Ihre Resultate zu erreichen. Hören Sie der Audio Version der Lektionen zu und tun Sie das Folgende.

Schritt 1: Zuhören und Wiederholen zur selben Zeit
Hören Sie sich die Audiodatei eines Kapitels an und wiederholen Sie, was Sie hören sofort. Warten Sie nicht bis zum Ende. Es ist in Ordnung, die ersten Male etwas zu versäumen. Machen Sie nur weiter ohne aufzuhören.

Schritt 2: Wiederholen Sie das komplette Kapitel
Hören Sie sich das komplette Kapitel von Anfang bis Ende an und wiederholen Sie dieses.

Schritt 3: Nehmen Sie Ihre Stimme auf
Nehmen Sie Ihre Stimme auf, wie Sie das Kapitel wiederholen. Dies ist wichtig. Überspringen Sie diesen Schritt *nicht*.

Suchen Sie sich ein Aufnahmegerät wie zum Beispiel Ihren Computer, ein Handy oder einen MP3 Recorder. Schließen Verwenden Sie ein Paar Kopfhörer und nehmen Sie Ihre Stimme auf während Sie das Kapitel vom Anfang bis zum Ende wiederholen.

Speichern Sie die Datei und fahren Sie mit Schritt 4 fort.

Schritt 4: Wiederholen Sie das Kapitel ein weiteres Mal
Hören Sie sich das Kapitel nochmals an und wiederholen Sie dies vom Anfang bis zum Ende.

Schritt 5: Kehren Sie direkt zurück zu den Wörtern, die Sie nicht sagen können und wiederholen Sie diese so oft wie es nötig ist
Wiederholen Sie das Kapitel nochmals. Dieses Mal aber, wenn es Wörter gibt, die Sie nicht korrekt aussprechen können, stoppen Sie direkt und kehren Sie zu ihnen zurück. Hören Sie sie sich noch einmal an und wiederholen Sie sie. Versuchen Sie es ein Mal, zwei Mal, drei Mal oder öfters. Versuchen Sie es so oft wie es nötig ist, bis Sie alle Wörter korrekt aussprechen können.

Schritt 6: Wiederholen Sie das Kapitel bis es flüssig ist
Jetzt da Sie Schritt 5 abgeschlossen haben können Sie jedes Wort korrekt aussprechen. Wiederholen Sie nun das komplette Kapitel vom Anfang bis zum Ende. Wiederholen Sie es so oft wie es nötig ist, bis Sie jeden Satz natürlich und fließend aussprechen können.

Schritt 7: Nehmen Sie Ihre Stimme auf
Jetzt da Sie Schritt 6 abgeschlossen haben können Sie jedes Wort korrekt und jeden Satz natürlich und fließend aussprechen. Nehmen Sie Ihre Stimme jetzt erneut auf. Nehmen Sie Ihre Stimme auf, wie Sie dasselbe Kapitel wiederholen. Speichern Sie die Datei.

Suchen Sie sich die erste Datei raus und spielen Sie sie ab. Machen Sie dasselbe mit der zweiten Datei.

Sprechen Sie in der zweiten Aufnahme besser als in der ersten Aufnahme?

      Ja? Weiter geht es mit Schritt 8.
      Nein? Weiter geht es mit Schritt 8.

Schritt 8: Machen Sie mit dem nächsten Kapitel weiter
Hören Sie sich die Audio Datei des nächsten Kapitels an und folgen Sie den Schritten 1 – 7.

Nachdem Sie alle Kapitel durchgearbeitet haben, kehren Sie zum ersten Kapitel zurück und fangen Sie von vorne an, bis Sie diese Lektion wie ein Einheimischer Sprecher beherrschen. Danach, verankern Sie dies in Ihrem Unterbewusstsein indem Sie weiter üben.

Sehen Sie sich die ersten paar Male das Buch an, aber wenn Sie mit dem Text vertraut sind, legen Sie das Buch weg. Konzentrieren Sie sich ausschließlich auf's Zuhören!

Jetzt hol sie Dir, Tiger!

FOCUS
Follow One Course Until Successful
Anonym

The English World

Rank	Word	Rank	Word
1	the	26	from
2	of	27	or
3	to	28	had
4	and	29	by
5	a	30	hot
6	in	31	but
7	is	32	some
8	it	33	what
9	you	34	there
10	that	35	we
11	he	36	can
12	was	37	out
13	for	38	other
14	on	39	were
15	are	40	all
16	with	41	your
17	as	42	when
18	I	43	up
19	his	44	use
20	they	45	word
21	be	46	how
22	at	47	said
23	one	48	an
24	have	49	each
25	this	50	she

Rank	Word	Rank	Word
51	which	76	more
52	do	77	day
53	their	78	could
54	time	79	go
55	if	80	come
56	will	81	did
57	way	82	my
58	about	83	sound
59	many	84	no
60	then	85	most
61	them	86	number
62	would	87	who
63	write	88	over
64	like	89	know
65	so	90	water
66	these	91	than
67	her	92	call
68	long	93	first
69	make	94	people
70	thing	95	may
71	see	96	down
72	him	97	side
73	two	98	been
74	has	99	now
75	look	100	find

Kapitel 7: 1 – 10, My First Day Of School In New York

#1, the
Das th in the wird betont. /TH/. Halten Sie Ihre Zungenspitze zwischen Ihre oberen und unteren Schneidezähne. Dann drücken Sie die Luft heraus. Fügen Sie Vibration hinzu. /TH/. The. The. The.

- The world.
- The book.
- The house.
- The tree.
- The computer.
- The best.
- The same.

- There are more than 7 billion people in the world.
- The tree is in front of the house.
- The book is next to the computer.
- The teacher is very happy to teach me.

Wenn das "the" vor einem Vokal ist (a, e, i, o, u), dann wird "the" als "thee" betont.
- The apple.
- The elephant
- The ice
- The other
- The umbrella
- The end.

- The apple tree is in the front of the house.
- The elephant is playing with the umbrella.
- The ice in this lake is melting, but the ice in the other lake is still frozen.

#2, of
Das f in of wird als v betont. /v/. /əv/. /əv/. /əv/.

- Of course.
- A lot of.
- In front of.
- Out of.
- Kind of.
- Because of.
- One of two.
- North of New York.
- The United States of America.
- A hundred of 500,000 English words.
- Chapter four of this book.

- The English language is one of the biggest languages in the world.
- One of my friends is an English teacher.
- Toronto is in the north of New York.
- English is the official language of the United States.
- If I follow the instructions in the book, I will pronounce every one of these words correctly.

#3, to

- To go.
- To do.
- To see.
- To learn.
- Due to.
- Want to.
- Come to.
- Go to.
- In order to

- I want to learn to speak English.
- To successfully learn to speak English, you must speak English.
- I asked her to come to my house, but she said she didn't want to.
- It's five to ten (It's five minutes to 10 O'clock).
- My car does 40 miles to the gallon.
- I'm nice to everybody.

#4, and
Das d in and ist betont. an/D/. Hören Sie die Vibration? An/D/. Es gibt eine Vibration. /D/. /D/. /D/. Es gibt keinen Vokal, aber es gibt Vibration. /D/. An/D/. Vergleichen Sie t mit d. T ist ohne Betonung wohingegen d betont ist. Nun t und d. /T/, /D/. /T/, /D/. /T/, /D/.

- And so on.
- And then.
- Hide and seek.
- Rock and roll.
- Back and forth.
- More and more.
- Better and better.
- Pen and paper.
- Milk and cheese.
- Love and marriage.
- Come and go.

- Do you have a pen and a paper?
- Milk and cheese help you grow tall.
- They say love and marriage are like horse and carriage.
- He turned around and left.
- The first one is a boy and the second one is a girl.
- My English is getting better and better.
- Three and seven make ten (3 + 7 = 10)

#5, a

- A train.
- A girl.
- A computer.
- A book.
- A seat.

- A train is coming.
- A girl walks on the train.
- She sits on a seat at the corner and takes out a book.
- She then takes out a computer.

#6, in

Nun passen Sie bitte auf. Das i in in ist ein kurzer Vokal. /IH/. Sagen Sie /IH/ und fügen dann ein n am Ende hinzu. In. In. In.
In wird nicht wie een betont. Vergleichen Sie den Unterschied zwischen in und een. In, een. In, een.

- In front.
- In fact.
- In the house.
- In English.
- Come in.
- Go in.
- Locked in.
- I'm in.

- In the year 2016, my one-year-old niece locked herself in the house by accident and no one had the key to go in.
- Do you want to play basketball in the afternoon? Sure! I'm in! See you in 15 minutes.
- She's in love with you. If you love her, go to her and say "I love you."
- It works like magic. I learned it in the book.

#7, is

Das s in is wird betont. /Z/. Lauschen Sie der Vibration.

- It is.
- This is.
- There is.
- She is.
- What is.
- This is wonderful.
- She's from Chicago.

- Chicago is 12 hours west of New York.
- She's from Chicago.
- He's in school. His school is PS 101.
- One and one is two. Two and two is four.
- Apples are on sale today. This apple is 25 cents.
- He loves her so much that she's everything to him.

#8, it

- In it.
- Get it.
- Like it.
- Take it.
- It is
- What time is it?
- It's OK.
- It's easy.
- We are it.

- The glass has water in it. It's half filled. How do you look at the water in the glass? Half full or half empty?
- It's half full! Keep looking at it this way and you'll be one happy person.
- Who is it?

- It's me.
- What time is it? It's 3:30.
- Sorry. It's my fault.
- It's OK.
- Did you finish the homework today?
- Yes. It's easy.
- Where is the rescue team?
- We're it.

#9, you

- How are you?
- I love you.
- Thank you.
- With you.
- For you.
- Have you.
- You are awesome!
- You students.
- You confident people.
- You get used to it.

- How are you?
- Fine, thanks.
- Are you OK?
- Yes. I'm fine.
- Do you take the subway train to work?
- Yes. I do.
- You're one awesome man!
- You students will take the SAT before entering college.

#10, that
Das th in that wird betont. /TH/. Halten Sie Ihre Zungenspitze

zwischen Ihre oberen und unteren Schneidezähne und erzeugen Sie den Ton, mit Vibration. /TH/. That.

- So that.
- After that.
- Like that.
- Who's that?
- That's a good idea?
- The word that you've just learned.
- The year that I came to America.
- I took the subway train at that time.
- Where's that boy of yours?
- Go that far.
- More than that.
- She said that.

- Who's that?
- That's a new student.
- Let's talk to him.
- That's a good idea.
- The word that you've just learned is you.
- The day that I came to America was a cold day.
- I took the subway train to school at that time.
- Where's that boy of yours?
- Not only would I go that far, I would even go beyond that.
- She said that she wanted to learn English.

Lassen Sie uns nun diese 10 Wörter anwenden!

- My name is Hassan.
- I came from Saudi Arabia.
- The day that I came to America it was snowing.
- There were two lakes near the house.
- The ice in the small lake was melting, but the ice in the other lake was still frozen.

- I took the subway train to school at that time.
- When I was waiting on the platform, I saw a beautiful girl wearing a pair of headphones.
- When a train came, the girl walked into the train.
- She sat on a seat at a corner and took out a book.
- She tapped on the screen of her cell phone and started reading.

- "Who's that?" When I entered the classroom, I heard someone said.
- "That's a new student." Someone else said.
- "Let's talk to him."
- "That's a good idea."
- So two people came to talk to me in English.
- I only knew a little bit of English, so it was hard for me to understand.
- "Do you have a pen and a paper?" One of them asked.
- "Pen? Paper?" I said.
- "Yes. Pen and paper."
- "Yes." I said and took out a pen and a notebook.
- They started talking to me and drawing pictures on the notebook for what I didn't understand.

- Class soon started.
- Mr. Xiao, the English teacher, taught me something that was shocking to me.
- He said, "the English language is one of the biggest

languages in the world. It has 500,000 words, but .1% (0.1%) make up 80% of the daily conversation."
- He then said, "to successfully learn to speak English, you must open your mouth and speak English no matter how much you know."

- I'd love to learn to speak English well, so I wanted to talk to the two classmates in English.
- Suddenly, I saw the beautiful girl whom I saw on the train.
- She was in the same class and I didn't notice that!
- I asked her to come to my house, but she said she didn't want to.

- Soon my English was getting better and better, and I felt more comfortable to talk in English.
- I felt so in love with the girl that I wanted to talk to her.
- "What's the word that we've just learned?" I asked.
- "The word that we've just learned is you," she said.
- "What time is it?" I asked.
- "It's five to three," she said.
- "Do you want to come to my house?" I asked.
- "No," she said.

Konzentrieren Sie sich auf was wie wollen,
nicht auf das, was Ihnen Angst macht.
Anthony Robbins

Kapitel 8: 11 – 20, My First Year In America
#11, he

- He is.
- He says.
- He also.
- Who is he?
- He's a good boy.

- He's an ESL student.
- He's a good kid.
- Hello, may I speak to Hassan, please? This is he.
- Everyone likes my father. He's a happy man.
- The boy knows he's loved.

#12, was
Heute → is
Gestern → was

- It was.
- That was.
- There was.
- The test was yesterday.
- The classroom was on the left.
- It was raining until 10.

- Our English test was yesterday.
- It was raining but there was a boy running to school.

- He walked past the classroom. It was on his left.
- The classroom was locked but there was a way in.

#13, for

Nochmals, es gibt einen /R/ Klang am Ende.

- Look for.
- For you.
- For them.
- For her.
- For ever.
- For example.
- For a while.
- For sure.
- This is for you.
- She's leaving for Houston.
- Three for a dollar.
- She's tall for her age.
- He was in school for eight hours.
- I run for three miles a day.

- What are you looking for?
- I'm looking for my eclipse glasses.
- They have been in your pocket for a whole day.
- How much are these postcards?
- They are three for a dollar.
- Oranges are a dollar for four.
- She stayed in school for eight hours yesterday and got 100 on the test for the third time.

#14, on

- On time.
- On hold.
- On the other hand.
- Come on.
- Hold on.
- Go on.
- Put on.
- Turn on.
- Carry on.
- On the stage.
- A smile on her face.
- The lid on the bottle.
- Write it down on paper.
- On the way.
- The test is on Wednesday.
- Lunch is on me.

- Which one is your kid performing on the stage?
- The one with a smile on her face.
- She drinks some water and puts the lid on the bottle.
- He writes down something on paper.
- They're on their way to becoming the next stars in the school performance team.

#15, are

Eins → is
Zwei oder mehr → are
Du / Sie → are
sie (Plural) → are

- There is.
- There are.
- She is running.

- They are running.
- How is she?
- How are they?

- There is a bus.
- There are two buses.
- She is running for president of the Success Impact Group.
- They are running for president of the Success Impact Group.
- There are many choices to make in life.
- Millions of people believe aliens are living among us.
- Scientists believe there are aliens living inside the moon. They don't live on the moon. They live in the moon.

#16, with
Wenn Sie th am Ende eines Wortes sehen, dann ist dieses th ohne Betonung.

- With you.
- With me.
- With love.
- With pleasure.
- Deal with.
- Along with.
- The girl with a flag.
- A book with a bookmark.
- Fill it with water.
- Fight with each other.
- Do it with pleasure.
- Angry with each other.
- Her students are still with her.

- The little girl with a flag is waving.

- She fills the bottle with water.
- Eighty percent of us work on a job we don't like. If we work on a job we enjoy doing, we do it with pleasure.
- When you're angry with each other, don't talk. Talk to each other when you're not angry with each other.
- After talking for 15 minutes, she looks at their facial expressions to see if her students are still with her.

#17, as

- Such as.
- As well as.
- As soon as.
- As long as.
- As far as.
- As many as.
- As a result.
- As you like.
- As usual
- Talk as you would if you were the winner.
- He worked as a chef.
- He works as a director.

- As many as 22 candidates are running for president of the Success Impact Group.
- All of them talk on the stage as if they had already won the election.
- Two hundred are watching as they're talking.
- America is the land of opportunities. Anything as wild as you can imagine is possible.
- Two years ago, he worked as a chef, but now he works as the director of business operations.
- Twenty years ago, Ken lived his life as a country boy, a middle school dropout, and a humble man. Now, he lives his life as a successful immigrant!

#18, I

- I'm Angela.
- I'm from Germany.
- I run for three miles a day.
- I'm a student.

#19, his

- His own.
- His family.
- His English.

- Victor came to America with his parents.
- This is his apartment.
- His school is PS101.
- His English is improving day-by-day.

#20, they
Eine Person → he/she
Zwei oder mehrere Personen → they
Ein Objekt → it
Zwei oder mehrere Objekte → they

- They are.
- They have.
- They say.
- They both.
- They looked confident.
- They are running for president.
- They set their goal years before.
- Ask someone if they wanted to vote.

- Two new students came today. They looked confident.
- Jessica and Virginia are successful leaders. They are running for president of the Success Impact Group.
- They set their goal years before to becoming president. They lay out their plan and take actions.
- Their supporters ask students if they wanted to vote for them.

Nun lassen Sie uns diese 10 Wörter anwenden.

- I'm Angela.
- I'm a student.
- I came from Germany.
- I came to America with my parents.
- Everyone likes my father. He's a happy person.
- I'm surprised to learn that food is very cheap in America.
- Apples are three for a dollar.
- Oranges are a dollar for four.

- I walk a mile to school.
- Our English test was yesterday.
- It was raining until 10, but there was a boy running to school.
- He walked pass the classroom. It was on his left.
- The classroom was locked, but there was a way in.
- He stayed in school for eight hours yesterday and got 100 on the test for the third time.

- April is the month to elect the next president of the Success Impact Group.
- As many as 22 candidates are running for president.
- All of them talk on the stage as if they had already won the election.
- Two hundred are watching as they're talking.
- Two new students came today. They looked confident.
- Jessica and Virginia are successful leaders. They are running for president of the Success Impact Group.
- They set their goal years before to becoming president. They lay out their plan and take actions.
- Their supporters ask students if they wanted to vote for them.
- America is the land of opportunities. Anything as wild as you can imagine is possible.
- Two years ago, he worked as a chef, but now he

works as the director of business operations.
- Twenty years ago, Ken lived his life as a country boy, a middle school dropout, and a humble man. Now, he lives his life as a successful immigrant!

Kapitel 9: 21 – 30, My First Job in Arizona

#21, be

- May be.
- Will be.
- Must be.
- Could be.
- Would be.
- Should be.
- Be careful.
- Be quiet.
- Be able to.
- Be right back.

- Six apples will be $2.
- I'll be there.
- It'll be this way.
- What will you be planning for life?
- What do you mean?
- We have plans for everything except for a plan for life.
- I don't have one yet. Now will be a good time to set one.

#22, at

- At home.
- At work.
- At least.
- At first.
- At last.
- At the same time
- Arrive at.

- Start at.
- Look at.
- Good at.

- I arrived at 250 Main Street at five o'clock.
- It was cooler at night, so I brought a jacket.
- I started to work at seven.
- I'm always learning at home, at work, and at school.
- I'm good at math. What are you good at?
- I'm good at nothing yet, but I'll be good at English in six months.

#23, one

- One day.
- One time.
- One more.
- One unit.
- One person.
- One of my plans.
- A good one.
- An unusual one.
- This one.
- That one.
- One in a million.

- One of my plans is to speak English like a native in six months.
- There is one good person who knows about my plan. Me.
- I practice my English with one of my friends. He wants to learn my native language. We help each other.
- Of all my friends, he's an unusual one.
- He's one of the people who have big dreams.

- He's one in a million who cares about the human race.

#24, have

Das v in have ist betont wie v mit Vibration. Berühren Sie Ihre Unterlippe mit ihren oberen Schneidezähnen und machen Sie dann das Geräusch, v. Wenn nun ein v am Ende ist, wird das /æ/ Geräusch länger. Have, have, have.

Vergleichen Sie den Unterschied zwischen half und have. Half, have, half, have.

Heute → have
Gestern → had
Länger her → have been

- Have fun.
- Have time.
- Have been.
- Have to.
- Have lunch.
- Have dinner.
- Have a good time.

- I have a new friend who is unusual.
- Do you have any brothers and sisters?
- We have two stores, one in Bellevue and one in Renton.
- They had lots of fun.
- He had twelve drinks and tried to drive home.
- I had to stop him and drove him home instead.
- We have been friends for 20 years. I felt like it was my duty to look after him.

#25, this

Das th in this wird betont als /TH/ mit Vibration. Das s in this wird als z betont, ebenfalls mit Vibration. This wird betont, hören Sie auf die Vibrationen, this, this, this.

Eins → this
Zwei oder mehr → these

- This time.
- This day.
- This week.
- This way.
- This one.
- This book.
- These books.

- Is this your book?
- No. It isn't.
- Whose books are these?
- This is mine. These are theirs.
- This will be an easy week since we've finished most of it.
- Who's this?
- This is Victor.

#26, from

- From here.
- From there.
- From now on.
- From Monday to Friday.
- From time to time.
- From no English to fluent English.
- Come from.
- Across from.

- Away from.
- Far from.
- Where are you from?

- Work hours are from nine to five.
- Work days are from Monday to Friday.
- From now on, I work eight hours a day.
- I've learned from speaking no English to speaking conversational English pretty easily.

#27, or

Hier gibt es einen /R/ Klang am Ende. Or, or, or.

- This or that.
- One or two.
- Use it or lose it.
- His or hers?
- More or less.
- Or not.
- Or else.
- To be or not to be.
- Now or never.
- Sooner or later.

- Would you like this one or that one?
- Would you like one pound or two pounds?
- Is this his or hers?
- Use it or lose it. We either use our skills or lose our skills.

#28, had
Heute → have
Gestern → had
Länger her → have been

- Had fun.
- Had time.
- Had been.
- Had to.
- Had lunch.
- Had dinner.
- Had a good time.
- I had water.
- She had tea.
- They had a few drinks.

- What did you have? I had water.
- What did she have? She had tea.
- How many books do you have today? I have two.
- How many books did you have yesterday? I had three.
- How much water did you have yesterday? I had eight bottles.

#29, by

- By myself.
- By noon.
- By hand.
- By the time.
- By the way.
- Go by.
- Stand by.
- Pass by.

- Day by day.
- Side by side.
- Step by step.
- A book by Ken Xiao.
- By bus. By train. By subway.

- This book is written by Ken Xiao.
- What do you go by? I go by Jack.
- How do you go to work? By bus.
- This project is due by Monday.
- I drove by your house this morning.
- I'll stop by later today.

#30, hot

- Hot day.
- Hot dish.
- Hot food.
- Hot spring.
- Hot water.
- Hot topic.
- Hot issue.
- Hot pepper.
- Hot potato.
- Very hot.
- Hot tub
- Hot stuff.
- Hot sauce.

- In Arizona, summer daytime temperatures range from 90 to 110 degrees. It's really hot for me.
- There is chili pepper in the soup. It's too hot for me. Is it hot for you?
- The Super Bowl is a hot game in America.
- House price was a hot issue in 2007.

- It's going to be a hot day today. It'll go up to 95.
- It's a hot dish. It's cooked with chili pepper.
- This is hot food. That is cold food.
- It's a hot topic everyone is talking about.
- If I were you, I would stay away from that project. It's a hot potato everyone is trying to avoid.

Es ist wieder soweit. Lassen Sie uns diese Wörter im Kontext erlernen.

- My name is Yoon-Jin.
- My parents and relatives called me Yoon-Jin.
- I go by Jack in school and at work.
- I came from Korea.
- In Arizona, summer is really cold at night and really hot during the day. Temperatures range from 50 to 110 degrees.
- In my first day of work, I arrived at 250 Main Street at eight o'clock.
- Work hours were from eight-thirty to five.
- Work days were from Monday to Friday.
- It has been this way, but from now on, work hours are from nine to five.
- It's cooler in the morning and at night, so I always bring a jacket.
- I work at a grocery store.
- One of my goals is to speak English fluently in six months.
- I practice every day by myself and with one of my friends.
- I'm sure I will speak English fluently.

> Entweder finden wir einen Weg oder wir werden einen bauen.
> **Hannibal**

Kapitel 10: 31 – 40, The World

#31, but

- But will.
- But then.
- But still.
- But also.
- Last but not least.

- Some countries are small, but some countries are big.
- She's new to our class, but she knows a lot of English words.
- I'm sorry. There is nothing I can do for you, but I can show you a way to get out of this.
- I would do nothing but laugh.
- Everyone but him wants to go to the party.

#32, some

- Some people.
- Some time.
- Some more.
- Some money.
- Some countries.
- Some of them.
- Some thirty students.
- Listen to some music.

- Most countries are small. Some countries are big.
- Some high school students work on a job after school to earn some money, but some parents encourage them to study instead.
- Some students joined a trip to Europe.
- Some thirty students were on that trip.
- Some of them listened to music and some of them listened to English lessons.

#33, what

- What about.
- What else.
- Whatever.
- What's your name?
- What?
- What time is it?
- What's up?
- What does it mean?
- What do you mean?

- What time is it?
- It's nine o'clock.
- What's your name?
- My name is Wei Ke.
- What?
- Wei Ke.
- What does it mean?
- It means a great scientist in Chinese.
- What a wonderful name!
- Thanks.
- What we need to do to become successful is a goal, actions, and persistence.

#34, there

Das th in there wird wie /TH/ mit Vibration betont. Platzieren Sie Ihre Zungenspitze zwischen Ihren oberen und unteren Schneidezähnen und pressen Sie die Luft heraus und erzeugen dann Vibration. /TH/. There.

- Stay there.
- Over there.
- Out there.
- Get there.
- Be there.
- There!
- Hi there!
- There is.
- There are.

- Where is Victor?
- He's over there.
- Where?
- There!
- There are about 200 countries in the world.
- There are 7000 languages in the world.

#35, we

- We are.
- We will.
- We shall.
- We would.
- We too.

- "We will either find a way or make a way."
- If we don't find the things we're looking for, make them!

- Shall we dance?
- Are we in the right time to study?

#36, can

- I can.
- We can.
- You can.
- Can you?
- It can.
- Trash can.
- Garbage can.

- Student: Can I go to the bathroom?
- Teacher: I don't know. Can you?
- Student: May I?
- Teacher: Yes. You may.

- What I can do is what I have the ability to do. What I will do is what I will take actions to get my results.
- Can you do it?
- Yes, I can, and I will.
- Out of the 7.6 billion people in the world, 795 million are hungry.
- There are many ways we can help these hungry people.

#37, out

- Take out.
- Carry out.

- Find out.
- Hang out.
- Figure out.
- Check out.
- Work out.
- Out of nowhere.
- Out there.
- A way out.

- Do you want to stay in or stay out?
- This is out of this world. I'll take two more.
- I'm sorry. I'm completely sold out.
- Is Victor home? No, he's out.
- Victor suddenly appears out of nowhere!
- There are many successful people out there we can learn something from.
- We'll either find a way out or make a way out.

#38, other
Das th in other wird als /TH/ mit Vibration betont. Platzieren Sie Ihre Zungenspitze zwischen Ihren oberen und unteren Schneidezähnen und pressen Sie die Luft heraus und erzeugen dann Vibration. /TH/. other.

Das o in other wird als /ə/ betont. Das o wird nicht betont wie /Ah/. Vergleichen Sie den Unterschied. /ə/ /Ah/, /ə/ /Ah/. /ə/ther.

- Other than.
- Other side.
- The other.
- In other words.
- On the other hand.
- One or the other.
- Any other.

- Each other.

- Which one would you like? This one or the other one?
- The other one.
- You can use this one or the other one.
- Let's try the other one.
- Another way to learn "other" is to learn from a friend who is a native speaker. Teach him or her your native language to help each other.
- Any other questions?

#39, were

Heute → are
Gestern → were

- There were.
- If I were you.
- As it were.
- As you were.

- There are 12 students here today.
- There were 11 students here yesterday.
- There were many opportunities.
- They were sitting right here.
- They were here until ten.
- You started when you were in preschool.
- There were many opportunities to raise my hands to ask questions in class.
- The teachers were sitting right here.
- They were here helping until ten.
- You were good friends when you were in preschool.

#40, all

- All of it.
- That's all.
- All of them.
- All I want.
- All we need.
- All right.
- After all.
- First of all.
- Above all.
- That's all.

- All of the students in the class came from different countries.
- All they want in class is to learn English. That's all.
- All of them want the same thing.
- All they need to do is to learn it and use it.

Hol sie Dir, Tiger!

- My name is Victor.
- I came from Russia.
- There are about 200 countries in the world.
- Most countries are small while some countries are big.
- Russia is the world's biggest country. The second biggest is Canada and the third is America.
- Russia is as big as Canada and America combined.
- All of the students in my class came from different countries.
- There were many opportunities to raise our hands to ask questions in class.
- We asked questions until the teachers were gone.
- There are many successful people out there we can learn from.
- There are many ways we can become successful.
- If we can dream it, we can achieve it.

- You can use this one or the other one.
- Which one would you like? This one or the other one?
- The other one.
- What I can do is what I have the ability to do. What I will do is what I will take actions to make things happen.
- Out of the 7.6 billion people in the world, 795 million are hungry.
- There are many ways we can help these hungry people.
- I won't be able to help all of them, but I can help some of them.

Wenn neun Hasen auf dem Boden sitzen und Sie einen fangen möchten, konzentrieren Sie sich nur auf einen.
Jack Ma

Kapitel 11: 41 – 50, English-Speaking Countries

#41, your

- Your book.
- Your name.
- Your car.
- Your English.
- Your energy.

- Is that your book?
- The story will make your heart smile.
- What is your name?
- My name is _____.
- What's your country of origin?
- What's your big dream?
- That's a wonderful dream you have.

#42, when

- When was the test?
- When I was a child.
- When did you come?
- Today is when I'll get my things done.
- When it's cold.

- When there are American, Australian, British and other accents to choose from, I need to choose one accent to learn.
- When you focus your attention on one thing, your energy will flow to it.
- When I was a child, I had many dreams.

#43, up

- Jump up.
- Go up.
- Get up.
- Kick up.
- Pick up.
- Wake up.
- Make up.
- Grow up.
- Stand up.

- Jumping up and down.
- Get up in the morning.
- The up escalator.
- Sales were up last month.
- What are you up to?

#44, use
Das s in use hat zwei Betonungen. Wenn use als Nomen verwendet wird, wird das s als s betont. Wenn use als Verb verwendet wird, wird das s als z mit Vibration betont.

Die folgenden drei Beispiele zeigen die Verwendung als Nomen. Hören Sie auf den s Klang.
- In use.
- Make use.
- For use.

Die folgenden drei Beispiele zeigen die Verwendung als Verb. Hören Sie auf den z Klang.
- Use for.
- Use up.
- Use to.

- We use a pen to write, we use a cup to drink, and we use our mind to think.
- If we use our mind and take actions until we become successful, we will become successful.
- Use My Fluent English formula to speak English like a native in six months.
- Like other languages, the English language used to be a small language, but it has become a big language today.
- Languages are like our muscles, we either use them or lose them.

#45, word

- Word processor.
- Word of mouth.
- Word order.
- Word list.
- One word.
- Two words.
- An English word.
- A Spanish word.
- A man of his word.

- "Excellent" is a wonderful word.
- A good way to build a vocabulary is to learn a word a day.
- My English teacher is a man of his word. He does what he says.

#46, how

- How to.
- How long.
- How nice!
- How many.
- How much.
- How come.
- How far.
- How are you?
- How does it work?
- How did it go?

- How do you say excellent in your language?
- If you know how to do something extremely well, someone will hire you.
- If you know how to do something extremely well and you use it to achieve a goal, you'll become successful.
- How nice it is to speak more than one language.
- How wonderful to see it happen!
- How did you like your trip to Europe?
- It was wonderful!

#47, said

Heute → say
Gestern → said

Said wird als sed betont. Es wird nicht als sad betont. Es wird als sed betont.

- He said.
- I said.
- As said.
- She said.
- They said.

- Easier said than done.
- When all is said and done.

- "What did she say when you asked her to go to your house?" She said, "no."
- Einstein said, "it's okay to make mistakes."
- It's easier said than done. It takes a big man admit a mistake.
- He also said, "the more mistakes you make, the more you learn."

#48, an

- A word.
- An English word.
- An umbrella.
- A yellow umbrella.
- A British accent.
- An American accent.
- A seventeen-day vacation.
- An eighteen-day vacation.
- Half an hour.
- Make an effort.
- Keep an eye on.
- Place an order.

#49, each

- Each day.
- Each book.
- Each one.
- Each time.
- Each other.
- For each.
- To each.

- Each and every one of us.

- Apples are 25 cents each.
- Each of us gets a textbook.
- Each day is a good opportunity to learn a new word.
- Each of us is unique.
- Each and every one of us can become successful.

#50, she

- She is.
- She does.
- She can.
- She will.
- She wants.
- She too.

- Who is she?
- She's Claire.
- What language does she speak?
- She speaks Spanish, but she wants to learn to speak English like a native speaker.

Holen wir sie uns!

- My name is Claire.
- Many people ask me where I came from by saying "Where are you from?"
- One person asked me this way, "What's your country of origin?"
- One person asked, "Where did you come from?"
- I came from Argentina.
- I came to America two years ago.
- Something I learned in my English class made my eyes open.

- The English language used to be a small language, but it has become a big language today.
- There are three major accents: the American accent with 250 million speakers, the British accent with 60 million speakers, and the Australian accent with 17 million speakers.

- I'm learning the American accent.
- A good way to build a vocabulary is to learn a word a day.
- My English teacher is a man of his word. He does what he says.
- He said, "if we use our mind and take actions until we become successful, we will become successful."
- How nice it is to speak more than one language.

Erinnern Sie sich immer daran, Ihr Focus definiert ihre Realität.
George Lucas

Kapitel 12: 51 – 60, Types of English

#51, which

- Which one?
- Which language?
- Which accent?
- Which is.

- Which one is your book?
- Which is yours?
- Which accent are you learning?

#52, do

- I do.
- You do.
- He does.
- She does.
- Do my best.

- I do my homework every day.
- Do your best.
- What do you do?
- Do you have any brothers and sisters?
- Which accent do you want to learn?

#53, their

- Their language.
- Their accent.
- Their book.
- Their children.
- Their friends.

- European immigrants brought their languages to America.
- They also brought their accents which contributed to the American English accent.
- Their children learned the new accent.

#54, time

- This time.
- Last time.
- The time.
- Time travel.
- Time to begin.

- What time is it?
- It's eight o'clock.
- What's the time?
- It's ten-thirty.
- It's time to begin our experiment.
- Last time it burned after 10 seconds. Let's see what happens this time.
- If you can travel back in time, where will you go?

#55, if

- If it rains, we'll bring an umbrella.
- If we use it, we'll keep it.
- If this, then that.
- If you do your homework, then you'll pass the test.

- If I set my goal, take action, and keep working on it, I will become successful.
- If you persevere, then you will become successful.

#56, will

- Will be.
- Will do.
- Willing to.
- I will.
- Will you?

- It will be 60 degrees tomorrow.
- I will bring a jacket.
- Will you do that again?
- Are you willing to practice for six months?
- You will become successful if you keep working on it.
- If you have faith, you will persevere.

#57, way

- One way.
- Two ways.
- Way to go.
- Make a way.
- A way in.

- A way out.

- One way to write is to use our right hand.
- Another way to write is to use our left hand.
- One way to learn English is to repeat what you hear again and again.
- There is a way in and there is a way out.
- We can either find a way or make a way.

#58, about

- What about?
- How about?
- Think about.

- How about you?
- What about me?
- We're going to the party. How about you?
- I'll think about it. What about you, George?
- I'm about to finish this book. I'm going stay home and finish it.
- These apples are about five pounds.
- There are about 20 trees in the garden.
- What are you talking about?
- We are talking about the party.

#59, many

- How many?
- So many.
- As many as.

- How many brothers and sisters do you have?
- Many students speak more than one language at

- home.
  - Immigrants brought many European accents to America.
  - There are as many as 7000 languages in the world.
  - We make so many mistakes in life, but we learn many lessons from our mistakes.

#60, then

  - If… then…
  - Back then.
  - Then again.

  - I set my goal and then achieve my goal.
  - The teacher came and then the students came.
  - She climbed one step and then another.
  - If you study for the test, then you'll pass the test.
  - If you do your homework, then you'll be OK.
  - Let's meet at noon. See you then.

Es ist wieder soweit. Lassen Sie es uns tun.

- Which one is your book?
- Which is yours?
- Which accent are you learning?
- I do my homework every day.
- Do your best.
- What do you do?
- Do you have any brothers and sisters?
- Which accent do you want to learn?
- European immigrants brought their languages to America.
- They also brought their accents which contributed to the American English accent.
- Their children learned the new accent.
- What time is it?
- It's eight o'clock.
- What's the time?
- It's ten-thirty.
- It's time to begin our experiment.
- Last time it burned after 10 seconds. Let's see what happens this time.
- If you can travel back in time, where will you go?
- If it rains, we'll bring an umbrella.
- If we use it, we'll keep it.
- If this, then that.
- If you do your homework, then you'll pass the test.
- If I set my goal, take action, and keep working on it, I will become successful.
- If you persevere, then you will become successful.
- It will be 60 degrees tomorrow.
- I will bring a jacket.
- Will you do that again?
- Are you willing to practice for six months?
- You will become successful if you keep working on it.
- If you have faith, you will persevere.

- One way to write is to use our right hand.
- Another way to write is to use our left hand.
- One way to learn English is to repeat what you hear again and again.
- There is a way in and there is a way out.
- We can either find a way or make a way.
- How about you?
- What about me?
- We're going to the party. How about you?
- I'll think about it. What about you, George?
- I'm about to finish this book. I'm going stay home and finish it.
- These apples are about five pounds.
- There are about 20 trees in the garden.
- What are you talking about?
- We are talking about the party.
- How many brothers and sisters do you have?
- Many students speak more than one language at home.
- Immigrants brought many European accents to America.
- There are as many as 7000 languages in the world.
- We make so many mistakes in life, but we learn many lessons from our mistakes.
- I set my goal and then achieve my goal.
- The teacher came and then the students came.
- She climbed one step and then another.
- If you study for the test, then you'll pass the test.
- If you do your homework, then you'll be OK.
- Let's meet at noon. See you then.

> Entscheiden Sie, was Sie wollen und glauben Sie daran, dass Sie es erreichen werden.
> **Anthony Robbins**

Kapitel 13: 61 – 70, American English

#61, them

Ich → me
Du / Sie → you
Er → him
sie (weiblich) → her
Wir → us
sie (Plural) → them

- It's them.
- Give them.
- Take them.
- Follow them.
- Tell them.

- Talk to native speakers and learn English from them.
- Give them what they want, talk about topics they like, and they'll be happy to talk to you.
- Find successful people, follow them, and you, too, will become successful.
- Do you know them? Talk to them and you will.
- They're good students. One of them is their team captain.
- If we hang out with them, we'll be good students, too.

#62, would

- I would.
- Would you?
- Would be.

- Would you like one?
- Yes, I would love to have one.
- The weather would be nice for a while.
- I would visit Arizona and Wyoming if I got two weeks off.
- If I were you, I would live on the west coast.
- If I have one more day, I will go to Yellowstone.
- If I had one more day, I would go to Yellowstone.
- It would be nice to see the sun at midnight.

#63, write

- Write a letter.
- Write an email.
- Write on a map.
- Write down your goal.

- Set our goal and write it down.
- Why do we write down our goals?
- Those who write down their goals become much more successful than those who don't write down their goals.

#64, like

- Like it.
- Like this.
- Like that.
- Likewise.
- Like attracts like.

- I like the warm weather of the west coast.
- Would you like to Tango?
- He can speak like a native.
- Living in Seattle makes me feel like living in nature.
- Do it like this.
- Eat it like that.
- Like attracts like. If you find one successful person, you will find more through that person.

#65, so

- So-so.
- So much.
- So well.
- So!
- So?
- So good.

- How is your English?
- So-so.
- How is her English?
- Her English is so good!
- Thank you so much!
- Do you think so?
- I think so.
- The temperature in eastern Canada is so cold in the winter.
- The temperature in western Canada is so warm in the winter.
- The equator is so hot and so is Phoenix.
- It was so hot in Phoenix, so I moved to Seattle.
- It's so effective to repeat what you hear again and again, so I'm using it.
- My pronunciation is improving so quickly, so I'm going

to continue practicing.

#66, these
Eins → this
Zwei oder mehr → these

- This book.
- These books.
- This is.
- These are.
- Is this your book?
- Are these your books?

- These cities are hot in the summer.
- These states are cold in the winter.
- These are useful words. Learn them and use them.

#67, her

Ich → me
Er → him
sie (weiblich) → her

Ich → my
Er → his
sie (weiblich) → her

- To her.
- For her.
- Respect her.

- Do you know her?
- Would you give this to her?

- Can you do this for her?
- She knows you like her.
- She always brings her phone and her book with her.

#68, long

- Long time.
- Long, long ago.
- A long moment.

- It's been a long time.
- She has long hair.
- Canada has long days in the summer.
- Canada has long nights in the winter.
- The Mississippi River is 2,202 miles long.
- The longest river in the US is the Missouri River. It's 2,341 miles long.
- When waiting in a long line, it's a great time to listen to an audiobook.

#69, make

- Make lunch.
- Make friends.
- Make money.
- Make a living.
- Make it on time.
- Make it happen.

- We'll make it on time.
- It's easy to make a living in America.
- You'll make more friends in a day by talking about the things they like than in a year by talking about the things you like.
- There are three types of people, those who don't

know what's happened, those who watch things happen, and those who make things happen.

#70, thing

- One thing.
- The thing.

- Location is one thing to think about.
- The other thing is the weather.
- One more thing to think about is the time zone.
- I'm thinking of learning to speak English well, but the thing is I don't have time.
- There are three types of people, those who don't know what's happened, those who watch things happen, and those who make things happen.
- Those who make things happen are usually the ones who become successful.

Sie wissen was kommt. Lassen Sie uns mit der Übung weitermachen.

- Talk to native speakers and learn English from them.
- Give them what they want, talk about topics they like, and they'll be happy to talk to you.
- Find successful people, follow them, and you, too, will become successful.
- Do you know them? Talk to them and you will.
- They're good students. One of them is their team captain.
- If we hang out with them, we'll be good students, too.
- Would you like one?
- Yes, I would love to have one.
- How nice would it be to learn to speak English like a native!
- The weather would be nice for a while.
- I would visit Arizona and Wyoming if I got two weeks off.
- If I were you, I would live on the west coast.
- If I have one more day, I will go to Yellowstone.
- If I had one more day, I would go to Yellowstone.
- It would be nice to see the sun at midnight.
- Set our goal and write it down.
- Why do we write down our goals?
- Those who write down their goals become much more successful than those who don't write down their goals.
- I like the warm weather of the west coast.
- Would you like to Tango?
- He can speak like a native.
- Living in Seattle makes me feel like living in nature.
- Do it like this.
- Eat it like that.
- Like attracts like. If you find one successful person, you will find more through that person.

- How is your English?
- So-so.
- How is her English?
- Her English is so good!
- Thank you so much!
- Do you think so?
- I think so.
- The temperature in eastern Canada is so cold in the winter.
- The temperature in western Canada is so warm in the winter.
- The equator is so hot and so is Phoenix.
- It was so hot in Phoenix, so I moved to Seattle.
- It's so effective to repeat what you hear again and again, so I'm using it.
- My pronunciation is improving so quickly, so I'm going to continue practicing.
- These cities are hot in the summer.
- These states are cold in the winter.
- These are useful words. Learn them and use them.
- Do you know her?
- Would you give this to her?
- She knows you like her.
- She always brings her phone and her book with her.
- It's been a long time.
- She has long hair.
- Canada has long days in the summer.
- Canada has long nights in the winter.
- The Mississippi River is 2,202 miles long.
- The longest river in the US is the Missouri River. It's 2,341 miles long.
- When waiting in a long line, it's a great time to listen to an audiobook.
- We'll make it on time.
- It's easy to make a living in America.
- You'll make more friends in a day by talking about the

- things they like than in a year by talking about the things you like.
- There are three types of people, those who don't know what's happened, those who watch things happen, and those who make things happen.
- Location is one thing to think about.
- The other thing is the weather.
- One more thing to think about is the time zone.
- I'm thinking of learning to speak English well, but the thing is I don't have time.
- There are three types of people, those who don't know what's happened, those who watch things happen, and those who make things happen.
- Those who make things happen are usually the ones who become successful.

Energie fließt in Richtung Aufmerksamkeit.
Hawaiianisches Sprichwort

Kapitel 14: 71 – 80, North America Climates

#71, see

- I see.
- See it for yourself.

- I see a frozen lake.
- They come to see a friend.
- If you go to Lake Michigan in the winter, you'll see a frozen lake.
- If you go to Yellowstone National Park, you'll see geysers shooting up hot water.
- Do you want to see how it works? It goes like this.
- I see.
- I'll go see it myself.

#72, him
Ich → me
sie (weiblich) → her
Er → him

- To him.
- For him.
- With him.

- Do you know him?
- Can you give this to him?

- Would you like to ask him to come with us?
- He knows she likes him.
- In California's Death Valley, summer is hot for him.
- California's mild winter is just right for him.

#73, two

- One and one is two.
- Two and four is six.
- Two times two is four.
- Two of my friends.

- The U.S. and Canada are two friendly countries in North America.
- I'll build my dreams with my own two hands.
- Two of my friends will join me.

#74, has

Er → has
sie (weiblich) → has
Es → has
Ich, Du / Sie, sie (plural) → have

- He has.
- She has.
- It has.
- Has it?

- Virginia has four seasons.
- Hawaii has one season.
- Alaska has a long and dark winter.
- Northern Canada has a long and bright summer.

- He has two children.
- She has a teacher's certificate.
- It has to be this way.
- It has been this way.

#75, look

- Look at.
- Look in.
- Look for.
- Look good
- Take a look.

- We can look through the clouds to see the stars.
- If you look around Seattle, you'll see lots of hiking trails.
- With 360 sunny days a year, I look at life differently in New Mexico.
- If you look for a warm place to live, go to California.
- Look! That's Mt. Denali, the highest mountain peak in North America.
- Look at the midnight sun! Welcome to Alaska!
- That looks good!
- Yes. It does look good!

#76, more

- One more.
- Two more.
- Some more.
- Take more.
- Do more.

- Would you like some more?
- Do you want some more?
- Want some more?
- If I have one more day, I will go to Yellowstone.
- There are more people in California than in any other state.
- Persistence is more important than talent. Do more than others.
- I like Seattle's cool summer days more than Houston's hot summer days.
- I'll be more than happy to help you.

#77, day

- One day.
- Two days.
- Day-by-day.
- Day after day.
- One more day.

- There are 24 hours a day. An average person sleeps eight hours a day and works eight hours a day. What we do with the remaining eight hours every day makes a huge difference 180 days later.
- Focus on a target day-by-day and keep working on it. You'll see the progress day after day.

#78, could

Gegenwart → can
Vergangenheit → could

- I could.
- Could you?
- It could be.
- It could have been.

- I could do this.
- Could you be more precise?
- They could be right.
- That could be the right answer.

#79, go

- Go to.
- Go on.
- Go ahead.
- Go around.
- Go straight.
- Go with.
- Get going.

- Go to a meeting.
- Go to school.
- I must go now.
- Let's give it a go to see what happens.
- Go head.
- We can go straight to our target or go around to get to our target.
- I go with the second. When there are obstacles in front of me, I'll go around them and then get back to my target.

#80, come

- Come up.
- Come to.
- Come with.
- Come on.
- Come in.
- Come around.
- Come along.

- Come to my house to get the book.
- Come to America to study.
- Come to Earth to get what you want.
- Tomorrow has yet to come.
- We come in peace.
- Your lunch comes with soup.
- Once you come up with a new idea, come into my office right away.
- Come on. Let's go.

Holen wir sie uns.

- I see a frozen lake.
- They come to see a friend.
- If you go to Lake Michigan in the winter, you'll see a frozen lake.
- If you go to Yellowstone National Park, you'll see geysers shooting up hot water.
- Do you want to see how it works? It goes like this.
- I see.
- I'll go see it myself.
- Do you know him?
- Can you give this to him?
- Would you like to ask him to come with us?
- He knows she likes him.
- In California's Death Valley, summer is hot for him.
- California's mild winter is just right for him.
- The U.S. and Canada are two friendly countries in North America.
- I'll build my dreams with my own two hands.
- Two of my friends will join me.
- Virginia has four seasons.
- Hawaii has one season.
- Alaska has a long and dark winter.
- Northern Canada has a long and bright summer.
- He has two children.
- She has a teacher's certificate.
- It has to be that way.
- It has been that way.
- We can look through the clouds to see the stars.
- If you look around Seattle, you'll see lots of hiking trails.
- With 360 sunny days a year, I look at life differently in New Mexico.
- If you look for a warm place to live, go to California.
- Look! That's Mt. Denali, the highest mountain peak in

North America.
- Look at the midnight sun! Welcome to Alaska!
- That looks good!
- Yes. It does look good!
- Would you like some more?
- Do you want some more?
- Want some more?
- If I have one more day, I will go to Yellowstone.
- There are more people in California than in any other state.
- Persistence is more important than talent. Do more than others.
- I like Seattle's cool summer days more than Houston's hot summer days.
- I'll be more than happy to help you.
- There are 24 hours a day. An average person sleeps eight hours a day and works eight hours a day. What we do with the remaining eight hours every day makes a huge difference 180 days later.
- Focus on a target day-by-day and keep working on it. You'll see the progress day after day.
- I could do this.
- Could you be more precise?
- They could be right.
- That could be the right answer.
- Go to a meeting.
- Go to school.
- I must go now.
- Let's give it a go to see what happens.
- Go head.
- We can go straight to our target or go around to get to our target.
- I go with the second. When there are obstacles in front of me, I'll go around them and then get back to my target.
- Come to my house to get the book.

- Come to America to study.
- Come to Earth to get what you want.
- Tomorrow has yet to come.
- We come in peace.
- Your lunch comes with soup.
- Once you come up with a new idea, come into my office right away.
- Come on. Let's go.

> Halten Sie Ihren Fokus gezielt wie ein Laser auf das, was Sie in Ihrem Leben erschaffen wollen.
> **Mike Basevic**

Kapitel 15: 81 – 90, 10 Largest Cities in America

#81, did

Heute → do
Gestern → did

- It did.
- What did?
- How did?
- Did it?

- Did it happen?
- Yes. It did.
- How did it go?
- It went crazy.
- Did you see that? Yes. I did.
- He did a good job.
- How long did it take you?
- They did it in three hours.
- What did you do?
- She did my hair last week.
- Why did you choose New York?
- Because New York is the largest city in America.
- I did 35 miles per hour in New York City and got pulled over by a cop.
- What's the speed limit in New York City? 30.
- When he was driving in New York, he made every right turn on red lights.

- Did he get pulled over by the police? Yes. He did.

#82, my

- My book.
- My phone.
- My name.
- Oh my God!

- My name is _____.
- My English is improving every day.
- My city is the second largest city in America.
- Oh my God! There is a bug in my phone.

#83, sound

- A sound.
- Soundwave.
- Soundtrack.
- Sound the alarm.
- Good sound.
- Sound good.

- What sound do you like the most, the sound of a subway train, the sound of your voice, or the sound of your heart?
- Let's listen to a soundtrack before we begin. How does that sound?
- That sounds like a plan.
- You had an exciting adventure in Chicago by the sound of your voice.
- With a population of 2.7 million, Chicago sounds like a big city.

- Yes, indeed. Chicago is the third biggest city in America after New York and Los Angeles.

#84, no

- Yes or no.
- No Smoking.
- No need.
- No way.
- No time.

- Are you a teacher? No. I'm a student.
- There is no need to bring a jacket. Unlike San Francisco, Houston's summer is not cold.
- Driving across Houston is no easy task, but I'll be back in no time.

#85, most

- The most.
- Most of.
- At the most.

- Philadelphia is the most populous city in Pennsylvania and the fifth most populous city in America.
- The most important day in my life is the day I discovered the formula for success.
- Most of everyone agreed that education is the most important factor to success. I disagreed.
- Thomas Edison, one of the most famous inventors who invented the electric light bulb, had only three months of formal education.
- According to Professor Duckworth, the most important

factor to success is not education. It's grit.

#86, number

- Number one.
- Number two.
- A phone number.
- The number of.

- What's your phone number?
- The number of residents of Phoenix is numbered more than 1.5 million.
- The number of visitors increases the number of jobs.
- Phoenix is the number one largest city in Arizona.
- With 1.6 million people, Phoenix is the number six largest city nationwide.
- With temperature often goes up to 105, Phoenix is the number one hottest city in America.

#87, who
- Who is?
- For who?
- To who?

- Who's that?
- That's the mayor of San Antonio.
- Who's this for?
- This is for the kid who got injured in the game.
- Who knows the population of San Antonio?
- One point five million.
- The number of visitors to San Antonio is almost 10 times of its population. Who wants to visit San Antonio?
- Home to one of the largest concentrations of military

bases, San Antonio has become known as "Military City, USA."
- Who wants to guess what the seventh largest city in America is?

#88, over

- Over there.
- Over here.
- Bring over.
- Sleepover.
- Over and out.

- What's that over there?
- It's an airplane.
- No. The round thing above it!
- Oh my God! It's a UFO!
- The White House is over in Washington DC.
- San Diego is over in California.
- There are rarely any clouds over San Diego.
- With a large naval base in San Diego, you can often see military aircraft flying over San Diego.
- I would stay in San Diego over Fairbanks in the winter.
- San Diego has a mild climate year-round while Fairbanks, Alaska's average winter temperature is -17 degrees Fahrenheit.

#89, know

- Know it.
- Know how.

- Tom knows how to build tree houses. Chris knows how to sell them.

- Do you know him? Yes. I know him. I've known him for 20 years.
- Do you know what state is Dallas in?
- Yes. It's in Texas.
- Do you know the population of Dallas?
- One point two million.

#90, water

- A glass of water.
- Hot water.
- Cold water.
- Surrounded by water.

- Most of our body is water.
- San Jose is a city close to water.
- Let's water the plants.
- They added water to their juice.
- Would you like some water?
- In San Jose, you get 15 inches of rain a year. Be sure to water your plants well.

Sie wissen es genau. Es ist wieder an der Zeit.

- Did it happen?
- Yes. It did.
- How did it go?
- It went crazy.
- Did you see that? Yes. I did.
- He did a good job.
- How long did it take you?
- They did it in three hours.
- What did you do?
- She did my hair last week.
- Why did you choose New York?
- Because New York is the largest city in America.
- I did 35 miles per hour in New York City and got pulled over by a cop.
- What's the speed limit in New York City? 30.
- When he was driving in New York, he made every right turn on red lights.
- Did he get pulled over by the police? Yes. He did.
- My name is _____.
- My English is improving every day.
- My city is the second largest city in America.
- Oh my God! There is a bug in my phone.
- What sound do you like the most, the sound of a subway train, the sound of your voice, or the sound of your heart?
- Let's listen to a soundtrack before we begin. How does that sound?
- That sounds like a plan.
- You had an exciting adventure in Chicago by the sound of your voice.
- With a population of 2.7 million, Chicago sounds like a big city.
- Yes, indeed. Chicago is the third biggest city in America after New York and Los Angeles.

- Is there anything wrong with it? No. Everything is fine.
- Are you a teacher? No. I'm a student.
- There is no need to bring a jacket. Unlike San Francisco, Houston's summer is not cold.
- Driving across Houston is no easy task, but I'll be back in no time.
- Philadelphia is the most populous city in Pennsylvania and the fifth most populous city in America.
- The most important day in my life is the day I discovered the formula to success.
- Most of everyone agreed that education is the most important factor to success. I disagreed.
- Thomas Edison, one of the most famous inventors who invented the electric light bulb, had only three months of formal education.
- According to Professor Duckworth, the most important factor to success is not education. It's grit.
- What's your phone number?
- The number of residents of Phoenix is numbered more than 1.5 million.
- The number of visitors increases the number of jobs.
- Phoenix is the number one largest city in Arizona.
- With 1.6 million people, Phoenix is the number six largest city nationwide.
- With temperature often goes up to 105, Phoenix is the number one hottest city in America.
- Who's that?
- That's the mayor of San Antonio.
- Who's this for?
- This is for the kid who got injured in the game.
- Who knows the population of San Antonio?
- One point five million.
- The number of visitors to San Antonio is almost 10 times of its population. Who wants to visit San Antonio?
- Home to one of the largest concentrations of military bases, San Antonio has become known as "Military

City, USA."
- Who wants to guess what the seventh largest city in America is?
- What's that over there?
- It's an airplane.
- No. The round thing above it!
- Oh my God! It's a UFO!
- The White House is over in Washington DC.
- San Diego is over in California.
- There are rarely any clouds over San Diego.
- With a large naval base in San Diego, you can often see military aircraft flying over San Diego.
- I would stay in San Diego over Fairbanks in the winter.
- San Diego has a mild climate year-round while Fairbanks, Alaska's average winter temperature is -17 degrees Fahrenheit.
- Tom knows how to build tree houses. Chris knows how to sell them.
- Do you know him? Yes. I know him. I've known him for 20 years.
- Do you know what state is Dallas in?
- Yes. It's in Texas.
- Do you know the population of Dallas?
- One point two million.
- Most of our body is water.
- San Jose is a city close to water.
- Let's water the plants.
- They added water to their juice.
- Would you like some water?
- In San Jose, you get 15 inches of rain a year. Be sure to water your plants well.

Was auch immer der Geist empfangen und glaube kann, kann er auch erreichen.
Napoleon Hill

Kapitel 16: 91 – 100, U.S. and Canada Culture

#91, than

- Bigger than.
- Longer than.
- More than.

- Rich is better than poor.
- Canada is a little bit bigger than America.
- America has a much bigger population than Canada.
- America has nine times more people than Canada.
- A gallon is heavier than a liter.

#92, call

- A phone call.
- Call back.
- Call it a day.

- I'll give you a call tonight.
- I'll call you tonight.
- Who made that phone call?
- Let's wrap it up and call it a day.
- They called their daughter Katie.
- The U.S. is called a melting pot.

#93, first

- First day.
- First job.
- The first.
- First grade.
- First time.

- What grade is your child in?
- He's in first grade.
- Have you seen snow before?
- No. This is my first time seeing snow.
- He's the first one to get there.

#94, people

Eins → person
Zwei oder mehr → people

- How many people?
- My people.
- For the people.

- My people have been working on this project since April.
- How many people signed up for the trip to Europe?
- Forty-six.
- When looking at a photo, what do you look at first? The people or the background?
- I always look at the people first.

#95, may

- The month of May.
- May I?
- You may.
- May be.

- May I use your pen?
- Yes. You may.
- **Think and Grow Rich** may have been an old book, but it has been the best-selling book in personal achievement.
- Learning to speak English may be easier than you think.
- Ken was born in May.

#96, down

- Sit down.
- Climb down.
- Fall down.
- Keep it down.
- Going down.
- The down escalator.
- Write down.
- A down payment.
- Walk down.

- Please sit down.
- Have you written down the VIN number of the car?
- Yes. I had it written down as I walked down the lot.
- How much down payment would you like to put down?
- I'll put down a $1000.

- Our finance department can help you keep the interest rate down.
- No. Thanks! I'll finance through my bank.

#97, side

- One side.
- The other side.
- Roadside
- Take a side.
- A side order.
- Both sides.

- No matter what decisions I make, my family always stands on my side.
- Having a supportive family on my side accelerates my success.
- In the UK, you drive on the left side of the road. In America, you drive on the right side.
- I'll take a house salad with the dressing on the side, please.
- The two sides agreed to start trading.

#98, been

Achtung: Been wird als bin oder ben betont anstatt been.

- Have been.
- Has been.

- How long have you been to the U.S.?
- Three years.
- How long have you been living in Canada?
- Two years.
- Your English is good! How long have you been

learning?
- I've been learning for three years.
- Where have you been lately?
- I have been visiting a friend in Canada.
- How have you been doing for the past three years?
- I have perfected my English!
- It has been a wonderful trip to Canada!
- Have you been there before?
- Yes. I've been there three times.

#99, now

- For now.
- From now on.
- Now is the time.

- If I start to practice my English now, I'll be speaking like a native six months from now.
- Now it's time to begin. Let's learn the first 100 words for now.
- I've been working here for three months now.
- It's been done. Now, what?
- Now let's relax.

#100, find

- Find it.
- Easy to find.

- Did you find the key?
- We need to find our way home.
- I turned around to find her smiling.
- We're on earth to find what we want. If we don't find what we want, make what we want!

Glückwunsch! Dies ist der letzte Zehner-Satz in Lektion Eins. Holen Sie sie sich.

- Rich is better than poor.
- Canada is a little bit bigger than America.
- America has a much bigger population than Canada.
- America has nine times more people than Canada.
- A gallon is heavier than a liter.
- I'll give you a call tonight.
- I'll call you tonight.
- Who made that phone call?
- Let's wrap it up and call it a day.
- My name is Yoon-Jin. My friends called me Jack.
- They called their daughter Katie.
- The U.S. is called a melting pot.
- What grade is your child in?
- He's in first grade.
- Have you seen snow before?
- No. This is my first time seeing snow.
- He's the first one to get there.
- My people have been working on this project since April.
- How many people signed up for the trip to Europe?
- Forty-six.
- There are 7.2 billion people in the world. Close to 90% have enough to eat.
- When looking at a photo, what do you look at first? The people or the background?
- I always look at the people first.
- May I use your pen?
- Yes. You may.
- ***Think and Grow Rich*** may have been an old book, but it has been the best-selling book in personal achievement.
- Learning to speak English may be easier than you think.

- Ken was born in May.
- Please sit down.
- Have you written down the VIN number of the car?
- Yes. I had it written down as I walked down the lot.
- How much down payment would you like to put down?
- I'll put down a $1000.
- Our finance department can help you keep the interest rate down.
- No. Thanks! I'll finance through my bank.
- No matter what decisions I make, my family always stands on my side.
- Having a supportive family on my side accelerates my success.
- In the UK, you drive on the left side of the road. In America, you drive on the right side.
- I'll take a house salad with the dressing on the side, please.
- The two sides agreed to start trading.
- How long have you been to the U.S.?
- Three years.
- How long have you been living in Canada?
- Two years.
- Your English is good! How long have you been learning?
- I've been learning for three years.
- Where have you been lately?
- I have been visiting a friend in Canada.
- How have you been doing for the past three years?
- I have perfected my English!
- It has been a wonderful trip to Canada!
- Have you been there before?
- Yes. I've been there three times.
- If I start to practice my English now, I'll be speaking like a native six months from now.
- Now it's time to begin. Let's learn the first 100 words

for now.
- I've been working here for three months now.
- It's been done. Now, what?
- Now let's relax.
- Did you find the key?
- We need to find our way home.
- I turned around to find her smiling.
- We're on earth to find what we want. If we don't find what we want, make what we want!

In the supermarket

Ein typischer Supermarkt ist in die folgenden zehn Abteilungen unterteilt. Jeder Satz zu zehn Wörtern ist auf eine dieser Abteilungen fokussiert.

1. The Produce Department (Achtung, es ist **Pro**duce Department)
2. The Floral Department
3. The Dairy Department
4. The Beverage Department
5. The General Supplies Department
6. The Pharmacy Department
7. The Health & Beauty Department
8. The Meat & Seafood Department
9. The Deli Department
10. The Bakery Department

Rank	Word	Rank	Word
101	any	126	name
102	new	127	very
103	work	128	through
104	part	129	just
105	take	130	form
106	get	131	much
107	place	132	great
108	made	133	think
109	live	134	say
110	where	135	help
111	after	136	low
112	back	137	line
113	little	138	before
114	only	139	turn
115	round	140	cause
116	man	141	same
117	year	142	mean
118	came	143	different
119	show	144	move
120	every	145	right
121	good	146	boy
122	me	147	old
123	give	148	too
124	our	149	does
125	under	150	tell

Rank	Word	Rank	Word
151	sentence	176	follow
152	set	177	act
153	three	178	why
154	want	179	ask
155	air	180	men
156	well	181	change
157	also	182	went
158	play	183	light
159	small	184	kind
160	end	185	off
161	put	186	need
162	home	187	house
163	read	188	picture
164	hand	189	try
165	port	190	us
166	large	191	again
167	spell	192	animal
168	add	193	point
169	even	194	mother
170	land	195	world
171	here	196	near
172	must	197	build
173	big	198	self
174	high	199	earth
175	such	200	father

Kapitel 17: 101 – 110, The Produce Department

Eingefügt 2/13/2017 von keywordsuggest.org

#101, any
Any wird wie eny betont. Es wird nicht wie Any betont. Es wird wie eny betont.

- Anyone.
- Anybody.
- Any time.
- Anything.
- Any choice.
- Any more.
- Any way.
- Any good.
- Any better.

- Does anyone have the time? It's 3:30.
- Do you have any potatoes?
- Yes, there are some potatoes left over there.
- I don't have any choice except to win.

- Anybody can do anything if they have a burning desire.
- This supermarket was unknown to any when it was first opened, but it's well known today to everyone in the neighborhood.
- He said his English isn't any better.
- Putting out a fire with gasoline isn't going to do any good.

#102, new

- New look.
- New life.
- New moon.
- New world.
- New book.
- New language.
- New York.
- Brand new.
- Something new.
- New potatoes.
- New to America.

- When I came to America, the English language was a new language to me.
- After listening to **The Strangest Secret**, I became a new person.
- The supermarket had a new look, so she went in and bought some new potatoes.
- Seeking for a new life, she bought her new car in New York.
- I was trying to look for new strategies to learn to speak English before I discovered what I needed was so simple and obvious.
- The local supermarket is hiring new assistants for its produce department.

- This supermarket is selling new potatoes this year.

#103, work

- Homework.
- Housework.
- After work.
- Good work!
- The complete works.
- Work from home.
- Work out.
- Work on.
- Work in progress.

- Fresh produce is from the hard work of farmers.
- "Heads up, guys. We've got work to do."
- School assignments to complete at home is your homework.
- Preparation before a job interview is also your homework.
- There are three ways to find work: wait for work opportunities, look for work opportunities, and create work opportunities. Creating work opportunities works better than the other two combined and then times 100.
- Where do you work? I work at Key Food.
- What do you do?
- I work as an assistant in the produce department.
- Work on something two hours a day every day for 20 years and you'll be the best in that area.
- Working from home is becoming more and more popular.
- How does it work?
- You get your work assignments from your company's website and work on them at home.

#104, part

- One Part.
- Two parts.
- Part one.
- Part two.
- Part of the family.
- Part of the store.
- Part of a movie.
- Parted.
- Depart.
- Department.

- Do your part and you'll be okay.
- My local supermarket has 10 departments.
- I work in the produce department.
- Part of my job is to make things look nice.

#105, take

Heute: take
Gestern: took
Länger her: taken

- Take care.
- Take out.
- Take on.
- Take up.
- Take along.
- Take over.
- Take place.
- Take it easy.
- Take a picture.
- Take two from six.

- Take blood pressure.
- Take notes.

- It'll just take five minutes to get to the supermarket. Just take I-90 West for three miles and take the exit on the right. I'll take you there.
- It takes time to do grocery shopping. I always take along a shopping list and quickly grab the things on the list. It takes half of the time to do shopping this way.
- I'll take your advice.

#106, get

Heute: get
Gestern: got
Länger her: gotten

- Get in.
- Get out.
- Get on.
- Get off.
- Get up.
- Get down.
- Get back.
- Get done.
- Get to.
- Get along.
- Get over.

- Let's get some lettuce and tomatoes to make our sandwiches.
- What do you mean? I didn't get you.
- For our potluck party tomorrow. We've got to bring something. I'm good at making sandwiches, so let's get some lettuce and tomatoes.

- Good idea! I've gotten into a habit of eating green vegetables and I'm getting healthier and healthier. Let's make some veggie sandwiches.
- This is just what I'm thinking about! Let's get in line.

#107, place

- In place.
- Take place.
- A place.
- Birthplace.
- My place.
- First place.
- To place.

- They place cucumbers and corns together.
- QFC is a good place for quality produce.
- The supermarket won first place in food quality and customer service.
- A 17-year-old high school student was offered a place in the produce department.

#108, made
Heute: make
Gestern: made
Länger her: made

- Made up.
- Made friends.
- Made sense.
- Made out.
- Made sure.
- Made money.
- Made a living.

- We made it!
- I made it on time to the movie and made a new friend today at work.
- I make money by working in the produce department of my local supermarket.
- It's easy to make a living in America.

#109, live

- Live in.
- Live on.
- Live for.
- Live up.
- Live with.
- To live.

- How long do turtles live? Turtles live for 150 years.
- Charles Darwin of England lived 200 years ago.
- Everyone in this neighborhood lives in harmony.
- Farmers in this neighborhood live by growing fresh produce.
- Galileo died 400 years ago, but his name lived on.
- A regular customer who lives in the neighborhood eats only vegetables and lives a healthy life.
- She said she's lived here all her life.

#110, where

- Where to?
- Where at?
- Where is?
- From where?
- To where?

- Where are alfalfa sprouts? The corner where the bean sprouts are.
- Where did you find that? I found this at that corner.
- Where do you live? I live around the corner.
- This is where I live.
- Where there's a will there's a way.

Lassen Sie uns nun diese 10 Wörter anwenden!

- Where do you live?
- I live around the corner. This is where I live.
- This is a very nice neighborhood.
- Yes, indeed. Everyone in this neighborhood lives in harmony.
- Where do you work?
- I work at QFC.
- QFC?
- Quality Foods Center.
- Is it your local supermarket?
- Yes. There two supermarkets in my neighborhood: Safeway and QFC.
- I also work at my local supermarket. It's Key Food. What do you do?
- An assistant in the produce department.
- What a coincidence! I also work in the produce department.
- The supermarket was unknown to any when it was first opened, but it's well known to everyone today in the neighborhood.
- It must have been doing a good job.
- Yes. It's a good place for quality produce. It won first place in food quality and customer service of the region last year.
- Nice! Farmers in my area live by growing fresh produce.
- My supermarket is selling new potatoes this year.
- Potatoes and yams are placed next to each in my store. I like to make them look nice.
- My manager is really nice.
- So is mine. He said if I'd just do my part, and I'd be okay.
- After listening to The Strangest Secret, I became a new person.
- You've listened to that, too?

- Yeah! You've listened to that, too?
- Yeah! Earl Nightingale said, "Don't just do your part. Do more than you're paid to do."
- Exactly! After I've been doing more than I'm paid to do, I was voted Employee of the Month!
- Hey, congratulations!
- Thanks!
- You know what? Me, too.
- Ha! Ha! We hold daily huddles in the morning, and the store manager always says, "There are three ways to earn a promotion: wait for a promotion opportunity, look for a promotion opportunity, and create a promotion opportunity. Creating a promotion opportunity works better than the other two combined and then times 1000."
- Yeah! When it's time for a promotion, we are next in line!

Englisch: Lernen Sie Englischsprechen wie ein Einheimischer in nur einem Kurs

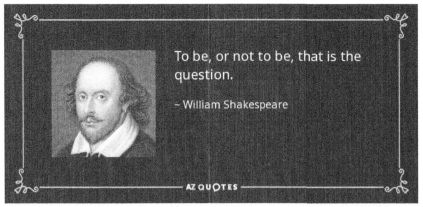

Eingefügt 1/29/2017 von http://www.azquotes.com/quote/267345.

Kapitel 18: 111 – 120, The Floral Department

#111, after

- After work.
- After school.
- After a while.
- After you.
- After all.
- Time after time.
- Day after day.
- The day after tomorrow.
- Go after.

- I bought two roses at the floral department after work.
- She always drinks a cup of tea after dinner.
- After a while, you get used to it.
- The floral department brings in fresh flowers day after day.
- Clean up after your dog. It's the law.
- They named the baby Charlie, after his grandfather.

#112, back

- Come back.
- Go back.
- Get back.
- Call back.
- Bring back.
- Sit back.
- Write back.
- Be right back.
- Got your back.
- Front or back?

- Lay on your back.
- Just go for it. I got your back.
- Is the floral department in the front or in the back?
- Floral is in the front. Dairy is in the back.
- The floral department has the local farmers backing it.
- This store started selling carnations back in the 90's.
- After three weeks, carnations are back in the store.
- I took some carnations after putting the roses back.
- If you'll be back in five minutes, your flowers will be ready.
- OK. I'll be back in five minutes.

#113, little

- Little flowers.
- Little bushes.
- Little one.
- Little bit.
- Little help.

- This plant will grow into a little bush.
- This plant will have little flowers.
- When I was little, I often played with my little brother.
- Shop for a little for some flower plants.
- There is a little problem. They sold out of rose plants.
- I got a little help from the florist. She found me some rose seeds.
- These giant blackberry plants were little known to local residents.
- The florist told me a little of the giant blackberries.

#114, only

- Only one.
- The only one.
- The one and only.
- Only if.
- If only.
- Not only.
- Only child.

- There are only five roses left.
- Flower sell in the winter has only declined by five percent.
- If you buy them by the bunch, roses are only a dollar each.
- We started selling jasmine plants only this year.
- She returned to get the last rose only to find that it was taken.
- The only lily in the store is waterlily.
- This supermarket is the only floral shop in town.

#115, round

- A round table.
- A round flower pot.
- Round One.
- Round Two.
- Round up.
- Round off.
- Round trip.

- Irises are on that round table.

- They're planted on round flower pots.
- I did two rounds of shopping today, a round for flowers and a round for plants.
- The first round of delivery was in early March.
- The florist's job is a daily round of helping customers and wrapping flowers.
- The New Horizon rounded the earth and sailed to Pluto.
- I was going to need nine irises, but I rounded it up to 10.
- I thought irises were only blue, but when the florist showed me some red irises, my eyes rounded in surprise.

#116, man

Eins → man
Zwei oder mehr → men

- A man.
- One man.
- Two men.
- Young man.
- Wise man.
- Man of his word.
- Man of the house.
- Man the station.

- A young man recently joined the floral department.
- The floral department is a three-man team.
- The man of the shop is a Harvard man.
- He always mans his station professionally.

#117, year

- This year.
- Last year.
- Every year.
- The year of 2018.
- Year after year.

- An Earth year is 365 days.
- A Martian year is 687 days.
- A Pluto year is 90,520 days.
- This plant is going to take years to grow.

#118, came

Heute → come
Gestern → came
Länger her → come

- Come on.
- Came down.
- Came in.
- Came out.
- Came to.
- Came back.
- Came from.
- Came over.
- Came into.
- Came with.

- I didn't speak any English when I came to America, but now I speak English like a native.
- Would you like to go to lunch with us?
- No, I just came from lunch.
- The sunflowers came in yesterday. Daisies will come

in today.
- They came and left.
- Two customers came into the store and bought all of our roses.
- The daisy baskets came with gift wraps.

#119, show

- A show.
- Show up.
- Show off.
- To show.
- Show to.

- The floral department had a flower show yesterday.
- Carnations were a big show-off.
- This is your show! Read out loud to show the class that you now can speak English like a native.
- The smart florist shows his work to his boss by decorating the floral department with colorful plants.
- The assistant showed the customer how to plant the bush.

#120, every

- Everyone.
- Every time.
- Every day.
- Everything.
- Everywhere.
- Everyone agrees.

- This store shows respect to each and every one of its customers every day.
- Every time I come, I see smiley faces.
- Everything in this store is fresh.
- There are supermarkets everywhere but I just like to come to this one. Everyone in the store is helpful and everything in the store is fresh.

Lassen Sie uns die zehn Wörter verwenden.

- Is the floral department in the front or back?
- It's in the back.
- This supermarket is the only floral shop in the neighborhood.
- The floral department has the local farmers backing it.
- The floral department brings in fresh flowers day after day.
- I was thinking to buy five roses after work.
- There were only three roses left.
- If you bought them by the bunch, roses were only a dollar each.
- Carnations were back in the store.
- This store started selling carnations back in the 90's.
- I took some carnations after putting the roses back.
- I returned to get the last roses only to find that they were taken.
- Two customers came in and bought all of the roses.
- The store started selling jasmine plants only this year.
- I was going to need nine irises, but I rounded it up to 10.
- I thought irises were only blue, but when the florist showed me some red irises, my eyes rounded in surprise.
- The sunflowers came in yesterday. Daisies will come in today.
- The daisy baskets came with gift wraps.
- The floral department just had a flower show yesterday.
- Carnations were a big show-off.
- The smart florist showed his work to his boss by decorating the floral department with colorful plants.
- I shopped for a little for some flower plants.
- There was a little problem. They sold out of rose plants.
- I got a little help from the florist. She found me some

rose seeds.
- The rose seeds would take some years to grow. It would have little flowers and would grow into little bushes.
- The assistant showed me how to plant the seeds.
- There were giant blackberry plants which were little known to local residents.
- The florist told me a little of the giant blackberries.
- "If you'll be back in five minutes," said the florist, "your flowers will be ready."
- "OK." I said, "I'll be back in five minutes."

> **Take small steps every day and you'll get there one day.**
> Anonymous

Kapitel 19: 121 – 130, The Dairy Department

#121, good

- A good thing.
- A good brand.
- Good or bad?
- For your own good.
- Storage area for goods.
- A good day.
- A good time.
- Good for 12 days.
- Good to go.

- Is it a good thing or a bad thing to drink milk?
- It's a good thing.
- Drink milk for your own good.
- What's a good brand?
- The milk here is good.
- It's good for 12 days.
- Please keep the goods storage area locked.
- Today is a good day to practice your English pronunciation.
- Practice every day and your English will be.
- You've been practicing for a good hour. You're looking good. Have a good time.
- You've already paid for that. You're good to go. Thank you for your business.

#122, me

- For me.
- Help me.
- It's me.
- Got me something.

- I got two chocolate milk. One for you and one for me.
- Here is your whole milk. I got me a skim milk.
- Could you help me with this?
- Who is it? It's me.

#123, give
Heute → give
Gestern → gave
Länger her → given

- Give and take.
- Give it a try.
- Give 100% and see what you'll get in return.
- Give me the police!
- Gave a relief.
- Give his name.
- Give in.
- Give up.
- Give out.
- Give off.
- give away.

- These stores are open for business. There is no give and take there.
- Milk or water? Give him milk, please.
- His parents didn't give the encouragement he needed to start his business.
- Give it a try and see what happens.
- Give 100% and you'll be surprised what you'll get in return.
- Successful people give. Unsuccessful people take.
- Give me the police!
- When the police arrived, she gave a relief.
- What was his name? He didn't give his name. He was tall and slender.
- When your children ask for soda instead of milk, do

not give in. Milk is good for them. Soda is bad for them.

#124, our

- Our customer.
- Our dairy department.
- Our body.
- Our promotion.
- Our brain.
- Our friend.
- Our own.

- Congratulations! You're our 100th customer today. You'll receive our free promotional item and a $100 gift card today. The gift card is good for anything in our dairy department.
- Our body contains mostly water.
- When we drink something, our brain quickly tells us the taste.

#125, under

Das u in under wird als uh betont. Es wird NICHT als ah betont, Ahn der. Es wird als Uhn der betont.

- Under way.
- Under consideration.
- Under review.
- Under the bridge.
- Under construction.
- Under pressure.
- Under 2%.
- Under contract.

- There is a creek under the bridge.
- The dairy department is under construction.
- The dairy department is under pressure for its delayed construction.
- Choose from whole milk, low-fat milk, and skim milk. Low-fat milk has 2% or under 2% fat. Skim milk has no fat.
- The milk and dairy products are supplied under contract by local farmers.

#126, name

Lassen Sie uns versuchen es von hinten zu betonen. M, A----me, Na----me. Das a wird als /A/ betont. Name. Es wird nicht als nem betont. Es wird als name betont. /N a-------me/.

- First name.
- Last name.
- Middle name.
- Full name.
- User name.
- A big name.
- Gain a name.
- Name the baby.

- What's your name?
- My name is _____.
- Dairy Queen is a big name.
- This is a big event. It'll lure the big names.
- iPhone gained a name for innovation.
- Have you named the baby yet?
- Have you given the baby a name yet?
- Donald was named Employee of the Month for excellent performance.

#127, very

Um das v in very zu betonen, beißen Sie sich sanft mit Ihren oberen Schneidezähnen auf die Unterlippe. Drücken Sie dann Luft heraus um den Klang zu betonen. Denken Sie daran, Ihre Unterlippe muss die oberen Schneidezähne berühren. Runden Sie die Lippen NICHT ab. Berühren Sie ausschließlich mit den oberen Schneidezähnen Ihre Unterlippe und pressen Sie die Luft zum Betonen des Klangs heraus. /V/, very. /V/, very.

- Very good.
- Very well.
- Very nice.
- Very funny
- Very much.
- Very important.
- Very easy.
- The very best.
- Very words.
- Very beginning.
- The very thought.

- Thank you very much.
- It's very important to drink a lot of fluid every day.
- It's very easy to forget about it.
- This milk is whole milk, fresh, and natural. It's the very best quality we have.
- These are the very words from our customers.
- Read the book from the very beginning.
- The very thought of killing small animals in his childhood life made him feel guilty.

#128, through

Es gibt hier keine Vibration im th. /TH/.

- Go through.

- Pass through.
- Come through.
- Look through.
- See through.
- Breakthrough.
- Walk through.
- Put through.
- Through traffic.

- The customer came in through the left door.
- Anthony Robbins teaches his students to walk through fire without getting hurt.
- Walk through the crowd to stand out.
- The heat is streaming through the window.
- Pass through Aisle 9 and the dairy department is at the end.
- We've finally gone through the busy hours.
- The dairy department is offering a discount from Monday through Friday. I heard it through a friend.
- Phone call for the dairy department. I'm putting it through.
- This street is under construction. No through traffic.

#129, just

- Just right.
- Just then.
- Just now.
- Just as.
- Just in case.
- Just in time.
- Just because.
- Just and fair.

- I just found it. This is just the right one.
- He was just here a moment ago.
- You came at just the right moment. These are on sale just now.
- They're just $1.99.
- How many would you like? Just one.
- America is a just and free society.

#130, form

- Form a company.
- Form a group.
- Form a habit.
- Into a form.
- Application form.
- Registration form.

- This company was formed in 1872.
- Three successful University of Washington students formed the Success Impact Group.
- Parents form the minds of their children. Your children will form good habits if unspoiled.
- Put the mixture into a form and let it dry.
- Water can exist in the forms of liquid, solid, and gas.
- We're hiring. Fill out an application form to join us.

Now, let's get them.

- The dairy department is offering a discount from Monday through Friday. I heard it through a friend.
- Where is the dairy department?
- Pass through Aisle 9 and the dairy department is at the end.
- Milk or water? Milk, please.
- Is it a good thing or a bad thing to drink milk?
- It's a good thing.
- Drink milk for your own good.
- What's a good brand?
- Dairy Queen is a big name.
- The milk here is good.
- It's good for 12 days.
- This milk is whole milk, fresh, and natural. It's the very best quality they have here.
- When is a good time to drink milk?
- Just like when is a good day to practice your English, today is a good day to drink milk.
- Could you help me to find a good one?
- I got two chocolate milk. One for you and one for me.
- Here is whole milk for you. I got me skim milk.
- When we drink something, our brain quickly tells us the taste.

- His parents didn't give the encouragement he needed to start his business.
- Give it a try and see what happens.
- Give 100% and you'll be surprised what you'll get in return.
- Successful people give. Unsuccessful people take.
- Give me the police!
- When the police arrived, she gave a relief.
- What was his name? He didn't give his name. He was tall and slender.

- When your children ask for soda instead of milk, do not give in. Milk is good for them. Soda is bad for them.
- Congratulations! You're our 100th customer today. You'll receive our free promotional item and a $100 gift card today. The gift card is good for anything in our dairy department.
- There is a creek under the bridge.
- The dairy department is under construction.
- The dairy department is under pressure for its delayed construction.
- Choose from whole milk, low-fat milk, and skim milk. Low-fat milk has 2% or under 2% fat. Skim milk has no fat.
- The milk and dairy products are supplied under contract by local farmers.
- This is a big event. It'll lure the big names.
- iPhone gained a name for innovation.
- Have you named the baby yet?
- Have you given the baby a name yet?
- Donald was named Employee of the Month for excellent performance.
- Thank you very much.
- It's very important to drink a lot of fluid every day.
- It's very easy to forget about it.
- These are the very words from the customers.
- Read the book from the very beginning.
- The customer came in through the left door.
- Anthony Robbins teaches his students to walk through fire without getting hurt.
- Walk through the crowd to stand out.
- The heat is streaming through the window.
- We've finally gone through the busy hours.
- Phone call for the dairy department. I'm putting it through.
- This street is under construction. No through traffic.
- I just found it. This is just the right one.

- He was just here a moment ago.
- You came at just the right moment. These are on sale just now.
- They're just $1.99.
- How many would you like? Just one.
- America is a just and free society.
- This company was formed in 1872.
- Three successful University of Washington students formed the Success Impact Group.
- Parents form the minds of their children.
- Put the mixture into a form and let it dry.
- Our body contains mostly water.
- Water can exist in the forms of liquid, solid, and gas.
- We're hiring. Fill out an application form to join us.
- You've been practicing for a good hour. You're looking good. Have a good time.
- You've already paid for that. You're good to go. Thank you for your business.

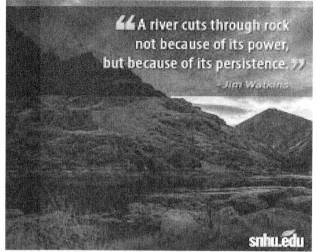

Retrieved 1/29/2017 from snhu.edu

Kapitel 20: 131 – 140, The Beverage Department

Eingefügt 2/13/2017 von tradefairny.com

#131, much

- Very much.
- So much.
- Too much.
- How much.
- Nothing much.
- As much.

- Thank you very much.
- Thank you so much.
- How much water should I drink a day?
- Eight glasses.
- Isn't it too much?
- No. That's just the minimum. Drink as much as you can after eight glasses.
- I had so much fun yesterday drinking Merlot. Would you join me today?
- I'm not much of a drinker. But thank you, though.
- Looks like you didn't get much sleep yesterday.
- Right! I partied overnight.

#132, great

- Great job!
- Great work!
- Great people.
- A great year.
- A great day.
- A great thing.

- Great job, guys! Keep up the good work!
- This has been a great year for the store.

- Have a great day.
- One of the great things about drinking water is it maintains your bodily fluid.
- This article about drinking water and avoiding coffee is of great interest.

#133, think

Heute → think
Gestern → thought
Länger her → thought

- Think about.
- Think of.
- Think like.
- Think over.
- Think twice.
- I think so.

- I'm just thinking about going to buy a case of bottled water.
- Are you thinking about spring water or purified water?
- Purified water. It's pure and much cheaper than spring water.
- I've thought about the same thing, too. A friend introduced to me to use a water filter. It's much cheaper than buying bottled water.
- I think that's a good idea! I've never thought of using a water filter. Where did you buy it?
- Home Depot.
- I'm thinking of saving money and eliminating plastics.
- You think like a winner!
- I can think of one more thing: saving a trip to the supermarket.

#134, say
Heute → say
Gestern → said
Länger her → said

- I say.
- You say.
- Have a say.
- Say hello.
- Say nothing.
- Say again.

- A Cola salesperson will have her say about the benefits of drinking soda.
- A wine salesperson will have his say about the benefits of drinking alcohol.
- A doctor will have his say about the benefits of drinking water.
- He said alcohol. I said soda. What do you say?
- I don't want to say too much. Doctors say water is good for us. I say water.
- What does the clock say?
- The clock says eight thirty.
- Let's say we leave at nine. We'll be there by noon.

#135, help

- Need help.
- Good help.
- Helper.
- Help out.
- Help yourself.
- Helpdesk.

- Do you need help?

- Yes. That would be great!
- That was a good help! Thanks.
- I run a corner store. She's my helper.
- Let me help you with this.
- Let me help you out.
- Speaking English like a native helped my confidence.
- Help yourself with the drinks.
- He's an alcoholic. He can't help drinking.

#136, low

- Low tone.
- Low point.
- Low ground.
- Low cost.
- Low fat.
- Low profile

- She spoke in a low tone.
- She bent down low to look at the ants.
- The supermarket is built on a low ground.
- The moon is low in the sky, but the tide is high on the shore.
- The highs and lows of the stock market.
- A low-income family in a high-income neighborhood.
- We're low on food. Let's go shop for grocery.
- These drinks are high in calories, and these are drinks that are low in calories.

#137, line

- Line up.

- Line out.
- Straight line.
- Country line.
- Line 1.
- Line 2.
- On the line.
- The line of work.
- Assembly line.

- If the police think you're drunk, they will ask you to walk in a straight line.
- The borderline between the U.S. and Canada.
- The equator is an invisible line.
- "There's a call for the beverage department on Line 2."
- "George, it's Bill on the line. Line 1."
- This is one of Amazon's shipping lines.
- We use a Ford production line.
- My line is production. (My line of work is production.)
- Each page has 25 lines.
- The line is that there will be no arguments with customers.
- Line up, guys! Let's form a straight line here. Please wait in line.

#138, before
Es ist vollkommen in Ordnung beefore zu sagen. Normalerweise konzentrieren wir uns auf "fore"und "be" klingt einfach wie der Klang von "b." Das ganze Wort wird zu "bfore".

- Before this.
- Before that.
- Before now.
- Before you.

- Before long.
- Before bed.
- The day before yesterday.
- Before or after.

- We can meet before lunch.
- I'm sorry. I can't make it before lunch. Can we meet before dinner?
- Keep your goal before you and keep working on it.
- Sorry, madam. I need to help him first. He was here before you.

#139, turn

- Turn on.
- Turn off.
- Turn in.
- Turn out.
- Turn up.
- Turn down.
- Turn left.
- Turn right.
- Turn around.
- Turn over.

- Should we take turns to take a break?
- Is it your turn or my turn?
- It's your turn.
- Turn left or turn right?
- Turn right. Then make a U-turn.
- Turn right then make a U-turn! That means turn left now!
- You're right, but if you turn left now, you'll need to wait three minutes to make the left turn. You can turn right now and then make a U-turn right away. It'll only take

about 10 seconds.
- My son just turned nine. How old is your son?
- He's nine. Ten! He just turned.
- Turn to page 20.
- She turned her attention to me.
- After years of working as a computer engineer, I turned to teaching English.
- Turn it over!
- Turn what over?
- The rocks. Many good things are hidden under rocks.
- Rob's face turned red.

#140, cause

- The cause.
- Main cause.
- To cause.
- Cause and effect.

- The cause was easy to identify.
- The cause of the accident was alcohol.
- Driving after drinking can easily cause accidents.

Verwenden wir sie im Kontext.

- How much water should I drink a day?
- Eight glasses.
- Isn't it too much?
- No. That's just the minimum. Drink as much as you can after eight glasses.
- Thank you very much.
- I had so much fun yesterday drinking Merlot. Would you join me today?
- No, thanks. I'm not much of a drinker. But thank you, though.
- Looks like you didn't get much sleep yesterday.
- Right! I partied overnight.
- This has been a great year for the store. We should celebrate.
- Do you need help?
- Yes. That would be great!
- Let me help you with this.
- That was a good help! Thanks.
- Have a great day.

- One of the great things about drinking water is it maintains your bodily fluid.
- This article about drinking water and avoiding coffee is of great interest.
- I'm just thinking about going to buy a case of bottled water.
- Are you thinking about spring water or purified water?
- Purified water. It's pure and much cheaper than spring water.
- I've thought about the same thing, too. A friend introduced to me to use a water filter. It's much cheaper than buying bottled water.
- I think that's a good idea! I've never thought of using a water filter. Where did you buy it?
- Home Depot.

- I'm thinking of saving money and eliminating plastics.
- You think like a winner!
- I can think of one more thing: saving a trip to the supermarket.
- A Cola salesperson will have her say about the benefits of drinking soda.
- A wine salesperson will have his say about the benefits of drinking alcohol.
- A doctor will have his say about the benefits of drinking water.
- He said alcohol. I said soda. What do you say?
- I don't want to say too much. Doctors say water is good for us. I say water.

- What does the clock say?
- The clock says eight thirty.
- Let's say we leave at nine. We'll be there by noon.
- Help yourself with the drinks.
- Nice drink. I can't help but drink it.
- These drinks are high in calories, and those are drinks that are low in calories.
- Should we take turns to drive?
- Is it your turn or my turn?
- It's your turn.
- There was an accident yesterday. The cause was easy to identify.
- The cause of the accident was alcohol.
- Driving after drinking can easily cause accidents.
- If the police think you're drunk, they will ask you to walk in a straight line.
- Thank goodness what you have here is not alcohol, or I would have to take a sip.
- Turn left or turn right?
- Turn right. Then make a U-turn.
- Turn right then make a U-turn! That means turn left now!

- You're right, but if you turn left now, you'll need to wait three minutes to make the left turn. You can turn right now and then make a U-turn right away. It'll only take you 10 seconds.

- She spoke in a low tone. She bent down low to look at the floor.
- The supermarket is built on a low ground, and occasionally, rain does find its way in.
- The moon is low in the sky, but the tide is high on the shore.
- The highs and lows of the stock market.
- A low-income family in a high-income neighborhood.
- We're low on food. Let's go shop for grocery.
- The borderline between the U.S. and Canada.
- The equator is an invisible line.
- "There's a call for the beverage department on Line 2."
- "George, it's Bill on the line. Line 1."
- This is one of Amazon's shipping lines.
- We use a Ford production line.
- My line is production. (My line of work is production.)
- Each page has 25 lines.
- The line is that there will be no arguments with customers.
- Line up, guys! Let's form a straight line here. Please wait in line.
- Let's meet before lunch.
- I'm sorry. I can't make it before lunch. Can we meet before dinner?
- Keep your goal before you and keep working it.
- Sorry, madam. I need to help him first. He was here before you.

- My son just turned nine. How old is your son?
- He's nine. Ten! He just turned.
- Turn to page 20.

- She turned her attention to me.
- After years of working as a computer engineer, I turned to teaching English.
- Turn it over!
- Turn what over?
- The rocks. Many good things are hidden under rocks.
- Rob's face turned red.
- Speaking English like a native helped my confidence.

Eingefügt 1/29/2017 von
http://www.azquotes.com/quotes/topics/persistence.html

Kapitel 21: 141 – 150, The General Supplies Department

Eingefügt 2/13/2017 von thebalance.com

#141, same

- Same thing.
- Same time.
- The same.
- Same as.
- Same here.
- Same to you.

- I'll do the same.
- I'll get the same thing.
- It's all the same.
- A customer has been shopping in the same place ever since she moved here.
- She moved here the same year I started to work here.
- The customer has been buying the same things over and over for the past 10 years.
- Treating children the same as adults will build their independence.

#142, mean

- The mean
- A mean person.
- A mean place.
- Meaning.
- In the meantime

- The mean of 3, 7, and 8 is 6.
- To find the mean, add the three numbers and divide it by three.
- The mean of 1, 2, 4, and 5 is 3.
- Seattle's mean summer temperature is 76 degrees F.
- She's so mean. She never shares her erasers with anybody.

- That must be because she came from a mean neighborhood.
- What's the meaning of being mean?
- The meaning of being mean is not generous.
- That's so hot, Jen!
- What do you mean?
- I mean the weather is hot today.
- Finish your homework and you'll earn your iPad back.
- Do you mean it?
- Of course, I mean it! I didn't mean to take your iPad. You were meant to finish your homework yesterday. I took your iPad so you can finish your homework. The iPad is meant for your use after you finish your homework. Finishing your homework means a lot to you.

#143, different

- Different time.
- Different ways.
- Different things.
- Different kind.
- Different from.
- Different than.

- Is it the same or different?
- Try something different.
- I've tried bleaching the cloth two different times and the stains just wouldn't go away.
- Try a different brand.
- This baking soda can be used in two different ways.

#144, move

- A different move.
- Make a move.
- Move from.
- Move to.
- Move on.
- Move up.
- Move in.
- Move out.
- Move along.
- Move forward.
- Move away.

- Moving from Virginia Beach to Seattle during a recession was a bold move.
- He just moved recently.
- My passion for space moved me to major in space studies.
- My first move is to do a market research. My second move is to write a plan. My next move is to take actions.
- The research tells me to move quickly with the plan.
- Detergent is a fast-moving item.
- Detergents are moving so fast that I often need to ask them for more.
- That is a touching story. I'm moved.

#145, right

- Left or right.
- Right or wrong?
- Right on.
- Right off.

- Right here.
- Right now.
- Right away.
- All right.
- Be right back.
- Copyright.
- Human right.

- Turn left or turn right?
- Turn right. Then make a U-turn.
- Turn right then make a U-turn! That means turn left now!
- You're right, but if you turn left now, you'll need to wait three minutes to make the left turn. You can turn right now and then make a U-turn right away. It'll only take you 10 seconds.
- Right on! We're on the right track.
- Is it right or wrong to send a birthday gift without a birthday card?
- There is no right or wrong to send a gift without a card. It's just better to send it with a card.
- You are right! I'll be right back.
- She's the right person to do the laundry.
- You got it right. This is the right answer.
- I hold the copyrights to this book. I sold the digital rights to Amazon and kept the audio rights and print rights. I have every right to sell the rights.
- Right. You're right on time!

#146, boy

- A boy.
- A baby boy.
- A little boy.

- Good boy.
- A boy's play.
- My boy (my son).
- A delivery boy.
- A country boy.
- Boy!

- A boy or a girl?
- A boy's play is very different than a girl's play.
- My boy is nine years old.
- The delivery boy just passed by.
- I am a country boy, but even a country boy can be highly successful. Can you be successful?
- Boy! That's a lot of work we've just finished.

#147, old

- Young and old.
- Old age.
- Old system.
- Old job.
- Old friend.
- Old days.
- Old times.
- How old are you?

- A young man standing in front of an old building.
- This young man always buys an old brand of dishwasher liquid.
- She washes her child's old clothes and gives them away.
- "Who said I'm old? I'm just 97!"
- "I may be 97 years old, but my heart is just 20."

- Successful people will tell you that you're never too young or too old to get started.
- The success formula is an old formula that worked in the old days and works today.
- Trying to get your old job back? Why not start your own business?

#148, too

- Too much.
- Too young.
- Too many.
- Too long.
- Too busy.
- Too far.
- Too expensive.
- Too late.
- Too good.
- Me too.

- Too little or too much information may not help you.
- Making decisions based on too little information is too risky.
- Successful people will tell you that you're never too young or too old to get started.
- He's a successful person, too.
- This is cane sugar, too.

#149, does

Ich, Du / Sie, sie (plural) → do
Er, sie (weiblich), es → does

Heute → do, does
Gestern → did
Länger her → done

- I do.
- He does.
- They do.
- She does.
- Doesn't matter.

- Do you have any napkins?
- Yes, I do.
- Does he have any napkins?
- Yes, he does.
- You do want to go there, don't you?
- A repair to the tire must be done before noon to deliver on time.
- Mom always does the cooking for breakfast.
- I always do the cooking for lunch.
- Dad always does the cooking for dinner.
- What do you do?
- I teach English.
- What does he do?
- He runs a grocery store.

#150, tell

Heute → tell
Gestern → told
Länger her – told

- Tell it.
- Can tell.
- Tell off.
- Tell about.
- Tell a story.
- Tell the truth.

- Tell a story.

- He just told a story.
- Did he tell the truth?
- Yes, he told the truth.
- A picture tells the truth.
- Can you tell me your plan?

Verwenden wir nun diese zehn Wörter.

- The mean of 3, 7, and 8 is 6.
- To find the mean, add the three numbers and divide it by three.
- The mean of 1, 2, 4, and 5 is 3.
- Seattle's mean summer temperature is 76 degrees F.
- She's so mean. She never shares her erasers with anybody.
- That must be because she came from a mean neighborhood.
- She's living in one of the best neighborhoods now. She will change her mean behavior.
- What's the meaning of being mean?
- What do you mean?
- I mean the weather is so hot today.
- Finish your homework and you'll earn your iPad back.
- Do you mean it?
- Of course, I mean it! I didn't mean to take your iPad. You were meant to finish your homework yesterday. I took your iPad so you can finish your homework. The iPad is meant for your use after you finish your homework. Finishing your homework means a lot to you.

- Is it the same or different?
- It's all the same.
- I'll do the same.
- Try something different.
- I've tried bleaching the cloth two different times and the stains just wouldn't go away.
- This baking soda can be used in two different ways.
- Try a different brand.
- I'll get the same thing.
- A customer has been shopping in the same place ever since she moved here.
- She moved here the same year I started to work here.

- The customer has been buying the same things over and over for the past 10 years.
- Treating children the same as adults will build their independence.

- He just moved recently.
- His recent move was just a move to three blocks away.
- My passion for space moved me to major in space studies.
- My first move is to do a market research. My second move is to write a plan. My next move is to take actions.
- The research tells me to move quickly with the plan.
- Detergent is a fast-moving item.
- Detergents are moving so fast that I often need to ask them for more.
- That is a touching story. I'm moved.
- Turn left or turn right?
- Turn right. Then make a U-turn.
- Turn right then make a U-turn! That means turn left now!
- You're right, but if you turn left now, you'll need to wait three minutes to make the left turn. You can turn right now and then make a U-turn right away. It'll only take you 10 seconds.
- Is it right or wrong to send a birthday gift without a birthday card?
- There is no right or wrong to send a gift without a card.
- You are right!
- You got it right.
- That is the right answer.
- I hold the copyright to my books. I sold the digital rights to Amazon and kept the audio rights and paperback rights. I have every right to sell the rights.
- You're right on time!

- He ran right off the track.
- I'll be right back.
- A boy or a girl?
- A boy's play is different than a girl's play.
- My boy is nine years old.
- The delivery boy just passed by.
- I am a country boy, but even a country boy can be highly successful. Can you be successful?
- Boy! That's going to take a lot of work to be successful!
- If you want it strong enough, nothing can stop you from getting it!

- A young man standing in front of an old building always buys an old brand of dishwasher liquid.
- "Who said I'm old? I'm just 97!"
- "I may be 97 years old, but my heart is just 20. That's why I'm a young man"
- Moving from Virginia Beach to Seattle during a recession was a bold move. It was a big decision to make.
- Trying to get your old job back? Why not start your own business? Successful people will tell you you're never too young or too old to get started.
- Follow your heart and keep working. Too little or too much information may not help you. The success formula is an old formula that worked 3000 years ago and works today.
- Follow the success formula, and you can be a successful person, too.

- This is cane sugar, too.
- Do you have any napkins?
- Yes, I do.
- Does he have any napkins?
- Yes, he does.
- You do want to go there, don't you? A repair to the tire

- must be done before noon to deliver on time.
- Mom always does the cooking for breakfast. I always do the cooking for lunch. Dad always does the cooking for dinner.
- What do you do?
- I teach English.
- What does he do?
- He runs a grocery store.
- Tell a story.
- He just told a story.
- Did he tell the truth?
- Yes, he told the truth.
- A picture tells the truth.
- Please tell him to bring the picture.
- Can you tell me your plan?
- Yes, you can tell by just looking at it.
- She's the right person to do the job.

Eingefügt 1/29/2017 von picturequotes.com.

Kapitel 22: 151 – 160, The Pharmacy Department

#151, sentence

- Useful sentence.
- One-word sentence.
- Daily sentence.
- Simple sentence.
- Complex sentence.
- Sentence to death.
- Death sentence.

- Learn English by learning useful words, phrases, and sentences.
- Use it or lose it! Learn and use daily conversation words, phrases, and sentences.
- Sometimes, a one-word sentence can be the best answer.
- Standing on Mars unprotected is better than sentencing to death. Anyone will die in seconds.
- Many states have stopped the death sentence.

#152, set
Heute → set
Gestern → set
Länger her → set

- Set up.
- Set down.
- Set on.
- Set off.
- Set in.
- Set out.
- Set sail.
- Set aside
- Set me thinking.

- Set a world record.
- Set the time.
- Set the volume.
- Set the price.
- Sunset.
- Set for a good night of sleep.

- She poured two teaspoons of the cough drops and set down the bottle.
- A set of numbers were printed on the bottle.
- The pharmacists have set up the equipment for a free blood pressure test.
- Nice! The store said yesterday that they would set it up and they did.
- The blood pressure test equipment was set on a table.
- The Titanic was ready to set sail for America.
- The sinking of the Titanic set me thinking.
- The discovery of penicillin set a world record in medicine.
- Take one tablet every four hours. Set the time to take the med (medicine).
- Take the med and set for a good night of sleep.
- When listening to this recording, set the volume high so you can hear it clearly.
- When the sun sets, the sky turns red. Enjoy the sunset.
- If I buy two, do I get a discount? I'm sorry but the price is set.

#153, three

- Three o'clock.
- Three hours.
- Three years.

- Three thousand.
- Three times.
- Three languages.

- What time is it? It's three o'clock.
- It's been three hours after you took the Tylenol. How do you feel?
- I feel great!
- Did you take two tablets?
- I took three. Three tablets a time, four times a day.
- The instructions were written in three languages.

#154, want

- Want to.
- Want for.
- Wanted.
- As you want.

- Do you want a pair of sunglasses?
- No. I want a ball cap.
- Mommy wants you to stay with me when we shop.
- No, mom! I want to sit on the cart.
- An assistant is wanted in the pharmacy.
- You should want for nothing except for rest since you're sick.

#155, air

- Aircraft.
- Airplane.
- Air traffic.
- Air transportation.
- Air conditioning.

- Airflow.
- Airforce.
- Fresh air.
- Aired on TV.

- Earth is protected by a thin layer of air.
- The air around the earth protects the earth from comets and asteroids.
- Open the windows and get some fresh air.
- Air traffic control directs aircraft on the ground and in the air.
- Airplanes will not fly on the moon because there is no air on the moon.
- Air transportation greatly increases transportation speed.
- The new TV program was aired on Channel 13 last night.

#156, well

- Very well.
- It went well.
- Speak English well.
- Rest well.
- Mix well.
- Sleep well.
- Get well.
- Quite well.
- Well known.
- Well?
- As well as.

- She slept well after taking the cough drops.
- If you rest well, your body will fight off the diseases

well.
- Add salt to warm water and mix well. Then gargle three times a day to reduce a sore throat.
- Well! Drink a glass of warm water every hour and take plenty of rests, and you'll feel well after three days.

#157, also

- I also.
- They also.
- And also.
- Also called.
- Also known as

- Where are Q-tips?
- They are also in the pharmacy department.
- I got some Tylenol, Motrin, and also some Ibuprofen.
- It's also a good idea to take some Nightquails at night.
- That's also a good idea.

#158, play

- A child's play.
- A child at play.
- Play games.
- Play football.
- Play a movie.
- Play a character in the movie.
- Play the piano.
- Play the violin.
- Play music.

- Riding a wooden horse is a child's play.
- A child at play actually thinks a wooden horse he's riding is a real horse.
- According to studies, when children are at play, they think the toy animals they're playing with are live animals.
- Children like to play games.
- Playing games is an important part of a child's life.
- He likes to play football.
- He's a football player.
- He played a character in a movie.
- She played Dorothy in The Wizard of The Oz.
- She plays the piano.
- I play the violin.

#159, small

- A small department.
- A small pharmacy.
- A small bottle.
- Small tablets.
- A small child.
- A small amount.
- A small voice.
- Small talk.
- Small town.
- Small business.

- The pharmacy is a small department in the supermarket.
- This is a small pharmacy.
- The pharmacy is small, but its business is big.
- A small bottle of Dayquails will stop your running

nose. Twelve glasses of water a day will help you recover.
- Give small children liquid medicines only. Even small tablets can be harmful to them.
- "Take a small amount," she said in a small voice.

#160, end

- The end of the movie.
- The end of the aisle.
- The end of the day.
- At the end.
- Front-end.
- Dead end.
- Till the end.
- End your day with a good thought.

- They watched the game all the way to the end.
- Band-Aids are at the end of the aisle.
- At the end of the conversation, he learned a lot of new words.
- All I heard was good things at my end.
- I heard happy ending at the other end.
- To build your happiness, end your days with good thoughts.

Lernen wir diese Wörter nun im Kontext.

- Learn English by learning useful words, phrases, and sentences. Learning English is like using your muscles. Use it or lose it! Learn it and use it by learning daily conversation words, phrases, and sentences.
- Sometimes, a one-word sentence can be the best answer.
- The air around the earth protects the earth from comets, asteroids, and radiation from the sun. Standing on Mars unprotected is better than sentencing to death.
- Many states have stopped the death sentence.
- She poured two teaspoons of the cough drops and set down the bottle.
- A set of numbers were printed on the bottle.
- The pharmacists have set up the equipment for a free blood pressure test.
- Nice! The store said yesterday that they would set it up and they did.
- The blood pressure test equipment was set on a table.
- The Titanic was ready to set sail for America.
- The sinking of the Titanic set me thinking.
- The discovery of penicillin set a world record in medicine.
- Take one tablet every four hours. Set the time to take the med (medicine).
- Take the med and set for a good night of sleep.
- When listening to this recording, set the volume high so you can hear it clearly.
- When the sun sets, the sky turns red. Enjoy the sunset.
- If I buy two, do I get a discount? I'm sorry, but the price is set.
- What time is it? It's three o'clock.

- It's been three hours after you took the Tylenol. How do you feel?
- I feel great!
- Did you take two tablets?
- I took three. Three tablets a time, four times a day.
- The instructions were written in three languages.
- Do you want a pair of sunglasses?
- No. I want a ball cap.
- An assistant is wanted in the pharmacy.
- You should want for nothing except for rest since you're sick.
- Open the windows and get some fresh air.
- Airplanes will not fly on the moon because there is no air on the moon.
- Air transportation greatly increases transportation speed.
- The new TV program was aired on Channel 13 last night.
- She slept well after taking the cough drops.
- If you rest well, your body will fight off the diseases well.
- Add salt to warm water and mix well. Then gargle three times a day to reduce a sore throat.
- The best treatment is to prepare well and not to get sick.
- I got some Tylenol, Motrin, and also some Ibuprofen.
- It's also a good idea to take some Nightquails at night.
- That's also a good idea.
- Where are Q-tips?
- They are in the pharmacy department also.

- Riding a wooden horse is a child's play.
- A child at play actually thinks a wooden horse he's riding is a real horse.
- According to studies, when children are at play, they think the toy animals they're playing with are live animals.

- Children like to play games.
- Playing games is an important part of a child's life.
- He likes to play football.
- He's a football player.
- He played a character in a movie.
- She played Dorothy in The Wizard of The Oz.
- She plays the piano.
- I play the violin.
- The pharmacy is a small department in the supermarket.
- This is a small pharmacy.
- The pharmacy is small, but its business is big.
- A small bottle of Dayquails will stop your running nose. Twelve glasses of water a day will help you recover.
- Give small children liquid medicines only. Even small tablets can be harmful to them.
- "Take a small amount," she said in a small voice.
- They watched the game all the way to the end.
- They ended the conversation with a goodbye.
- At the end of the conversation, he learned a lot of new words.
- All I heard was good things at my end.
- I heard happy ending at the other end.
- To build your happiness, end your days with good thoughts.

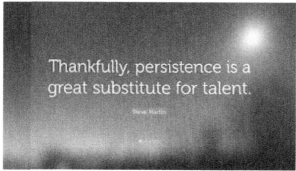

Steve Martin
Eingefügt 1/29/2017 von quotefancy.com.

Kapitel 23: 161 – 170, The Health & Beauty Department

Retrieved 2/13/2017 from Amazon.com

#161, put

- Put up.
- Put down.
- Put in.
- Put out.
- Put on.
- Put at.
- Put off.
- Put away.
- Put forward

- Put up a fight with this virus.
- She has put in extra effort to win the beauty contest.
- Which one are you going to get, a lipstick or a lip balm? A lip balm. I've already put it in the shopping cart.
- Put me in your situation, I would get the same thing.
- Lip balms put me at ease. They don't make me look too shiny.
- The new rule was put out yesterday at the meeting.
- Health & beauty magazines normally put pictures of beautiful models on their cover pages.

#162, home

- Go home.
- Get home.
- Stay home.
- Come home.
- At home.
- Home, sweet home!
- Leave home for college.
- Welcome home!

- Home team.
- Home office.
- Work from home.
- Homepage.

- Let's go home.
- Home, sweet home!
- You're back!
- No, I'm home!
- Welcome home!
- For the first time, I'm going to leave home for college.
- What's your home address?
- This store is known to locals as the home of lip balms.
- My home is also my office.
- Which one is your home team?
- The Seahawks.

#163, read

Heute → read
Gestern → read
Länger her → read

- Read a book.
- Read a letter.
- Read an email.
- Read to a child.
- Readout.
- Read up.
- Read on
- Read through.
- Read and write
- Read aloud.
- Read out loud.
- Do you read me?

- Excuse me. Where is the health and beauty department?
- Three aisles down where the sign reads H & B.
- Thanks.
- You're welcome.
- This book is a good read. It's one of the best books I've read. I've read all of the stories to my son.
- To improve your English pronunciation, read out loud.
- This is Captain Oscar of the fishing boat Titanic. Do you read me? Over.

#164, hand

- At hand.
- Hold hands.
- Lend a hand.
- Need a hand.
- Give a hand.
- Give a big hand.
- In good hands.
- On the one hand.
- On the other hand.
- Hand in.
- Hand out.
- Handoff.
- Hand down.
- Hand over.
- First hand.
- Second hand.
- Left hand.
- Right hand.

- On busy streets, moms hold the hands of their children for their safety.

- In supermarkets, moms let go of the hands of their children to give them freedom.
- Do you need a hand?
- Yes, I need some help. Would you lend me a hand?
- Good job, Evan! You deserve a big hand.
- Who are you learning English from?
- I'm learning English from Ken.
- Ken is a successful teacher. You're in good hands.
- Michelle Phan is a good hand at makeup. She's one of the best in the world. We have her products here.
- Would you hand over the towel?
- Can you hand over the towel?

#165, port

- Seaport.
- Airport.
- Homeport.
- USB port.
- Serial port.
- Parallel port.
- Loading port.
- The Seattle Port.
- Port forwarding.
- Port side.

- The cosmetics came from the seaport.
- The Atlanta Airport is the busiest airport in America.
- The Port of Seattle is the third busiest port in America.
- When you're facing the front, the left side of the boat is the port side of the boat.
- Norfolk Naval Base is home port to five aircraft carriers.
- A computer's USB port transfers data 7,000 times

faster than a serial port.

#166, large

- A large building.
- A large ship.
- A large department.
- A large order.
- A large investment.
- A large view.
- At large.
- Very large.
- Extra large.
- Large-scale.
- Large amount.

- The health & beauty department is inside this large building.
- Health & beauty is a large department in this supermarket.
- Do you have any more Michelle Phan blushes? I'd like to do a large order.
- Yes, we do. They're excellent blushes.
- Yes. It's a large investment.
- Please come with me. They're under the window with a large view.

#167, spell

- Spell check.
- Spell out.
- Dry spell.
- Cold spell.

- Warm spell.
- Break the spell.
- Put a spell.
- Magic spell.

- Your name, please?
- Ken Xiao.
- How do you spell your last name?
- X-I-A-O.
- Applying poisoned makeup on the face will spell disaster.
- As I arrived Texas, I felt an early warm spell in spring.
- After staying 40 minutes in the sauna, I felt a spell of dizziness.

#168, add

- Add up.
- Add to.
- Add on.
- Add in.
- Add more.
- Add water to flour.
- Add sugar to water.
- Add oil to fire.

- To apply makeup, add blush on top of the foundation.
- Add sugar to water and steam the broccoli. This will be a healthy lunch.
- Add up the numbers to find the total.
- The numbers have added up to a total of $20.
- Making $5,000 a month but spending $6,000 just doesn't add up.
- "I have another part-time job," she later added.

#169, even

- Even up.
- Even better.
- Even though.
- Even if.
- Even so.
- Even more.
- Even now.
- Even after
- Even or odd?
- Even number.
- Make it even.
- Even chance.
- Not even.
- Break even.

- Is it an even number or an odd number?
- It's an even number. It's 12.
- You helped me yesterday. Let me help you today to make it even.
- If I help you today, we'll be even.
- We have an even chance at the beauty contest.
- How much is this?
- Ten dollars even.
- We can even up the shelves to make it look better.
- What's the brand of the blush?
- Michelle Phan.
- Excellent!
- It's a new brand and most have never even heard of it.
- That's even better. There's a large market for it.

#170, land

- Dryland.
- Wetland.
- Flatland.
- Farmland.
- Homeland.
- Foreign land.

- Except for two hills, most of my homeland is farmland.
- After leaving my homeland, I landed in a foreign land.
- America is the land of opportunities. Anything you can imagine is possible. Even if you're just a 16-year-old girl.
- A hippo can run at 19 mph on land, but it's not a land animal. It's too heavy to live on land.
- "KW2315, Atlanta Tower, you are clear for landing."
- The Wright brothers landed the world's first airplane in Kitty Hawk, North Carolina.

Jetzt erlernen wir diese Wörter im Kontext.

- Excuse me. Where is the health and beauty department?
- Three aisles down where the sign reads H & B.
- Thanks.
- You're welcome.

- Put up a fight with this virus.
- She has put in extra effort to win the beauty contest.
- Which one are you going to get, a lipstick or a lip balm? A lip balm. I've already put it in the shopping cart.
- Put me in your situation, I would get the same thing.
- Lip balms put me at ease. They don't make me look too shiny.
- The new rule was put out yesterday at the meeting.
- Health & beauty magazines normally put pictures of beautiful models on their cover pages.

- Your name, please?
- Ken Xiao.
- How do you spell your last name?
- X-I-A-O.
- You're back!
- No, I'm home!
- Welcome home!
- Except for two hills, most of my homeland is farmland.
- After leaving my homeland, I landed on a foreign land.
- For the first time, I'm going to leave home for college.
- What's your home address?
- This store is known to locals as the home of lip balms.
- My home is also my office. I've been working from home for the past two years.
- Which one is your home team?
- The Seahawks.

- This book is a good read. It's one of the best books I've read. I've read all of the stories to my son.
- To improve your English pronunciation, read out loud.
- This is Captain Oscar of the fishing boat Titanic. Do you read me?
- On busy streets, moms hold the hands of their children for their safety.
- In supermarkets, moms let go of the hands of their children to give them freedom.
- Do you need a hand?
- Yes, I need some help. Would you lend me a hand?
- Good job, Evan! You deserve a big hand.
- Who are you learning English from?
- I'm learning English from Ken.
- Ken is a successful teacher. You're in good hands.

- Would you hand over the towel?
- Can you hand over the towel?
- The cosmetics came from the seaport.
- The Atlanta Airport is the busiest airport in America.
- The Port of Seattle is the third busiest port in America.
- When you're facing the front, the left side of the boat is the port side of the boat.
- Norfolk Naval Base is home port to five aircraft carriers.
- A computer's USB port transfers data 7,000 times faster than a serial port.
- The health & beauty department is inside this large building.
- Health & beauty is a large department in this supermarket.
- Do you have anymore Michelle Phan blushes? I'd like to do a large order.
- Yes, we do. They're excellent blushes.
- Yes. It's a large investment.
- Please come with me. They're under the window with

a large view.
- A hippo can run at 19 mph on land, but it's not a land animal. It's too heavy to live on land.
- "KW2315, Atlanta Tower, you are clear for landing."
- The Wright brothers landed the world's first airplane in Kitty Hawk, North Carolina.

- Driving at 100 mph would spell disaster.
- Applying poisoned makeup on the face would also spell disaster.
- As I arrived Texas, I felt an early warm spell in spring.
- After staying 40 minutes in the sauna, I felt a spell of dizziness.
- Add sugar to water and steam the broccoli. This will be a healthy lunch.
- Add up the numbers to find the total.
- The numbers have added up to a total of $20.
- Making $5,000 a month but spending $6,000 just doesn't add up.
- "I have another part-time job," she later added.
- Is it an even number or an odd number?
- It's an even number. It's 12.
- You helped me yesterday. Let me help you today to make it even.
- If I help you today, we'll be even.
- We have an even chance at the beauty contest.
- We can even up the shelves to make it look better.

- To apply makeup, add blush on top of the foundation.
- What's the brand of the blush?
- Michelle Phan.
- Excellent!
- Michelle Phan is a good hand at makeup. She's one of the best in the world. We have her products here.
- It's a new brand and most have never even heard of it.
- That's even better. There's a large market for it.

- America is the land of opportunities. Anything you can imagine is possible. Even if you're just a 16-year-old girl.

Dream in light years
challenge miles
walk step by step
William Shakespeare

Kapitel 24: 171 – 180, The Meat & Seafood Department

#171, here

- Here!
- Come here.
- Same here.
- Over here.
- Right here.
- Near here.
- Stay here.
- Still here.
- From here.
- Here we go.
- Here you are.
- Here it is.

- Excuse me. Where are lamb chops?
- They're over here.
- I'm here to pick up an order for Ken.
- Here is your order, Ken. Please sign here.
- I'm here to pick up some shrimp.
- Here is your shrimp.
- And here is the money.
- Excellent. Thanks.

#172, must

- Must be.
- Must have.
- Must go.
- Must do.
- Must see.
- I must.
- One must.

- To speak English well, you must open your mouth to practice English.
- You must be kidding! No, I'm serious!
- This lobster is a must try. It's so good!
- Water is a must-have for any hiker.
- If you want to be there on time, you must go now.
- Studying before the test is something I must do.
- If you visit Seattle, the Space Needle is something you must see.

#173, big

- Big eyes.
- A big boy.
- A big project.
- A big store.
- A big lunch.
- A big decision.

- May I help you?
- Yes, I'd like to have a salmon, please.
- Is this salmon OK? No, the one with big eyes.
- You are a big boy now.
- Moving the meat department to the back is a big project.
- This is a big store with a cafeteria.
- Let's have a big lunch.
- It's a big decision to make.

#174, high

- High season.

- High tide.
- High up the mountain.
- High temperatures.
- High summer.
- High school.
- High office.
- High principles.
- High price.
- Highs and lows.
- High heels.
- High quality.
- High speed.
- High tech.
- High performance.
- High five.

- Salmons are in high season right now.
- It's a good time to go fishing at high tides.
- These are not farmed fish. These are wild fish caught in the streams high up in the mountains.
- Keep the meat at low temperatures below 41. A temperature above 41 will spoil it.
- The high school graduate who takes the high office leads the company by high principles.
- Selling his seafood at a high price is certainly not one of his principles.
- The company had its highs and lows. It had made a million dollars a day at its highest point.

#175, such

- Such lesson
- Such book.
- Such a.

- Such thing.
- Such as.
- Such that.
- As such.

- What is this? I've never seen such thing before.
- That's such a big shrimp. What kind is it? It's a Pacific lobster.
- May I ask a stupid question?
- There is no such thing as a stupid question. The stupid thing is you don't ask when you have a question.
- This is such an easy lesson.

#176, follow

- Follow up.
- Follow me.
- To follow.
- Follow the leader.
- Examples to follow.
- Follow through.
- Follow by.
- Follow suit.
- Follow on
- Follow your plan.
- Follow your heart.
- A plan to follow.

- Following are sentences for the word "Follow."
- Follow your heart to do what you want to do.
- Follow your heart, write out a plan to follow, and follow the plan to succeed.
- Follow your plan and make sure your plan is followed.

- Are you a follower or a leader?
- Be a leader and a follower to succeed.
- Be a leader to find out what you want, be a leader to write out a plan, and be a follower to follow your plan.

#177, act

- Act out.
- Act up.
- Act on.
- Act for.
- Act as.
- Act upon.
- In the act.
- The power to act.
- Act as if someone is watching.
- Act like a winner.
- An acting principal.
- A hero act.

- The power to act is now.
- Act as someone is watching.
- Act like a winner to be a winner.
- In the absence of the principal, the assistant principal takes on the role of an acting principal.
- Bacteria act on sugar left on the teeth.
- Watching how animals are killed in the slaughterhouse is an act to stop eating meat.

#178, why

- Why?
- Why not.

- That's why.
- Why is that?
- Why so?
- I wonder why.
- The reason why.
- Why would you do that?
- Why don't you get this instead?

- Why would you do that?
- Why do you do that?
- Why don't you get two instead?
- Why is that?
- If you get two, you get a 50% discount.

#179, ask

- Ask for.
- Ask about.
- Ask to.
- Ask questions.
- Ask out.

- May I ask a stupid question? There is no stupid question. The stupid thing is you don't ask when you have a question.
- The staff in the meat department are very friendly. Ask for help at any time.
- I'm going to ask for James. I know him by name.
- Let me ask him the difference between this New York steak and that T-bone steak.
- Andrea is just 12 years old. It's too early to ask her out to dinner.

#180, men

Eins → man
Zwei oder mehr → men

- One man.
- Two men.
- Most men.
- For men.
- Men and women.
- A gentleman.
- Three gentlemen.
- A man of his word.
- The man of the shop.
- Man the station.

- Two young men recently joined the meat department.
- The seafood department is a two-man team.
- The Man of the Month is from the seafood department.
- He always mans his station professionally.

Lassen Sie uns nun Ihre Muskeln trainieren. Es geht los.

- Excuse me. Where are lamb chops?
- They're over here.
- May I help you?
- Yes, I'm here to pick up an order for Ken.
- Here is your order, Ken. Please sign here.
- What are you doing here, Jen?
- I'm here to pick up some shrimp.
- Here is your shrimp.
- And here is the money.
- Excellent. Thanks.
- This lobster is a must try. It's so good!
- May I help you?
- Yes, I'd like to have a salmon, please.
- Is this salmon OK? No, the one with big eyes.
- Why don't you get two instead?
- Why is that?
- If you get two, you get a 50% discount.
- These are not farmed fish. These are wild fish caught in the streams high up in the mountains.

- Water is a must-have for any hiker.
- You must be kidding!
- No, I'm serious! You must bring water if you want to go hiking.
- If you want to be there on time, you must go now.
- Studying before the test is something I must do.
- If you visit Seattle, the Space Needle is something you must see.

- You are a big boy now.
- Moving the meat department to the back is a big project.
- This is a big store with a cafeteria.
- Let's have a big lunch.

- That's a big decision to make.
- Salmons are in high season right now.
- It's a good time to go fishing at high tides.

- Keep the meat at low temperatures below 41. A temperature above 41 will spoil it.
- The high school graduate who takes the high office of the W3 Seafood Company leads the company by high principles.
- The company had its highs and lows. It had made a million dollars a day at its highest point.
- What is this? I've never seen such thing before.
- That's such a big shrimp. What kind is it? It's a Pacific lobster.
- May I ask a stupid question?
- There is no such thing as a stupid question. The stupid thing is you don't ask when you have a question.
- This is such an easy lesson.
- Following are sentences for the word "Follow."
- Follow your heart to do what you want to do.
- Follow your heart, write out a plan to follow, and follow the plan to succeed.
- Follow your plan and make sure your plan is followed.
- Are you a follower or a leader?
- Be a leader and a follower to succeed.
- Be a leader to find out what you want, be a leader to write out a plan, and be a follower to follow your plan.
- The power to act is now.
- Act as someone is watching.
- Act like a winner to be a winner.
- In the absence of the principal, the assistant principal takes on the role of an acting principal.
- Bacteria act on sugar left on the teeth.
- Watching how animals are killed in the slaughterhouse is an act to stop eating meat.
- Why would you do that?

- Why do you do that?

- May I ask a stupid question? There is no stupid question. The stupid thing is you don't ask when you have a question.
- Why are chickens so cheap this week?

- The staff in the meat department are very friendly. Ask for help at any time.
- I'm going to ask for James. I know him by name.
- Let me ask him the difference between this New York steak and that T-bone steak.
- Andrea is just 12 years old. It's too early to ask her out to dinner.
- Two young men recently joined the meat department.
- The seafood department is a two-man team.
- The Man of the Month is from the seafood department.
- He always mans his station professionally.

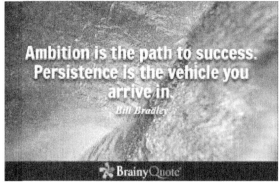
Eingefügt 1/29/2017 von brainyquote.com.

Kapitel 25: 181 – 190, The Deli Department

#181, change

- The change.
- To change.
- No change.
- For a change.
- Change to.
- Change color.
- Change order.
- Keep the change.
- What a change.
- Change the rule.
- Change the menu.
- Change the light bulb.
- Change of management.

- A dollar fifty is your change.
- Keep the change.
- What a change. The whole menu is changed.
- What's today's special? Turkey and meatball on mashed potatoes.
- What a change! Looks like a holiday menu.
- Brandon, two light bulbs burned out today. Can you change them?
- Seattle has just changed the residential speed limit from 25 to 20.

#182, went
Heute – go
Gestern – went
Länger her – gone

- Go to.
- Went to.

- Go out.
- Went out.
- Go ahead.
- Went ahead.
- Go straight.
- Went straight.
- Went on.
- Went back.
- Went away.
- Went to bed.
- As time went on.

- Where did Sophia go? She went to the deli.
- Did you go out yesterday? Yes, I went out with her.
- Sophia went to the Deli Department.
- She went straight to the new items yesterday.
- She went ahead to try the turkey and meatball on mashed potatoes.
- Time went by quickly. It's been two weeks since they changed their menu.
- Five minutes went by, and they didn't say a word.
- Sophia talks to another girl when she comes in every day, but today, they went for five minutes without talking.
- She went a long way.
- Lunch price went up by 10%, but food quantity went up by 10%, too.
- When I returned, they were gone.
- When I came back for more, the whole case of hot food was gone.
- Since there was no more food to buy, the rest of the money went to my savings.
- What went wrong? Nothing went wrong. I just got richer by saving more lunch money.
- Did you come to the deli for an interview yesterday? How did it go? It went well. I got hired.

#183, light

Today – light
Yesterday – lit
For some time – lighted

- Daylight.
- Sunlight.
- Headlight.
- Traffic lights.
- Light bulb.
- Streetlight.
- Light it up.
- Light up.
- Light green.
- Light blue.
- Light rain.
- Light truck.
- Light breakfast.

- Street lights, traffic lights, and vehicle lights light up the night sky.
- The lights in the supermarket are as bright as daylight.
- Although they've never seen sunlight, these green leaves look as healthy as if they had.
- The heat lamps use light bulbs that are designed to generate heat.
- The heat lamps lit up; the food stayed hot.
- These green leaves are as light as feathers.
- These green leaf lettuces are delivered by a light truck every morning.
- I had a light breakfast and a big lunch.

#184, kind

- Kind of.
- What kind.
- Very kind.
- A kind customer.
- A kind clerk.
- Kind enough.
- Kind to the stomach.

- The deli used to have one kind of fried chicken, but now they have two kinds.
- They serve pizza once a week. Once in a while, they serve a homemade pizza that's different in kind from any other.
- Every one of the clerks is kind and polite.
- Once a clerk was kind enough to make a meatball "fall" into my order.
- They sometimes serve spicy food, but it's kind to the stomach.

#185, off

- Turn off.
- Get off.
- Runoff.
- Take off.
- Cut off.
- Lay off.
- Put off.
- Set off.
- Show off.
- Kick off.
- On or off.

- Is Brandon here? No, he's off. He gets off at 1.

- Jessica, can you turn off the heat lamps, please?
- Jessica has run off with Alisa.
- Turkey and meatball are on sale today. If you buy both of them, you get $2 off.
- Excellent! I'll take them.
- Good deal! I'll take $2 off.
- Hi, Alisa. I haven't heard from you about the project. Are we on or off?

#186, need

- In need.
- Need help,.
- No need.
- Basic need.
- A friend in need is a friend indeed

- Do you need help?
- Need any help?
- Do you need any help?
- Yes, I need some help. I'd like six fried chicken wings, please.
- There's no need to wrap them up. I'm going to eat them right here.
- Workers and supplies are deli's basic needs for daily operation.
- The basic human need for food.
- The basic human need for shelter.
- Basic human needs for food and shelter.

#187, house

- A single-family house.

- A big house.
- A townhouse.
- A birdhouse.
- The White House.
- House wine.
- On house.
- A full house.
- House the poor and the homeless.

- In crowded cities, houses are usually townhouses.
- A birdhouse in the backyard is a safe house for birds.
- The White House is the house where the president lives.
- The deli is not a restaurant. They don't have a house salad, but they do have an excellent salad.
- In a restaurant, if they say "on house," it means you get it for free. For example, "This is our house wine. On house." It means the restaurant is giving you their regular wine for free.
- Seattle is doing so much to house the poor and the homeless.

#188, picture

- Take a picture.
- Paint a picture.
- Draw a picture.
- Motion picture.
- In the picture.
- A good picture.
- Picture frame.
- Big picture.

- Harry Potter was named the best picture of the year.
- I showed the clerk a picture of the salad I wanted to

order, and she instantly knew what it was and made it for me.
- Pictured here is the salad.
- I pictured myself eating the salad while she was making it.

#189, try

- Try again.
- Keep trying.
- Try on.
- Try out.
- Try to.
- Try hard.
- Give it a try.

- You should try this sandwich. It's really good.
- Try again and again and again.
- Keep trying until you succeed.
- She passed the job interview for the clerk position and liked the job after a tryout.
- I tried the deli, but their phone was busy.
- Now we know what to do. Let's give it a try.

#190, us
Ich → me
Du / Sie → you
Wir → us

- To us.
- With us.
- For us.
- All of us.
- Between us.

- Both of us.
- Let us.

- Let me know.
- Let us know.
- Let's give it a try.
- Let's go.
- Let's get something hot.
- Are you with us?
- Yes. Let both of us get some hot food from the deli.
- This is between us, I got a whole pizza for all of us.

Jetzt werden die Muskeln trainiert, Tiger!

- What a change. The whole menu is changed.
- What's today's special? Turkey and meatball on mashed potatoes.
- What a change! Looks like a holiday menu.
- Lunch price went up by 10%, but food quantity went up by 10%, too.
- Deli changed its management last week. The rule has changed, too.
- Sophia went to the Deli Department.
- Sophia normally talks to another girl when she comes in every day, but today, they went for five minutes without talking.
- They went straight to the new items yesterday.
- They went ahead to tried the turkey and meatball on mashed potatoes.
- Five minutes went by, and they didn't say a word.
- They went a long way. When I returned, they were gone. When I came back for more, the whole case of hot food was gone.
- Since there was no more food to buy, the rest of the money went to my savings.
- Time went by quickly. It's been two weeks since they changed their menu.
- These green leaves are as light as feathers. They are delivered by a light truck every morning.
- I had a light breakfast and a big lunch.
- The deli used to have one kind of fried chicken, but now they have two kinds.
- They serve pizza once a week. Once in a while, they serve a homemade pizza that's different in kind from any other.
- Every one of the clerks is kind and polite.
- Once a clerk was kind enough to make a meatball "fall" into my order.
- They sometimes serve spicy food, but it's kind to the

stomach.

- Brandon, two light bulbs burned out today. Can you change them? Is Brandon here?
- No, he's off. He gets off at 1 today.
- Seattle has just changed the residential speed limit from 25 to 20.
- Where did Sophia go? She went to the deli.
- Did you go out yesterday? Yes, I went out with her.
- What went wrong? Nothing went wrong. I just got richer by saving more lunch money.
- Did you come to the deli for an interview yesterday? How did it go? It went well. I got hired.
- Street lights, traffic lights, and vehicle lights light up the night sky.
- The lights in the supermarket are as bright as daylight.
- Although they've never seen sunlight, these green leaves look as healthy as if they have.
- The heat lamps use light bulbs that are designed to generate heat.
- The heat lamps light up the hot food bar.
- The heat lamps lit up; the food stayed hot.
- The heat lamps have lighted up the hot food bar.
- Jessica, can you turn off the heat lamps, please?
- Jessica has run off with Alisa.
- Turkey and meatballs are on sale today. If you buy both of them, you get $2 off.
- Excellent! I'll take them.
- Good deal! I'll take $2 off.
- Hi, Alisa. I haven't heard from you about the project. Are we on or off?

- Do you need help?
- Need any help?
- Do you need any help?
- Yes, I need some help. I'd like six fried chicken wings,

- please.
- There's no need to wrap them up. I'm going to eat them right here.
- Workers and supplies are deli's basic needs for daily operation.
- The basic human need for food.
- The basic human need for shelter.
- Basic human needs for food and shelter.
- Most houses in America's rural areas are single-family houses.
- In cities, houses are small. In suburbs, houses are big.
- In crowded cities, houses are usually townhouses.
- A birdhouse in the backyard is a safe house for birds.
- The White House is the house where the president lives.
- The deli is not a restaurant. They don't have a house salad, but they do have an excellent salad.
- In a restaurant, if they say "on house," it means you get it for free. For example, "This is our house wine. On house." It means the restaurant is giving you their regular wine for free.
- Seattle is doing so much to house the poor and the homeless.
- Take a picture of me ordering lunch at the deli.
- Paint a picture of the picture taken at the deli ordering lunch.
- Harry Potter was named the best picture of the year.
- I showed the clerk a picture of the salad I wanted to order, and she instantly knew what it was and made it for me.
- Pictured here is the salad.
- I pictured myself eating the salad while she was making it.
- You should try this sandwich. It's really good.
- Try again and again and again.
- I tried again and again and successfully ordered the

- perfect chicken sandwich at the deli.
- Keep trying until you succeed.
- She passed the job interview for the clerk position and liked the job after a tryout.
- I tried the deli, but their phone was busy.
- Now we know what to do. Let's give it a try.
- Let me know.
- Let us know.
- Let's give it a try.
- Let's go.
- Let's get something hot.
- Let's get some hot food from the deli.
- We got us some hot food from the deli.
- A dollar fifty is your change.
- Keep the change.

Englisch: Lernen Sie Englischsprechen wie ein Einheimischer in nur einem Kurs

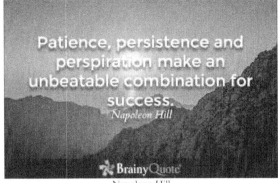

Napoleon Hill
Eingefügt 1/29/2017 von brainyquote.com.

Kapitel 26: 191 – 200, The Bakery Department

#191, again

Again wird als agen betont. Es wird nicht wie again oder agan betont. Es wird als agen betont.

- Try again.
- Do again.
- Say again.
- Not again.
- Then again.
- Meet again.
- Come again.
- Once again.
- Never again.
- Over again.
- Again and again.
- Over and over again.

- That's amazing! Can you do it again?
- Do you have any naan?
- What was it again?
- Naan. An Indian bread.
- Do you have any croissants?
- Say it again?
- Croissants.
- We bake croissants every day, but then again, they can be sold out in the morning.
- Try again and again and again.
- I tried again and again and successfully ordered the perfect cake at the bakery.
- Thank you for your help.
- See you again.
- Come again.

#192, animal

- An animal.
- A wild animal.
- A small animal.
- A stuffed animal.
- Land animals.
- Sea animals.
- Flying animals.

- Cats are animals welcomed in Petco.
- Cheetahs are the fastest land animals on earth. They can run 70 miles per hour.
- Blue whales are the largest animals in the world.
- The very thought of killing small animals in his childhood life made him feel guilty.

#193, point

- Point out.
- Point to.
- Point at.
- The point.
- Turning point.
- Melting point.
- Boiling point.
- Focal point.
- Starting point.
- Point of view.

- How big is this cake?
- This is a 15.8- inch cake.
- The point of the mountain peak is in the center of the cake.

- Put the point of the knife at the point of the mountain peak and cut it there.
- Excuse me. Where is the bakery department?
- Go straight to the point where you see a coffee shop. That's where the bakery department is.
- When I ordered a birthday cake for my kid, the baker pointed out a few points.
- What's the point of adding a toy on the cake?
- The point is for kids to get excited about the cake.
- Good idea! Five points for the bakery department.

#194, mother

- Mother and baby.
- Mother bear.
- Mother Teresa.
- Mothership.
- Motherland.
- Mother tongue.
- Mother language.
- Mother in law.
- Mothered two children.

- A kid came to the baker with his mother and asked for a sample cookie.
- The kid ordered a cake with a decorative picture of a mother bear and a baby bear.
- The mother ordered a cake with a picture of Mother Teresa.
- Failure is the mother of success.
- She said she mothered two children.

#195, world

- My world.
- Our world.
- Around the world.
- Other worlds.
- All over the world.
- The whole world.
- The music world.
- The bakery world.
- The English-speaking world.
- New world.
- Out of this world.

- Earth is our world.
- People travel here from around the world.
- Scientists suggest that there must be life on other worlds.
- I found my world on Facebook.
- Technology has completely changed the music world.
- Technology has also changed the bakery world. Customers place their cookie orders on the World Wide Web.
- The bakery department is an English-speaking world, but the deli department is a completely different world.

#196, near

- Near to.
- Near here.
- Near future.
- Come near.
- Draw near.
- Quite near.
- Very near.
- Nowhere near

- Near the bakery.

- The cookie tables are near the coffee shop.
- The current baking cycle is drawing near.
- A sample cookie stand is placed near the entrance of the store.
- Cream cheesecakes are near the end of the season.
- If I round it up to the nearest thousand, I would have sold 2,000 cookies today.
- Baking related items are placed near the bakery.
- As technology advances quickly, a self-baking machine will be available in the near future.

#197, build

Heute – build
Gestern – built
Länger her – built

- Build up.
- Build in.
- Build on.
- Build upon.
- Build into.
- Build a house.
- Build a bridge.
- Build a fire.
- Build a baking oven.
- Build your fluency.
- Medium build.
- Muscular build.

- The house was built two years ago.
- The bridge was built 50 years ago.
- After the baking oven was built, baking cookies was

so easy.
- I've built up my English fluency in six months.
- By talking to hundreds of customers a day, every day, one of my students has built up her confidence in English fluency.
- He's strong and muscular build.

#198, self
Eins – self
Zwei oder mehr – selves

- Yourself.
- Your outer self.
- Myself.
- My inner self.
- Self-confidence.
- Self-esteem.
- Self-driving cars.
- Self-baking machines.
- Self-conscious
- Self-employed.

- Help yourself!
- If there was only one choice between my inner self and my outer self, I'd rather choose my inner self.
- Building your outer self will build your attractiveness.
- Building your inner self will build your success.
- Self-driving cars can be used to deliver cookies.
- Self-baking machines can greatly reduce the department's manpower and enhance its quality.

#199, earth

- The earth.
- On earth.
- Planet Earth.
- Down to earth.
- The Earth's orbit.
- Orbit around the Earth.
- Dig up tons of earth.

- Earth is our world.
- We have one place to live – Planet Earth.
- Earth's nearest neighbor is Venus.
- The earth's orbit is surrounded by thousands of satellites.
- The moon orbits around the earth.
- They dug up tons of earth to build the new house.
- We're on Earth to find what we want. If we don't find what we want, make what we want!

#200, father

- My father.
- Father and son.
- Father figure.
- Like father, like son.
- Founding father.
- Fathered two children.

- The father teaches the son.
- The son learns from the father.
- Like father, like son.
- The daughter models the father.
- He's the founding father of this bakery shop.
- They're the founding fathers of the country.
- He said he fathered two children.

Herzlichen Glückwunsch! Dies ist der letzte Zehner-Satz in Lektion zwei. Verwenden wir die Wörter im Kontext.

- Excuse me. Where is the bakery department?
- Go straight to the point where you see a coffee shop. That's where the bakery department is.
- How big is this cake?
- This is a 15.8- inch cake.
- The point of the mountain peak is the center of the cake.
- Put the point of the knife at the point of the mountain peak and cut it there.
- When I ordered the birthday cake for my kid, the baker pointed out a few points.
- What's the point of adding a toy on the cake?
- The point is for kids to get excited about the cake.
- Good idea! Five points for the bakery department.
- Technology has completely changed the music world.
- Technology has also changed the bakery world. Customers place their orders on the World Wide Web.
- The bakery department is an English-speaking world, but the deli department is a completely different world.
- The cookie tables are near the coffee shop.
- The current baking cycle is drawing near.
- A sample cookie stand is placed near the entrance of the store.
- Cream cheesecakes are near the end of the season.
- If I round it up to the nearest thousand, I would have sold 2,000 cookies today.
- Baking related items are placed near the bakery.
- As technology advances quickly, a self-baking machine will be available in the near future.
- A kid came to the bakery with his mother asked for a sample cookie.
- The kid ordered a cake with a decorative picture of a mother bear and a baby bear.
- The mother ordered a cake with a picture of Mother

Teresa.
- That's amazing! Can you do it again?
- Do you have any naan?
- What was it again?
- Naan. An Indian bread.
- Do you have any croissants?
- Say it again?
- Croissants.
- We bake croissants every day, but then again, they can be sold out in the morning.
- I tried again and again and successfully ordered the perfect cake at the bakery.
- Thank you for your help.
- See you again.
- Come again.

- Cats are animals welcomed in Petco, but they're not welcomed in the supermarket.
- Spiders are animals of the wild.
- Cheetahs are the fastest land animals on Earth. They can run 70 miles per hour.
- The very thought of killing small animals in his childhood life made him feel guilty.
- Failure is the mother of success.
- She said she mothered two children.
- People travel here from around the world.
- Scientists suggest that there must be life on other worlds.
- I found my world on Facebook.
- The house was built two years ago.
- The bridge was built 50 years ago.
- After the baking oven was built, baking cookies was so easy.
- I've built up my English fluency in six months.
- By talking to hundreds of customers a day, every day, one of my students has built up her confidence in

English fluency.
- He's strong and muscular build.
- If there was only one choice between my inner self and my outer self, I'd rather choose my inner self.
- Building your outer self will build your attractiveness.
- Building your inner self will build your success.
- Self-driving cars can be used to deliver cookies.
- Self-baking machines can greatly reduce the department's manpower and enhance its quality.
- Earth is our world.
- We have one place to live – Planet Earth.
- The earth's orbit is surrounded by thousands of satellites.
- The moon orbits around the Earth.
- They dug up tons of earth to build the new house.
- We're on Earth to find what we want. If we don't find what we want, make what we want!
- The father teaches the son.
- The son learns from the father.
- Like father, like son.
- The daughter models the father.
- He's the founding father of this bakery shop.
- They're the founding fathers of the country.
- He said he fathered two children.

> **Niemals aufgeben. Gewinner geben niemals auf und Verlierer gewinnen niemals.**
> Vince Lombardi

School, Work, Society

Rank	Word	Rank	Word
201	head	226	between
202	stand	227	city
203	own	228	tree
204	page	229	cross
205	should	230	since
206	country	231	hard
207	found	232	start
208	answer	233	might
209	school	234	story
210	grow	235	saw
211	study	236	far
212	still	237	sea
213	learn	238	draw
214	plant	239	left
215	cover	240	late
216	food	241	run
217	sun	242	don't
218	four	243	while
219	thought	244	press
220	let	245	close
221	keep	246	night
222	eye	247	real
223	never	248	life
224	last	249	few
225	door	250	stop

Rank	Word	Rank	Word
251	open	276	care
252	seem	277	second
253	together	278	group
254	next	279	carry
255	white	280	took
256	children	281	rain
257	begin	282	eat
258	got	283	room
259	walk	284	friend
260	example	285	began
261	ease	286	idea
262	paper	287	fish
263	often	288	mountain
264	always	289	north
265	music	290	once
266	those	291	base
267	both	292	hear
268	mark	293	horse
269	book	294	cut
270	letter	295	sure
271	until	296	watch
272	mile	297	color
273	river	298	face
274	car	299	wood
275	feet	300	main

Kapitel 27: 201 – 210, In High School
#201, head

- Head up.
- Head for.
- Head on.
- Head office.
- Head and shoulder
- Head to toe.
- Head to school!
- Head of the school football team.
- Headphones
- Headband
- Headlight
- Headquarter
- Headset
- Headwind
- A head of lettuce.

- Where's Head and Shoulder?
- What?
- The shampoo.
- Use Head and Shoulder to wash from head to toe and then look at people from head to toe.
- How much is a head of lettuce?
- A dollar.
- Jack and Johnny are heading to school together after a fight yesterday.
- Do you want to head to the supermarket after school?
- Let's head to the park after school.
- He's the head of the school football team.
- Do you want to buy a headphone or a headset?
- I'm going to buy a headlight.

#202, stand

Heute → stand
Gestern → stood
Länger her → stood

- Stand in.
- Stand out.
- Stand up.
- Stand down.
- Stand for.
- Stand by.
- Stand it.
- Stand-alone.
- A microphone stand.
- A light stand.
- A stand on immigration law.

- What's your stand on the new immigration law?
- Stand up from your seat after you've been sitting for a while.
- She was attacked during the meeting, but she stood up for herself.
- While we were standing in line to get our movie tickets, a young man stood up for his friend who was in trouble.
- We should stand here to wait for our parents.

#203, own

- Your own.
- My own.
- Our own.
- His own.
- Own it.
- On its own.

- Your own business.
- Of my own.

- I own the same book as him.
- Do you have your own computer at school?
- I own a guitar. He owns a picture of my guitar.
- Jake washes his own shirt at home. I clean up my own mess at home.
- The students expressed their own opinions. I encouraged them to talk.
- Kids own their dreams. Happy parents share them.

#204, page

- Page one.
- Page two.
- First page.
- Next page.
- Front page.
- Cover page.
- Web page.
- Homepage.
- Current page.
- Turn the page.
- Page number.
- What page?

- The first page is about your own dreams.
- The second page is about your own life.
- What page are you up to in Chemistry class?
- How many pages do you have?
- Can you make me a copy of this page?
- I will write three more pages.
- Turn your book to page 24.

- I wrote three more pages yesterday.

#205, should

- I should.
- She should.
- You should.
- Should be.
- Should not.
- Should have.

- I think I should help him with his homework.
- Should I go to the park alone?
- You should be successful.
- He should feed his pet daily.
- Children should own their dreams.
- You should tell him the truth.
- Bob should pay for his class now.
- You know how to read and write English. You should learn how to speak English as well.

#206, country

- Cross country.
- In the country.
- Home country.
- Country code.
- Country house.
- Foreign country.
- Country of origin.
- Country music.

- What country were you born in?
- What country did you come from?

- My parents were born in a different country.
- What country would you like to travel to if you want to listen to country music?
- Although Ken is a country boy, he's proud of it. He has learned a great deal of nature from living in the country.
- Even people came from the countryside can be successful. I can be successful, too.

#207, found
Heute → find
Gestern → found
Länger her → found

- Have found.
- Be found.
- Found out.
- Found guilty.
- Lost and found.
- Founding fathers.

- He found his textbook in his book bag.
- Josh found the subject interesting.
- I think Henry found a job by now.
- She found her purse under her bed.
- I found it easy to lift this table.
- She found it funny to solve the math problem.
- He found it comfortable to get along with her friends.
- He's the founding father of this school.
- George Washington is the founding father of a country.

#208, answer

- Answer me.

- Answer him.
- Answer back.
- Answer sheet.
- Answer the phone.
- Answer the question.
- The correct answer.

- Please answer this question, Johnny.
- Who wants to answer this question?
- These math questions are really easy to answer!
- Active students want to answer questions.
- Do you have an answer?
- Yes. I do have an answer!
- There are many answers to a question that asks for your opinion.

#209, school

- Elementary school.
- Primary school.
- Secondary school.
- Middle school.
- High school.
- At school.
- After school.
- Go to school.
- A good school.
- A school of fish.

- I am leaving high school tomorrow for college.
- She loves her teachers at her current school.
- Do you know what school John attends?
- What subject do you like best at school?
- Do you like to go to school?
- Sally really likes to go to school.

- Some subjects are really interesting at school.
- A school of fish is swimming together for protection.

#210, grow

Heute → grow
Gestern → grew
Länger her → grown

- Grow up.
- Grow on.
- Grow out.
- Grow apart.
- Grow into
- Grow plants
- Room to grow.

- Where did you grow up?
- I grew up in Brooklyn.
- The wind grows stronger at night. Josh's mustache grows faster at night.
- These bamboos will continue to grow at two feet per day.
- I grew up in a different country.
- Haven't seen you in 10 years. You've grown.

Holen wir sie uns!

- Where's Head and Shoulder?
- What?
- The shampoo.
- Use Head and Shoulder to wash from head to toe and then look at people from head to toe.
- How much is a head of lettuce?
- A dollar.
- Jack and Johnny are heading to school together after a fight yesterday.
- Do you want to head to the supermarket after school?
- Let's head to the park after school.
- He's the head of the school football team.
- Do you want to buy a headphone or a headset?
- I'm going to buy a headlight.
- What's your stand on the new immigration law?
- Stand up from your seat after you've been sitting for a while.
- She was attacked during the meeting, but she stood up for herself.
- While we were standing in line to get our movie tickets, a young man stood up for his friend who was in trouble.
- We should stand here to wait for our parents.
- I own the same book as him.
- Do you have your own computer at school?
- I own a guitar. He owns a picture of my guitar.
- Jake washes his own shirt at home. I clean up my own mess at home.
- The students expressed their own opinions. I encouraged them to talk.
- Kids own their dreams. Happy parents share them.
- The first page is about your own dreams.
- The second page is about your own life.
- What page are you up to in Chemistry class?

- How many pages do you have?
- Can you make me a copy of this page?
- I will write three more pages.
- Turn your book to page 24.
- I wrote three more pages yesterday.
- I think I should help him with his homework.
- Should I go to the park alone?
- You should be successful.
- He should feed his pet daily.
- Children should own their dreams.
- You should tell him the truth.
- Bob should pay for his class now.
- You know how to read and write English. You should learn how to speak English as well.
- Although Ken is a country boy, he's proud of it. He has learned a great deal of nature living in the country.
- Even people came from the countryside can be successful. I can be successful, too.
- The country's economy is good.
- What country were you born in?
- My parents were born in a different country.
- What country would you like to travel to if you want to listen to country music?
- He found his textbook in his book bag.
- Josh found the subject interesting.
- I think Henry found a job by now.
- She found her purse under her bed.
- I found it easy to lift this table.
- She found it funny to solve the math problem.
- He found it comfortable to get along with her friends.
- He's the founding father of this school.
- George Washington is the founding father of a country.
- Please answer this question, Johnny.
- Who wants to answer this question?

- These math questions are really easy to answer!
- Active students want to answer questions.
- Do you have an answer?
- Yes. I do have an answer!
- There are many answers to a question that asks for your opinion.
- I am leaving high school tomorrow for college.
- She loves her teachers at her current school.
- Do you know what school John attends?
- What subject do you like best at school?
- Do you like to go to school?
- Sally really likes to go to school.
- Some subjects are really interesting at school.
- A school of fish is swimming together for protection.
- Where did you grow up?
- I grew up in Brooklyn.
- The wind grows stronger at night. Josh's mustache grows faster at night.
- These bamboos will continue to grow at two feet per day.
- I grew up in a different country.
- Haven't seen you in 10 years. You've grown.

Kapitel 28: 211 – 220, More High school!

#211, study

- A study.
- To study.
- Study room.
- Study hall.
- Study skills.
- Study science.
- Case study.
- Field study.

- What are you studying?
- I'm studying music.
- Can I study with you?
- Okay. Let's study together.
- According to studies, many who study very hard get a Ph. D. degree and then work for high school dropouts.
- She will get into the study of happiness this semester.

#212, still

- Stand still.
- Sit still.
- Lie still.
- Hold still.
- Still care.
- Still hungry.
- Still here.
- Still water.

- I still remember winning the game.
- I've tried 68 times and I'm still trying.

- Please sit still for this exam.
- We can still win this soccer game if you keeping singing.
- He is still singing that happy song.
- Is she still studying?
- Josh is still here to help.

#213, learn

- To learn.
- Live and learn.
- Learn more.
- Learn about.
- Learn from.
- Learn by heart.
- Lifelong learning.
- Lessons learned.

- I need to learn a foreign language.
- What's easier to learn, English or rocket science?
- We learn our lessons from failing.
- "Tell me and I forget. Teach me and I remember. Involve me and I learn."
- I want to learn how to cook.
- I want to learn how to speak English.
- You teach me how to cook. I teach you how to speak English. Deal?
- Deal!
- What did you learn today?
- Get involved to learn.

#214, plant

- A plant.
- To plant.
- Power plant.
- Plant a seed.
- Plant a tree.
- Plant a bug.
- Plant an idea.

- I've learned how to plant tomato seeds today by doing it myself.
- They're planting trees around the power plant.
- Did you water the plants?
- When did you plant the idea in your mind to become a musician?
- What are you going plant in your garden?
- I'm going to plant roses.

#215, cover

- Cover letter.
- Cover page.
- Cover up.
- Cover down.
- Front cover.
- Back cover.
- Take cover.
- Book cover.
- Cover me.

- We often judge a book by its cover.
- Look at the cover of that book!
- We have a lot of ground to cover.

- I'm happy to cover your job for you.
- The snow covered the town.
- The floor was covered with dust, so I covered the bed with a blanket.
- We've already covered that topic in school.

#216, food

- Fast food.
- Junk food.
- Fresh food.
- Frozen food.
- Canned food.
- Good food.
- Food court.
- Food chain.

- Tom likes to eat hot food for lunch.
- Let's prepare some food for the party.
- There's plenty of food to go around at school!
- We still have some food left.
- Do you like spicy food?
- Do you want to share your food with me?
- There is plenty of food in the cafeteria.

#217, sun

- Sunrise.
- Sunset.
- Sunlight.
- Sunshine.
- Sunday.
- Morning sun.

- Rising sun.
- In the sun.
- Under the sun.

- Earth goes around the sun at 18.5 miles per second.
- Earth takes 365 days to rotate around the sun.
- The sun is about to rise. Let's start before the sun rises.
- The sun is warm and they enjoy it.
- The sun is shining bright today. It's a good idea to bring a pair of sunglasses.
- It's okay to sit on the sunny side. The water evaporated when the sun rose.
- It'll be sunny this Sunday. Do you want to go see the sunset?

#218, four

- The number four.
- Four languages.
- Four seasons.
- Forty-four.
- Four hundred
- Four billion.

- Let's split the bill four ways.
- This drink is $4.
- They have four children living with them.
- Four is a lucky number in America.
- He has been excited for four days.
- My apartment is on the fourth floor.
- Ken speaks four languages perfectly.

#219, thought

Heute → think
Gestern → thought
Länger her → thought

- My thoughts.
- I thought.
- Food for thought.
- What are your thoughts?
- Thought about.
- Lost in thought.
- Thought out.
- A thought.
- Second thought.
- Well thought.
- Deep thought.

- I thought I would finish this in a month, but after I wrote out a plan and followed it, I finished it in a week.
- She pushed the thought from her mind.
- The thought never crossed her mind.
- I've failed so many times that the thoughts of pain can no longer hurt my brain.
- Speaking English like a native was easier than I thought.

#220, let

Heute → let
Gestern → let
Länger her → let

- Let go.
- Let out.
- Let it go.
- Let's go!

- Let's party.
- Let me see.
- Let me know.
- You can let your past play two roles.
- I will let my past stay behind me.

- Let go of your past so you can succeed now.
- It's hard to let go of the past, but the choice is yours.
- You can let your past do two things to you: let it destroy you or let it help you.
- My past is so humble that it feels much better to hide it, but I choose to face it and let it help me all the way to my success.
- I will let my past become my friend.
- Let me help you with your pronunciation. Just follow my steps and let's party after that.

Auf geht's!

- What are you studying?
- I'm studying music.
- Can I study with you?
- Okay. Let's study together.
- According to studies, many who study very hard get a Ph.D. degree and then work for high school dropouts.
- She will get into the study of happiness this semester.
- I still remember winning the game.
- I've tried 68 times and I'm still trying.
- Please sit still for this exam.
- We can still win this soccer game if you keeping singing.
- He is still singing that happy song.
- Is she still studying?
- Josh is still here to help.
- I need to learn a foreign language.
- What's easier to learn, English or rocket science?
- We learn our lessons from failing.
- "Tell me and I forget. Teach me and I remember. Involve me and I learn."
- I want to learn how to cook.
- I want to learn how to speak English.
- You teach me how to cook. I teach you how to speak English. Deal?
- Deal!
- What did you learn today?
- Get involved to learn.
- I've learned how to plant tomato seeds today by doing it myself.
- They're planting trees around the power plant.
- Would you like to plant these eggplants together?
- Did you water the plants?
- When did you plant the idea in your mind to become a musician?

- What are you going plant in your garden?
- I'm going to plant roses.
- We often judge a book by its cover.
- Look at the cover of that book!
- We have a lot of ground to cover.
- I'm happy to cover your job for you.
- The snow covered the town.
- The floor was covered with dust, so I covered the bed with a blanket.
- We've already covered that topic in school.
- Tom likes to eat hot food for lunch.
- Let's prepare some food for the party.
- There's plenty of food to go around at school!
- We still have some food left.
- Do you like spicy food?
- Do you want to share your food with me?
- There is plenty of food in the cafeteria.
- Earth goes around the sun at 18.5 miles per second.
- Earth takes 365 days to rotate around the sun.
- The sun is about to rise. Let's start before the sun rises.
- The sun is warm and they enjoy it.
- The sun is shining bright today. It's a good idea to bring a pair of sunglasses.
- It's okay to sit on the sunny side. The water evaporated when the sun rose.
- It'll be sunny this Sunday. Do you want to go see the sunset?
- Let's split the bill four ways.
- This drink is $4.
- They have four children living with them.
- Four is a lucky number in America.
- He has been excited for four days.
- My apartment is on the fourth floor.
- Ken speaks four languages perfectly.
- I thought I would finish this in a month, but after I

wrote out a plan and followed it, I finished it in a week.
- She pushed the thought from her mind.
- The thought never crossed her mind.
- I've failed so many times that the thoughts of pain can no longer hurt my brain.
- Speaking English like a native was easier than I thought.
- Let go so you can succeed.
- It's hard to let go of the past, but the choice is yours.
- You can let your past do two things to you: let it destroy you or let it help you.
- My past is so humble that most people will try to hide it, but I will face it and let it help me all the way to my success.
- I will let my past become my friend.
- Let me help you with your pronunciation. Just follow my steps and let's party after that.

Kapitel 29: 221 – 230, College

#221, keep

- Keep it.
- Keep in.
- Keep out.
- Keep on.
- Keep up.
- Keep fit.
- Keep going.
- Keep warm.
- Keep practicing.
- Keep the change.
- Keep away.
- Keep in touch.

- Keep trying and you will succeed.
- Just keep practicing to improve your pronunciation.
- They say "use it or lose it." I say "use it to keep it."
- I'll keep what I've learned by using what I've learned.
- She likes to keep her room really organized while he likes to keep his room really messy.
- Bob keeps trying to help everybody to make more friends.
- They stay together to keep warm.
- Keep practicing and you will speak like a native!

#222, eye

- Eyesight.
- Eye on.
- Eye drop.
- Eye contact.
- Eyeshadow.

- Left eye.
- Right eye.
- Evil eye.
- An eye for an eye.

- Open your eyes to see the outer world. Close your eyes to see the inner world.
- The show was so good that kept my eyes open.
- I can see the surprise in your eyes during math.
- She has really attractive eyes. I saw happy tears in her eyes.
- Keep an eye out for the children.
- "An eye for an eye makes the world blind."
- What you eye on is what you see. What you sow is what you reap.

#223, never

- Never try, never know.
- Never ever.
- Never give up.
- Never mind.
- Never again.
- Never ending.
- Better than never.

- Making $1 million a month may seem impossible, but you never try, you never know.
- Start today. It's never too late.
- Never give up. If what you're doing is what you want to do, keep doing it until you succeed.
- Bob never needs to study for his tests and he always passes them. I never want to know why.

#224, last

- Last one.
- Last time.
- Last minute.
- Last day.
- Last month.
- Last person.
- Last name.
- Last resort.
- Last but not least.
- At last.

- I finished my homework last night. I tried to finish the last one by 10 but I finished it by nine.
- We were the last ones to arrive at the party but we were the first ones to enjoy it.
- The last meal we had was breakfast yesterday.
- They say that some friendships last forever.
- These batteries last for eight hours.
- Who's the last person to land on the moon?

#225, door

- Front door.
- Backdoor.
- Sliding door.
- Next door.
- Hold the door.
- Open the door.
- Close the door.
- Walk through the door.
- Look for the door.
- Door to English fluency.

- Leave the door open. I am coming back.
- The door is open. Please come in.
- You can find the door to the left of the aquarium.
- Please hold the door for the professor. He's got a lot of stuff.
- If you find famous quotes in this book, you're right. I'm showing you the door to success.

#226, between

- In between.
- Choose between.
- Stay between.
- Get between.
- Relax between.
- Sat between.
- Far between.
- Between us.
- Between them.

- Decide between these two schools on which one will get you to your destination.
- Just between you and me, how did you do that?
- There is a three-minute wait between trains.
- It's easy to tell the difference between them.
- Things worked out between Tom and Jerry.

#227, city

- City hall.
- City tour.
- City center.
- City block.
- City life.

- Capital city.
- Around the city.
- New York City.
- The city of Toronto.
- A huge city.
- Country or city?

- He plans to meet his relatives in the city.
- Boston is a big city. It's also one of the oldest cities in America.
- I can show you around the city after school.
- It's easy for me to adjust living in the city.
- The biggest city in America is New York City.
- The last city that I would visit is Chicago.

#228, tree

- Tall tree.
- Peachtree.
- Plumtree.
- Family tree.
- Climb a tree.
- Under the tree.
- Tree branch.
- Treehouse.

- They tied their horses to a tree and planted 10 more trees in the yard.
- Ken likes to sit under the tree in the fall to enjoy the change of colors.
- Kids enjoy climbing trees. Most parents stop them. Some parents let them fall to learn a lesson.

#229, cross

- Crossroad.
- Cross out.
- Cross section.
- Crossover.
- Crisscross.
- Across from.
- Cross the street.
- Cross the bridge.
- Cross the road.
- Cross the border.

- Children should cross the street with care, but I saw a child crossed the street with his eyes glued on his cell phone.
- Look at the train crossing the bridge. It looks like a train from the 1800s.
- Where will you go in front of a crossroad?
- Across from your left is money. Across from your right is love. Which way will you cross?

#230, since

- Since then.
- Since when.
- Since yesterday.
- Since last year.
- Since that.
- Ever since.
- Since I'm here.

- What a hungry day. I've eaten two more meals since breakfast.
- I've known Tom since he was a kid.
- We knew Jack lived in California since he was born.

- Since the task is important, I will take care of it.
- It's been sunny since Sunday.
- Since I did a good job finishing all of this, I should give me a big reward.

Hol sie Dir, Tiger!

- Keep trying and you will succeed.
- Just keep practicing to improve your pronunciation.
- They say "use it or lose it." I say "use it to keep it."
- I'll keep what I've learned by using what I've learned.
- Bob keeps trying to help everybody to make more friends.
- They stay together to keep warm.
- Keep practicing and you will speak like a native!
- Open your eyes to see the outer world. Close your eyes to see the inner world.
- The show was so good that kept my eyes open.
- I can see the surprise in your eyes during math.
- She has really attractive eyes. I saw happy tears in her eyes.
- Keep an eye out for the children.
- "An eye for an eye makes the world blind."
- What you eye on is what you see. What you sow is what you reap.
- Making $1 million a month may seem impossible, but you never try, you never know.
- Start today. It's never too late.
- Never give up. If what you're doing is what you want to do, keep doing it until you succeed.
- Bob never needs to study for his tests and he always passes them. I never want to know why.
- I finished my homework last night. I tried to finish the last one by 10 but I finished it by nine.
- We were the last ones to arrive at the party but we were the first ones to enjoy it.
- The last meal we had was breakfast yesterday.
- They say that some friendships last forever.
- These batteries last for eight hours.
- Who's the last person to land on the moon?
- Leave the door open. I am coming back.

- The door is open. Please come in.
- You can find the door to the left of the aquarium.
- Please hold the door for the professor. He's got a lot of stuff.
- If you find famous quotes in this book, you're right. I'm showing you the door to success.
- Decide between these two schools on which one will get you to your destination.
- Just between you and me, how did you do that?
- There is a three-minute wait between trains.
- Things worked out between Tom and Jerry.
- He plans to meet his relatives in the city.
- Boston is a big city. It's also one of the oldest cities in America.
- I can show you around the city after school.
- It's easy for me to adjust living in the city.
- The biggest city in America is New York City.
- The last city that I would visit is Chicago.
- They tied their horses to a tree and planted 10 more trees in the yard.
- Ken likes to sit under the tree in the fall to enjoy the change of colors.
- Kids enjoy climbing trees. Most parents stop them. Some parents let them fall to learn a lesson.
- Children should cross the street with care, but I saw a child crossed the street with his eyes glued on his cell phone.
- Look at the train crossing the bridge. It looks like a train from the 1800s.
- Where will you go in front of a crossroad?
- Across from your left is money. Across from your right is love. Which way will you cross?
- What a hungry day. I've eaten two more meals since breakfast.
- I've known Tom since he was a kid.
- We knew Jack lived in California since he was born.
- Since the task is important, I will take care of it.

- It's been sunny since Sunday.
- Since I have a lot of energy, I'll get it done now.
- Since I did a good job finishing all of this, I should give me a big reward.

Kapitel 30: 231 – 240, More College

#231, hard

- Hard drive.
- Hard disk.
- Hard copy.
- Work hard.
- Hard work.
- Hard object.
- Hard or easy.
- Learn it the hard way.

- Getting an A in this computer course is hard, but if I work hard, I can do it.
- Passing that math class seems hard, but it's actually very easy.
- It can be hard to take many courses at once.
- If you pick up a piece of rock, put it next to your ear and hear music, what music is that?
- Hard rock music.
- I can learn things the easy way or the hard way.
- The easy way is to make mistakes when I'm a kid. The hard way is to make mistakes when I'm an adult.

#232, start

- Startup.
- Start over.
- Start out.
- Start off.
- Start again.
- Start with.
- Start from.

- At start
- To start.
- A head start.
- A good start.

- When does school start next semester?
- This class will start in 15 minutes. Do you want to start going there now?
- Give me a head start when you're ready to start your homework.
- I will also start going to my classes in June.
- A good start is half done.
- I'll give you a head start before I begin.

#233, might

- Might be.
- Might have.
- Might as well.
- Might is right.
- Pigs might fly.
- Might have been.
- Might win.
- Might come.

- This might be the right answer.
- The invention of the internet might be the best thing ever happened in communications.
- She might have to ask her professor for help if she does not understand this topic.
- They might pass by each other on campus today.
- You might get lost on the campus if you don't have a map.
- The professor might give us a surprise quiz tomorrow.

#234, story

- Love story.
- True story.
- Long story.
- Bedtime story.
- A story.
- Tell a story.
- Read a story.
- Long story short.
- A 10-story building.

- Let me tell you a story of Thomas Edison.
- Did you read the story before answering the questions on the test?
- How many stories were there on the test you took?
- I read all two of the stories that were recommended by the professor.
- This class is in a 10-story building.

#235, saw

Heute → see
Gestern → saw
Länger her → seen

- I saw it.
- Never saw it.
- She saw the movie.
- I know what I saw.

- Did you see that?
- Yes, I saw it.
- Do you believe it then?

- Yes. I know what I saw.
- I saw all the textbooks that are needed for the course.
- It would be great if you tell me what you saw in class.
- I only saw the last bits of the lesson from the professor.
- He said he saw great opportunities for growth in this school.
- She wanted to move to this school after she saw the student performance around here.
- He felt relaxed after he saw his improvement at school.

#236, far

- So far.
- How far.
- Too far.
- By far.
- As far as.
- So far, so good.
- Far down the road.
- Far or close?
- Far from.
- Far away.
- The far corner.
- The far side.

- Speaking like a native seems far away, but it will be mine if I have the will to get it.
- How's the progress so far?
- We are so far, so good and looking so darn good!
- I saw my friend from school from far down the road.
- My campus is pretty far from my house, but the good thing is I can exercise by running to school.
- The bus stop is at the far corner of this building.

- The train station is at the far side of the campus.
- There might be something beyond our imagination on the far side of the moon.

#237, sea

- The sea.
- At sea.
- By sea
- The Red Sea.
- The Black Sea.
- The Mediterranean Sea.
- Overseas.
- Sea level.
- Seabass.
- Seafood.
- Sea waves.
- Sea lion.

- Do you want to go swimming? In the sea?
- Yeah. I want to go swimming in the Dead Sea.
- Why is that?
- Because everyone will float in the Dead Sea.
- After the final exam, I went to the Mediterranean Sea to have some fun.
- The sea is looking pretty rough today, but it's usually calm.
- How far above sea level are we?
- Many students study overseas.
- What sea do you like, the Red Sea, the Black Sea, or the Mediterranean Sea?

#238, draw

Heute → draw

Gestern → drew
Länger her → drawn

- Draw in.
- Draw out.
- Draw on.
- Draw off
- Draw up.
- Draw close.
- Draw a picture.
- Draw a house.
- Draw attention.
- Draw him aside.
- Drawn by horse.

- I'm going to draw a big house for our art class. What are you going to draw?
- I have a friend who draws really well.
- Did you have to draw diagrams in English class?
- No. You draw diagrams in math class. You can draw the attention of the girl sitting next to you in English class.
- The doctor will draw your blood or the nurse will do it.
- The teacher can draw their own conclusions.
- Drawing pictures on a moving cart drawn by a horse can be challenging but fun!
- The finals were drawing close. Johnny quickly drew him aside and asked questions about the drawing class.
- The ball game ended in a draw. Everyone is a winner!

#239, left

Heute → leave
Gestern → left

Länger her → left

- Turn left.
- On the left.
- To the left.
- Left out.
- Left behind.
- Left hand.
- Left side.
- Left arm.
- Left school.

- Turn left or turn right?
- Turn left.
- Where is he?
- He left after school.
- Did you leave a message?
- Yes. I left a note for him.
- All that's left is the final exam!
- We've left no one behind. Everyone sat on the left side, wrote with their left hand, and left school altogether.

#240, late

- Running late.
- Arrived late.
- Stay up late.
- Very late.
- Too late.
- Better late than never.
- The latest news.

- Why was the student late to class?

- Because the bus left early today.
- Do you know why Robert came late to math class?
- If you're running late to class, copy your notes from someone else.
- I have the latest news: The exam will have 10 questions.
- See you later.

Und es ist wieder soweit!

- Getting an A in this computer course is hard, but if I work hard, I can do it.
- Passing that math class seems hard, but it's actually very easy.
- It can be hard to take many courses at once.
- If you pick up a piece of rock, put it next to your ear and hear music, what music is that?
- Hard rock music.
- I can learn things the easy way or the hard way.
- The easy way is to make mistakes when I'm a kid. The hard way is to make mistakes when I'm an adult.
- When does school start next semester?
- This class will start in 15 minutes. Do you want to start going there now?
- Give me a head start when you're ready to start your homework.
- I will also start going to my classes in June.
- A good start is half done.
- I'll give you a head start before I begin.
- This might be the right answer.
- The invention of the internet might be the best thing ever happened in communications.
- She might have to ask her professor for help if she does not understand this topic.
- They might pass by each other on campus today.
- You might get lost on the campus if you don't have a map.
- The professor might give us a surprise quiz tomorrow.
- Let me tell you a story of Thomas Edison.
- Did you read the story before answering the questions on the test?
- There was a great story about how a farmer became a hero.
- I read all two of the stories that were recommended by the professor.

- This class is in a 10-story building.
- Did you see that?
- Yes, I saw it.
- Do you believe it then?
- Yes. I know what I saw.
- I saw all the textbooks that are needed for the course.
- It'd be great if you tell me what you saw in class.
- I only saw the last bits of the lesson from the professor.
- He said he saw great opportunities for growth in this school.
- She wanted to move to this school after she saw the student performance around here.
- He felt relaxed after he saw his improvement at school.
- Speaking like a native seems far away, but it will be mine if I have the will to get it.
- How's the progress so far?
- We are so far, so good and looking so darn good!
- I saw my friend from school from far down the road.
- My campus is pretty far from my house, but the good thing is I can exercise by running to school.
- The bus stop is at the far corner of this building.
- The train station is at the far side of the campus.
- There might be something beyond our imagination on the far side of the moon.
- Do you want to go swimming? In the sea?
- Yeah. I want to go swimming in the Dead Sea.
- Why is that?
- Because everyone will float in the Dead Sea.
- After the final exam, I went to the Mediterranean Sea to have some fun.
- The sea is looking pretty rough today, but it's usually calm.
- How far above sea level are we?
- Many students study overseas.

- What sea do you like, the Red Sea, the Black Sea, or the Mediterranean Sea?
- I'm going to draw a big house for our art class. What are you going to draw?
- I have a friend who draws really well.
- Did you have to draw diagrams in English class?
- No. You draw diagrams in math class. You can draw the attention of the girl sitting next to you in English class.
- The doctor will draw your blood or the nurse will do it.
- The teacher can draw their own conclusions.
- The finals were drawing close. Johnny quickly drew him aside and asked questions about the drawing class.
- The ball game ended in a draw. Everyone is a winner!
- Turn left or turn right?
- Turn left.
- Where is he?
- He left after school.
- Did you leave a message?
- Yes. I left a note for him.
- All that's left is the final exam!
- We left for the movies after we finished our math class.
- Why was the student late to class?
- Because the bus left early today.
- Do you know why Robert came late to math class?
- Because the train arrived late.
- If you're running late to class, copy your notes from someone.
- I have the latest news: The exam will have 10 questions.
- See you later.

**Alles ist möglich wenn Sie ausreichend Geduld haben.
J. K. Rowling**

Kapitel 31: 241 – 250, In the Society

#241, run

Heute → run
Gestern → ran
Länger her → run

- Run up.
- Run down.
- Run out.
- Runoff.
- Run into.
- Run for.
- Runaway.
- Run over.
- A runway.
- Run around.
- Run a store.
- In the long run

- Why are you running home?
- I'm trying to run away from fear.
- There is one way to run away from fear—overcome it.
- If you run away from your projects, you will face them later. Face them now.
- Let's run to the store to get our art supplies.
- Max runs a store around the corner. We can go to his store so we don't go running around looking for them.
- Do you want to run for President of the club?
- Andrea is running for the president of the Success Impact Group.

#242, don't

- Don't ask.
- Don't talk!
- Don't worry.
- Don't care.
- Don't touch it.

- Don't worry. Be happy.
- Don't worry. Just get it done.
- The professor said don't talk or ask questions during the exam. Just take it.
- I don't care if it rains. I have to go to the movies.

#243, while

- A while.
- The while.
- Meanwhile.
- For a while.
- A while ago.
- Once in a while.
- After a while.
- A while ago.
- Wait a while
- Repeat while I listen.

- I haven't eaten in a while but I still have lots of energy.
- Let's repeat our lesson while we listen.
- I usually relax while I eat.
- The train took a while to come, but I still got to the office on time.
- I felt I had full of energy while listening to my boss.
- I haven't seen James in a while. I should go call him.
- Study right away after class while the memory is still

fresh.

#244, press

- Press on!
- Press down.
- Press it.
- Press the button.
- Press hard.
- Press conference.
- The L.A. Daily Press.

- Henry has his trousers pressed every day to make them look nice.
- Where can I get my suit pressed around the city?
- Press five. It'll get you there.
- Press your hand on your forehead to check if you're okay.
- The company issued a press release to the public.
- The press pressed hard trying to confirm the rumors.

#245, close

- Close up.
- Close down.
- Close to.
- Close by.
- Close in.
- Closeout.
- Close friend.
- Close-talk.
- Close enough.
- Open or close.

- Close the door.
- Close to the window.

- Can you close the window, please?
- Yes. If you'd close the door.
- That store is closing early today because of a holiday. It's closed now. We've walked close enough to see it.
- Anna and Sarah are close friends. They keep each other's secrets.
- She closed her eyes to feel the breeze since her seat was close to the window.
- The project due day is closing in. The IT team holds close talks daily.

#246, night

- Day or night.
- Day and night.
- Last night.
- At night.
- Nightfall.
- Good night.
- A moonless night.
- Night sky.

- If you go to Arizona, you'll see beautiful night skies.
- Visitors can come day or night. The park is open day and night.
- It was a moonless night that night when I went stargazing. I saw Venus and Jupiter since I arrived before nightfall.
- Good night!

#247, real

- For real.
- Get real.
- Keep it real.
- Real person.
- Real thing.
- Real gold.
- Real love.
- Real-time.
- Real life.
- Real estate agent.

- He's in real need for help. If you help him out now, you'll be his real friend.
- It was really hard to get this internship during college, but I worked really hard and got it.
- I've had a really good day at work because there were lots of snacks.
- The worker who helped us goes by CJ. He never told us his real name.

#248, life

- Full life.
- Half-life.
- Way of life.
- Full of life.
- New life.
- Shelf life.
- For life.
- An entire life.
- Life on Earth.
- Life jacket

- Do you have a life insurance?
- No, but I have a life.
- What's your aim in life?
- My aim in life is to change life on Earth within my lifetime. What do you want from life?
- I just want a simple and quiet life.
- Einstein spent his entire life in science.
- The ocean is full of life.
- Life on Earth is beautiful! I'll guard this planet with my life.

#249, few

- A few.
- The few.
- Very few.
- Quite a few.
- Too few.
- Fewer.
- Fewer than.
- A few minutes.
- A few days.
- A few years ago

- I had a few dollars last year, but now I have a lot more.
- Give me a few minutes to finish this.
- I bought a few stamps a few days ago.
- He has very few friends, but all his friends are good friends.
- I have fewer friends, but all of them can trust me with their lives.

#250, stop

- Bus stop.
- Stop sign.
- Non-stop.
- Full stop.
- Stop by.
- Stop moving.
- Stop right here.

- With a strong enough faith, no one can stop you from reaching your dreams.
- Do you see the stop sign? That's where the bus stop is.
- Please stop right here. I need to stop the squirrels from eating my corns.

Bringen wir es hinter uns!

- Why are you running home?
- I'm trying to run away from fear.
- There is one way to run away from fear—overcome it.
- If you run away from your projects, you will face them later. Face them now.
- Let's run to the store to get our art supplies.
- Max runs a store around the corner. We can go to his store so we don't go running around looking for them.
- Do you want to run for President of the club?
- Andrea is running for the president of the Success Impact Group.
- Don't worry. Be happy.
- Don't worry. Just get it done.
- The professor said don't talk or ask questions during the exam. Just take it.
- I don't care if it rains. I have to go to the movies.
- I haven't eaten in a while but I still have lots of energy.
- Let's repeat our lesson while we listen.
- I usually relax while I eat.
- The train took a while to come, but I still got to the office on time.
- I felt I had full of energy while listening to my boss.
- I haven't seen James in a while. I should go call him.
- Study right away after class while the memory is still fresh.
- Henry has his trousers pressed every day to make them look nice.
- Where can I get my suit pressed around the city?
- Press five. It'll get you there.
- Press your hand on your forehead to check if you're okay.
- The company issued a press release to the public.
- The press pressed hard trying to confirm the rumors.
- Can you close the window, please?

- Yes. If you'd close the door.
- That store is closing early today because of a holiday. It's closed now. We've walked close enough to see it.
- Anna and Sarah are close friends. They keep each other's secrets.
- She closed her eyes to feel the breeze since her seat was close to the window.
- The project due day is closing in. The IT team holds close talks daily.
- If you go to Arizona, you'll see beautiful night skies.
- Visitors can come day or night. The park is open day and night.
- It was a moonless night that night when I went stargazing. I saw Venus and Jupiter since I arrived before nightfall.
- Good night!
- He is in real need for help. If you help him out now, you'll be his real friend.
- It was really hard to get this internship during college, but I worked really hard and got it.
- I've had a really good day at work because there were lots of snacks.
- The worker who helped us goes by CJ. He never told us his real name.
- Do you have a life insurance?
- No, but I have a life.
- What's your aim in life?
- My aim in life is to change life on Earth within my lifetime. What do you want from life?
- I just want a simple and quiet life.
- Einstein spent his entire life in science.
- The ocean is full of life.
- Life on Earth is beautiful! I'll guard this planet with my life.
- I had a few dollars last year, but now I have a lot more.
- Give me a few minutes to finish this.

- I bought a few stamps a few days ago.
- He has very few friends, but all his friends are good friends.
- I have fewer friends, but all of them can trust me with their lives.
- With a strong enough faith, no one can stop you from reaching your dreams.
- Do you see the stop sign? That's where the bus stop is.
- Please stop right here. I need to stop the squirrels from eating my corns.

Es erscheint immer unmöglich bis es getan ist.
Nelson Mandela

Kapitel 32: 251 – 260, More in the Society!

#251, open

- Open up.
- Open mind.
- Open air.
- Open space.
- Open house.
- Open relationship.
- Open the door.
- Leave it open.
- Open to suggestions.
- Open and honest.
- Open until filled.

- Is it okay to open the window?
- Yes, if it's okay to leave the door open.
- I can barely keep my eyes open in the desert.
- He's about to open another store on the other side of the town. That will open up new opportunities on the other side of the town.
- There are more open spots on the other side of the town. These spots are open until filled. Any ideas? I'm open to suggestions.

#252, seem

- Seem to.
- Seem like.
- Seem right.
- Would seem.

- Seem okay.
- Seem happy.
- Seem excited.
- Seem to get it.

- He seems to be in good health.
- It seems important to check that item out.
- Tom seems a lot happier since you showed up.
- He seems to enjoy himself at college.
- Tim seemed to be having lots of fun today.

#253, together

- Stay together.
- Work together.
- Come together.
- Go together.
- Put together.
- Get together.
- All together.
- Stick together.
- Bring together.

- Tom likes to rub his hands together during cold days.
- The Red Team had lots of fun together in the forest. They're returning to the forest together.
- Two brothers set out on a journey together.
- They remember the happy childhood days they played together.
- They seem to get together on everything.
- Now they came in together and donated more money than the rest of the class added together.

#254, next

- Next to.
- Next door.
- Next time.
- Next week.
- Next year.
- Next of kin.
- What next?
- What's next?
- Who's next?
- The next.

- Tom happened to sit next to Mary at the corner during the contest.
- What happened next?
- They passed the contest and went on to the next level together.
- Next March, Tom will be going to Australia for one year to study.
- Who's next?
- You're next.
- Once I achieve this goal, I'll write down my next goal.
- Where is the shoe store?
- Next door.

#255, white

- Black and white.
- Off-white.
- White wine.
- White pepper.
- White bread.
- White flower.
- White color.

- White Collar.

- The white horse was prancing around the fence while the lady in white bent over to pick up the white flower from the ground.
- The dress she was wearing contained both red and white roses. That was why the horse tried to eat her dress.
- How do you order a vegetable sandwich on white bread?
- Just say vegetable sandwich on white.

#256, children

- The children.
- For children.
- Little children.
- Small children.
- Raise children.
- Like a child.
- Such a child.
- Childish.

- A child's play seems childish to us, but children enjoy it.
- Children like to play in the park.
- Children should obey their parents.

#257, begin
Heute → begin
Gestern → began
Länger her → begun

- Begin to.
- Begin with.
- Begin on.
- Begin work.
- Begin at the beginning.
- Begin again.
- To begin.
- Will begin.

- This has been your advantage from the beginning.
- Tom read the whole book yesterday from beginning to end and learned a great deal from it.
- We were about to start when it began to rain.
- He began to laugh when he saw the beginning of the movie.
- The word atrium begins with the A vowel sound.

#258, got

Heute → get
Gestern → got
Länger her → got
Länger her → gotten

- Got up.
- Got off.
- Got in.
- Got out.
- Got it.
- Got there.
- Got to go.
- Got married.

- I got to the bus stop just in time to get on the bus.
- When I got home, I noticed that I had a visitor.

- Bill got up early in order to catch the first train.
- When I got to school, the race had just begun.
- He got into Harvard. I got to go meet him.

#259, walk

- Walk on.
- Walk up.
- Walk-in.
- Walk out.
- Walk around.
- Walk away.
- A sidewalk.
- Go for a walk.

- Three beautiful ladies just walked into the lobby when Tom was ready to go for a walk.
- Jason stopped talking when Mary walked into the classroom.
- I walked 30 miles home yesterday after work. Was I crazy?
- Mark can walk to his office in thirty minutes or less.

#260, example

Example wird als ig'zampəl mit Vibration betont. Zzzzz, ig'zampəl. Es wird nicht als ig'sampəl betont. Mit Vibration wird es als ig'zampəl betont. ig'zampəl. ig'zampəl.

- An example.
- For example.
- As an example.
- Show an example.
- Set an example.

- Make an example.
- Give an example.
- Follow an example.

- You ought to set an example for the others.
- What you do becomes examples to your children.
- Your children will follow your examples.
- Can someone show me an example of a good person?
- Sure! Mother Teresa is an example of a good person.
- Thomas Edison is an example of success through persistence.

Setzen wir unsere Reise fort.

- Is it okay to open the window?
- Yes, if it's okay to leave the door open.
- I can barely keep my eyes open in the desert.
- He's about to open another store on the other side of the town. That will open up new opportunities on the other side of the town.
- There are more open spots on the other side of the town. These spots are open until filled. Any ideas? I'm open to suggestions.
- It seems important to check that item out.
- Tom seems a lot happier since you showed up.
- He seems to enjoy himself at college.
- Tim seemed to be having lots of fun today.
- Tom likes to rub his hands together during cold days.
- The Red Team had lots of fun together in the forest. They're returning to the forest together.
- Two brothers set out on a journey together.
- They remember the happy childhood days they played together.
- They seem to get together on everything.
- Now they came in together and donated more money than the rest of the class added together.
- Tom happened to sit next to Mary at the corner during the contest.
- What happened next?
- They passed contest and went on to the next level together.
- Next March, Tom will be going to Australia for one year to study.
- Who's next?
- You're next.
- Once I achieve this goal, I'll write down my next goal.
- Where is the shoe store?
- Next door.
- The white horse was prancing around the fence while

- the lady in white bent over to pick up the white flower from the ground.
- The dress she was wearing contained both red and white roses. That was why the horse tried to eat her dress.
- How do you order a vegetable sandwich on white bread?
- Just say vegetable sandwich on white.
- A child's play seems childish to us, but children enjoy it.
- Under the care of their parents, children like to play in the park.
- Children should obey their parents.
- This has been your advantage from the beginning.
- Tom read the whole book yesterday from beginning to end and learned a great deal from it.
- We were about to start when it began to rain.
- I'm beginning to getting results from my practices.
- He began to laugh when he saw the beginning of the movie.
- The word atrium begins with the A vowel sound.
- I got to the bus stop just on time to get on the bus.
- When I got home, I noticed that I had a visitor.
- Bill got up early in order to catch the first train.
- When I got to school, the race had just begun.
- He got into Harvard. I got to go meet him.
- Three beautiful ladies just walked into the lobby when Tom was ready to go for a walk.
- Tom got to his feet just before the chair collapsed.
- Jason stopped talking when Mary walked into the classroom.
- I walked 30 miles home yesterday after work. Was I crazy?
- Mark can walk to his office in thirty minutes or less.
- You ought to set an example for the others.
- What you do becomes examples to your children.
- Your children will follow your examples.

- Can someone show me an example of a good person?
- Sure! Mother Teresa is an example of a good person.
- Thomas Edison is an example of success through persistence.

Alles wird mit einem Verlangen erschaffen.
Earl Nightingale

Kapitel 33: 261 – 270, a Job or a Career

#261, ease

Das s in ease wird als ein z betont mit Vibration. Ease wird als eaze betont.

- Ease up.
- Ease off.
- Feel ease.
- At ease.
- With ease.

- It's easy for me to feel at ease when I meditate.
- When I meditate, my mind is empty. That sets my mind at ease.
- An empty mind eases up my body.
- I can meditate with ease.
- When you want peace, meditate.

#262, paper

- A paper.
- The paper.
- On paper.
- A piece of paper.
- Term papers.
- Paper clip.
- Paper towel.
- Paper bag.
- Paper plane

- Children like to make paper airplanes. It's childish to us, but it's amazing to them. A paper airplane is a paper to us, but it's a plane to them.
- Please look at this paper carefully. Everything we've talked about is on the paper.
- Our term papers are due by next Saturday. I've finished two term papers so far.

#263, often

- How often.
- Very often.
- More often.
- Quite often.
- Come often.
- Speak often.
- Laugh often.
- Eat often.
- As often as.
- Every so often

- James often laughs when he watches movies.
- Laugh often to stay healthy.
- I practice my English often. How often do you practice?
- I practice more often. I practice every available moment I have.
- Right! I often hear him practice.

#264, always

- Always on.
- Always try.

- Always be.
- Always stay happy.
- always on top.
- As always.

- Jenny always seems to be happy.
- Helen is always at the top of her class.
- I've always tried to do the right things.
- I always eat a big meal when I celebrate.
- Billy always feels happy when he sees Mary.
- Try this and when you get tired, you can always take a break.
- Always learn something when you're in your car.
- Never say never. Always say always.

#265, music

- Read music.
- Write music.
- Listen to music.
- Country music.
- Rock music.

- Sam has a great talent in music and he's determined to pursue a music career.
- He really enjoys playing classical music. He always listens to it.
- Last night, we attended a country music concert in London, but a rock music star suddenly showed up.
- The music we listened to last night was wonderful.
- Learn to read music first and then learn to write music.

#266, those

- To those.
- For those.
- Of those.
- As those.
- All those.
- Those days.
- Those who.
- Those flowers.
- Those positive people.
- Those who practiced.
- Those who are positive.

- She looks good in those red clothes.
- He devoted himself to music in those days.
- He's one of those people who seems to be good at everything.
- All of those students are happy since all of them are positive.
- Those who are positive will stay happy.

#267, both

- Both side.
- Both end.
- Both of.
- Both ways.
- Both parties.
- Both hands.

- Jenny and Mary are both positive people.
- Both of them went to the window to look outside.
- They both laughed while watching.
- Both America and Canada are large countries.

- Both sides are friendly.

#268, mark

- A mark.
- Birthmark.
- Trademark.
- Quotation mark.
- Make a mark.
- Leave a mark.
- Mark up.
- Markdown.
- Mark out.
- Mark off.

- "Mark my words" is often used as something will definitely happen.
- She put her hair down to hide her birthmark.
- The dog left a mark on his favorite tree.
- I marked all the important details of the story.
- What's his name?
- His name is Mark.

#269, book

- Textbook.
- Read a book.
- Address book.
- Instruction book.
- Phonebook.
- Bookstore.
- Bookbag.

- Bookmark.
- Bookkeeper.

- Do you know which book is our textbook?
- The book with the blue cover is our textbook.
- He's about to finish reading the book.
- I borrowed the book from this library and got a free bookmark.
- Our bookkeeper will book a ticket for you.

#270, letter

- Cover letter.
- Capital letter.
- Love letter.
- Write a letter.
- Mail a letter.
- Letter of appreciation.

- Should I use capital letters for this drawing?
- Capital letters would be a great choice.
- I'm going to write a letter with this invisible ink pen.
- How are they going to read the letter?
- They're going to read the letter with a pair of invisible glasses.
- Letters are delivered here at noon.
- I haven't received any letters from friends in the last 10 years because they all send emails instead.

Verwenden wir diese Wörter!

- It's easy for me to feel at ease when I meditate.
- When I meditate, my mind is empty. That sets my mind at ease.
- An empty mind eases up my body.
- I can meditate with ease.
- When you want peace, meditate.
- Children like to make paper airplanes. A paper airplane is a paper to us, but it's a plane to them.
- Please look at this paper carefully. Everything we've talked about is on the paper.
- Our term papers are due by next Saturday. I've finished two term papers so far.
- James often laughs when he watches movies.
- Laugh often to stay healthy.
- I practice my English often. How often do you practice?
- I practice more often. I practice every available moment I have.
- Right! I often hear him practice.
- Jenny always seems to be happy.
- Helen is always at the top of her class.
- I've always tried to do the right things.
- I always eat a big meal when I celebrate.
- Billy always feels happy when he sees Mary.
- Always learn something when you're in your car.
- Never say never. Always say always.
- Sam has a great talent in music and he's determined to pursue a music career.
- He really enjoys playing classical music. No matter where he goes, he always listens to it.
- Last night, we attended a country music concert in London, but a rock music star suddenly showed up.
- The music we listened to last night was wonderful.
- Learn to read music first and then learn to write music.

- She looks good in those red clothes.
- He devoted himself to music in those days.
- He's one of those people who seems to be good at everything.
- All of those students are happy since all of them are positive.
- Those who are positive will stay happy.
- Jenny and Mary are both positive people.
- Both of them went to the window to look outside.
- They both laughed while watching.
- Both America and Canada are large countries.
- Both sides are friendly.
- "Mark my words" is often used as something will definitely happen.
- She put her hair down to hide her birthmark.
- The dog left a mark on his favorite tree.
- I marked all the important details of this story.
- What's his name?
- His name is Mark.
- Do you know which book is our textbook?
- The book with the blue cover is our textbook.
- He's about to finish reading the book.
- I borrowed the book from this library and got a free bookmark.
- Our bookkeeper will book a ticket for you.
- Should I use capital letters for this drawing?
- Capital letters would be a great choice.
- I'm going to write a letter with this invisible ink pen.
- How are they going to read the letter?
- They're going to read the letter with a pair of invisible glasses.
- Letters are delivered here at noon.
- I haven't received any letters from friends in the last 10 years because they all send emails instead.

Sie sind zu mehr fähig als Sie erahnen.
E. O. Wilson

Kapitel 34: 271 – 280, More a Job or a Career

#271, until

- Until now.
- Until then.
- Until morning.
- Until dark.
- Until finished.
- Until done.
- Until recently.
- Until further notice.
- Wait until.
- Work until.

- Let's wait until dark to stargaze.
- I'll wait until morning to get up.
- If you keep working, it's just a matter of time until you succeed.
- What will you choose, work on a job until it is time to retire or work on your passion until you succeed?

#272, mile

- One mile.
- Walk a mile.
- Miles away.
- Miles better.
- Square mile.
- Last mile.
- Stand out a mile.

- Go the extra mile.

- I walk a mile to get to work every day.
- A mile is 1.6 km.
- Those who go the extra mile will stand out from the crowd.
- Going the extra mile is miles better than not going the extra mile.
- If you want just a job, do what you're supposed to do. If you want a career, do more than what you're supposed to do. The extra mile you've walked will gain you unimaginable benefits.

#273, river

- A river.
- Clean river.
- The Mississippi River.
- The Missouri River.

- Bizarre! A man swam across the river to go to a job interview.
- Did he get the job?
- Yes. He showed up soaking wet at the interview.
- And then?
- He said he swam across the river because the job was important to him.
- Rivers flow to the sea. Treat others like family.
- The Missouri River is 2,341 miles long. It's the longest river in America.

#274, car

- A car.
- Hybrid car.

- Electric car.
- Family car.
- New car.
- Used car.
- Fast car.
- By car.
- Car park.
- Car rental.
- Car wash.

- Josh drove his new car to New Jersey so that he could interview for a job.
- I went to the interview for a job by taking the train instead of driving my car.
- If you get this job, you will be able to buy a car. If you don't get this job, you will be able to work on something bigger than doing a job.
- Her parents bought her an electric car after seeing her putting endless energy into the renewable energy program.

#275, feet

- One foot.
- Two feet.
- My feet.
- Bare feet.
- Both feet.
- Square feet.
- Stand on your feet.
- Three feet from gold.

- Set a target and start walking on your feet if you want a career rather than a job!
- After barely making it through the job interview, he

was barely on his feet.
- He had been on his feet all day looking for a job. He didn't get a job but learned a lesson. He started to stand on his feet to build his company rather than looking for a job.
- Josh jumped to his feet when he knew he got the job.
- She fell down on her feet after realizing she didn't prepare for the job interview.
- I'll stand on my feet, stop looking for a job, and create my own opportunities.
- **Three Feet from Gold** is a book about why I should continue to work on my goal. I can be three feet away from success.

#276, care

- With care.
- To care.
- Take care.
- Healthcare.
- Skin care.
- Customer care.
- Care of.
- Care for.
- Care about.

- Do you care if you get the job?
- Look around you, 95% of people care about having a job, 80% don't like their job, and 30% hate their job.
- Now, do you still care for a job? How about care for your passion and make your passion work for you?
- He's an exception, he doesn't care about finding a job. He creates jobs. Anyone, including me, can be like him.
- I treat my parents with love and care! If I don't, I'll be

sorry when see their empty chair.

#277, second

- One second.
- Two seconds.
- Wait a second.
- Every second.
- Second chance.
- Second hand.
- Second floor.
- Second to none.

- If you like science, make it work for you. You can make more money in 60 seconds inventing a new technology than you can in 60 days doing a job you don't like.
- He was getting a second thought on whether to continue looking for a job or start working on his passion.
- His interview for the job didn't last a second because he didn't care. He had something much better to do.
- Decide what you want first, then decide what you do second.

#278, group

- Big group.
- That group.
- Ethnic group.
- Focus group.
- Age group.

- Follow the group.
- Lead the group.
- Walk with the group.
- Group work.
- Group leader.
- Group them together.

- I followed the group of people into the room for the interview.
- We were interviewed in groups instead of one at a time.
- Make sure you work well in groups because it is needed for a job.
- Be brave. Lead the group. Anyone can be a leader, including me!
- If you group the successful and the unsuccessful people together, which group do you belong to?
- I can be in the successful group if I'll just do one thing: go get what I want until I succeed!

#279, carry

- To carry.
- Carry on.
- Carry out.
- Carry with.
- Carryover.
- Carry away.
- Carry forward.

- Do you carry a pen?
- Yes.
- Can I borrow your pen?
- Sure! Here it is. It's an ink pen but it's out of ink today.

- Do you carry a backpack to school?
- Yes. I carry a laptop in the backpack.
- If I carry on my daily business with a specific target in sight, I can carry out the result at a specific time.

#280, took
Heute → take
Gestern → took
Länger her → taken

- Took care.
- Took away.
- Took off.
- Took out.
- Took place.
- Took over.
- Took a long time.
- Took the long way.
- Took a picture.
- Took notes.
- Took my advice.
- Took some time.
- Took my time.

- I once took an exam after a job interview and saw the interviewer exchanged a smile with yet another interviewer. Their body language sent me a clear message.
- There were people in line who already took the exam for the job. They took notes while they took the exam.
- The person he was interviewing with took his time with his questions. He took my advice by staying positive on all answers.
- He took a picture before going to interview for the job. That took away five minutes.

Üben Sie weiter.

- Let's wait until dark to stargaze.
- I'll wait until morning to get up.
- If you keep working, it's just a matter of time until you succeed.
- What will you choose, work on a job until it is time to retire or work on your passion until you succeed?
- I walk a mile to get to work every day.
- A mile is 1.6 km.
- Those who go the extra mile will stand out from the crowd.
- Going the extra mile is miles better than not going the extra mile.
- If you want just a job, do what you're supposed to do. If you want a career, do more than what you're supposed to do. The extra mile you've walked will gain you unimaginable benefits.
- Bizarre! A man swam across the river to go to a job interview.
- Did he get the job?
- Yes. He showed up soaking wet at the interview.
- And then?
- He said he swam across the river because the job was important to him.
- Rivers flow to the sea. Treat others like family.
- The Missouri River is 2,341 miles long. It's the longest river in America.
- I went to the interview for a job by taking the train instead of driving my car.
- If you get this job, you will be able to buy a car. If you don't get this job, you will be able to work on something bigger than doing a job.
- Her parents bought her an electric car after seeing her putting endless energy into the renewable energy program.
- Set a target and start walking on your feet if you want

a career rather than a job!
- After barely making it through the job interview, he was barely on his feet.
- He had been on his feet all day looking for a job. He didn't get a job but learned a lesson. He started to stand on his feet to build his company rather than looking for a job.
- She fell down on her feet after realizing she didn't prepare for the job interview.
- I'll stop looking for a job, and create my own opportunities.
- **Three Feet from Gold** is a book about why I should continue to work on my goal. I can be three feet away from success.
- Do you care if you get the job?
- Look around you, 95% of people care about having a job, 80% don't like their job, and 30% hate their job.
- Now, do you still care for a job? How about care for your passion and make your passion work for you?
- He's an exception, he doesn't care about finding a job. He creates jobs. Anyone, including me, can be like him.
- I treat my parents with love and care! If I don't, I'll be sorry when I see their empty chair.
- If you like science, make it work for you. You can make more money in 60 seconds inventing a new technology than you can in 60 days doing a job you don't like.
- He was getting a second thought on whether to continue looking for a job or start working on his passion.
- His interview for the job didn't last a second because he didn't care. He had something much better to do.
- Decide what you want first, then decide what you do second.
- There were a group of people waiting in line for the interview.

- I followed the group of people into the room for the interview.
- We were interviewed in groups instead of one at a time.
- Make sure you work well in groups because it is needed for a job.
- Be brave. Lead the group. Anyone can be a leader, including me!
- If you group the successful and the unsuccessful people together, which group do you belong to?
- I can be in the successful group if I'll just do one thing: go get what I want until I succeed!
- Do you carry a pen?
- Yes.
- Can I borrow your pen?
- Sure! Here it is. It's an ink pen but it's out of ink today.
- Do you carry a backpack to school?
- Yes. I carry a laptop in the backpack.
- If I carry on my daily business with a specific target in sight, I can carry out the result at the specific time.
- I once took an exam after a job interview and saw the interviewer exchanged a smile with yet another interviewer. Their body language sent me a clear message.
- There were people in line who already took the exam for the job. They took notes while they took the exam.
- The person he was interviewing with took his time. He took my advice by staying positive on all answers.
- He took a picture before going to the interview for the job. That took away five minutes.

**Wenn Sie es träumen können, können Sie es auch tun.
Walt Disney**

Kapitel 35: 281 – 290, Making Friends

#281, rain

- Rain or dry.
- Pouring rain.
- Heavy rain.
- Light rain.
- In the rain.
- Rainy day.
- Rainy season.
- Rainforest.

- We'll meet here next week. Rain or dry.
- A pouring rain is just what's needed in the dry summer months.
- It's been raining all day, easing the drought.
- Rainy season is the perfect time to harvest mushrooms in the rainforest.

#282, eat

Heute → eat
Gestern → ate
Länger her → eaten

- To eat.
- Eat out.
- Eat up.
- Eat away.
- Eat well.
- Eat a lot.
- Eat three meals a day.

- Eat the difficult meals.
- Something to eat.

- It tastes better to eat with friends.
- Make friends by eating with a new group of people.
- If you try to eat with people and socialize, you have a better chance of making friends.
- Which of these is the healthiest meal to eat, steam vegetables, raw fish, or fried chicken?
- Which one do you choose to eat, an easy meal or a difficult meal?

#283, room

- Living room.
- Bedroom.
- Classroom.
- Emergency room.
- Locker room.
- Fitting room.
- Room service.
- Room to grow.

- Open up to make room for making new friends.
- There is enough room to take two more people.
- The classroom is filled with teachers today.
- Your college roommate knows a great deal about you.

#284, friend

- A friend.
- My friend.

- Close friend.
- Good friend.
- True friend.
- Boyfriend.
- Girlfriend.
- Old friend.
- Long-lost friend.
- A friend of mine.
- A friend in need is a friend indeed

- A friend in need is a friend indeed.
- Friendly smiles will make you a lot of new friends.
- Do you want to make friends? If so, help people.
- Do you enjoy making friends? If so, help more people.
- Which one do you choose, 1000 new friends or one true friend?

#285, began
Heute → begin
Gestern → began
Länger her → begun

- Began with.
- Began to.
- Began on.
- Began work.
- Began again.
- Began at the beginning.
- Began my journey.

- He began making friends by listening to people and helping people.
- We all began somewhere when we tried to make friends.
- After the internet began, it was easy to make friends with people from around the world.

- When I began my hard work, I began with one idea.
- After I began my journey, I began to enjoy the feeling of success.

#286, idea

- An idea.
- Good idea.
- Main idea.
- No idea.
- The idea of.

- If you want to become successful in selling, you must get the idea of helping people.
- What's your idea? I'm open to suggestions.
- My idea is to go swimming in Lake Michigan in December.
- Good idea! We can make some friends who also go swimming there.

#287, fish

- A fish.
- Goldfish.
- Big fish.
- To fish.
- A school of fish.
- Fishing for something.

- "Give a man a fish, feed home for a day; teach a man to fish, feed home for a lifetime."
- A dolphin is a fish that likes to make friends.
- A school of fish is swimming in the ocean. If you have to choose one, which one will you choose, one that's in the crowd or one that leads the crowd?

- If a friend keeps fishing for your secret, is he a real friend?

#288, mountain

- A mountain.
- The mountain.
- High mountain.
- Mountain range.
- Mountain bike.
- Mountain dew.
- Climb a mountain.
- Walk on the mountain.
- Gaze at the mountain.
- A mountain of work.

- I went hiking with my friends on the mountain, and we had a great time.
- Let us go climb the mountains together to make some friends.
- Do you want to go to the mountains and gaze down from above?
- The highest mountain on Earth is Mount Everest.
- Would you rather eat a mountain of food or finish a mountain of work?

#289, north

- The north.
- Head north.
- Up north.
- Go north.
- Due north.
- The North Pole.

- The north stars.
- North America.
- In the north.
- To the north.

- Our ancestors used the north stars to find their directions.
- Where do you want to go on your next road trip, north or south?
- Head north to the forest to enjoy the peace of nature.
- In the North Pole, it's easy to see an aurora.
- North Africa's climate is very different than North America's climate.

#290, once

- Once upon a time.
- At once.
- Once again.
- Once more.
- Once in a while.
- All at once.
- Measure once, cut twice.
- Measure twice, cut once.

- Once I got a really high score on my math test, and everyone in the class wanted to become my friend. I made everyone my friend at once.
- Once I made a big mistake, but I learned something big from it.
- Once in a while, I'd face the same situation again, but I will not make the same mistake again.
- It's easy to make friends once you've mastered how to communicate with people.
- Would you rather measure once and cut twice or measure twice and cut once?

Bleiben Sie auf dem Laufenden!

- We'll meet here next week. Rain or dry.
- A pouring rain is just what's needed in the dry summer months.
- It's been raining all day, easing the drought.
- Rainy season is the perfect time to harvest mushrooms in the rainforest.
- It tastes better to eat with friends.
- Make friends by eating with a new group of people.
- If you try to eat with people and socialize, you have a better chance of making friends.
- Which of these is the healthiest meal to eat, steam vegetables, raw fish, or fried chicken?
- Which one do you choose to eat, an easy meal or a difficult meal?
- Open up to make room for making new friends.
- There is enough room to take two more people.
- The classroom is filled with teachers today.
- Your college roommate knows a great deal about you.
- A friend in need is a friend indeed.
- Friendly smiles will make you a lot of new friends.
- Do you want to make friends? If so, help people.
- Do you enjoy making friends? If so, help more people.
- Which one do you choose, 1000 new friends or one true friend?
- He began making friends by listening to people and helping people.
- We all began somewhere when we tried to make friends.
- After the internet began, it was easy to make friends with people from around the world.
- When I began my hard work, I began with one idea.
- After I began my journey, I began to enjoy the feeling of success.
- If you want to become successful in selling, you must get the idea of helping people.

- What's your idea? I'm open to suggestions.
- My idea is to go swimming in Lake Michigan in December.
- Good idea! We can make some friends who also go swimming there.
- "Give a man a fish, feed home for a day; teach a man to fish, feed home for a lifetime."
- A dolphin is a fish that likes to make friends.
- A school of fish is swimming in the ocean. If you have to choose one, which one will you choose, one that's in the crowd or one that leads the crowd?
- If a friend keeps fishing for your secret, is he a real friend?
- I went hiking with my friends on the mountain, and we had a great time.
- Let us go climb the mountains together to make some friends.
- Do you want to go to the mountains and gaze down from above?
- The highest mountain on Earth is Mount Everest.
- Would you rather eat a mountain of food or finish a mountain of work?
- Our ancestors used the north stars to find their directions.
- Where do you want to go on your next road trip, north or south?
- Head north to the forest to enjoy the peace of nature.
- In the North Pole, it's easy to see an aurora.
- North Africa's climate is very different than North America's climate.
- Once I got a really high score on my math test, and everyone in the class wanted to become my friend. I made everyone my friend at once.
- Once I made a big mistake, but I learned something big from it.
- Once in a while, I'd face the same situation again, but I will not make the same mistake again.

- It's easy to make friends once you've mastered how to communicate with people.
- Would you rather measure once and cut twice or measure twice and cut once?

Kapitel 36: 291 – 300, More Making Friends

#291, base

- A base.
- The base.
- Basement.
- Home base.
- Military base.
- Knowledge base.
- Customer base.
- Second base.
- Base on.
- Baseball.
- Base form.

- Do you believe the moon is an alien base?
- Based on my research, I do believe that the moon is the home base of an alien race.
- The basement of your house is a great place to store your old electronic gadgets. Bring them out 200 years later, and they'll become priceless antiques.
- The knowledge base is a good place to look for answers.
- With a large customer base, starting a new business is halfway done.

#292, hear

Heute → hear
Gestern → heard
Länger her → heard

- To hear.
- Hear music.
- Heard the news.
- Hear from.
- Hear about.
- Hear out.

- If you press your ear against a rock and hear music, what music do you hear?
- Rock music.
- Did you hear the news?
- Yes, I heard the news. The news is no news is good news.
- Where did you hear about that?
- I heard that from the doctor.
- If you want to say something, say it so that they hear you out, and if you'd like to donate $2 million, we would love to hear from you.
- OK. I heard you.

#293, horse

- A horse.
- Seahorse.
- Rocking horse.
- Ride a horse.
- Horse race.
- Horseback riding.
- Horsepower.

- What do you learn first, to walk or to ride a horse?
- Would you rather ride a horse or a cow?
- How many horsepower does your car have?
- 200.
- What horse you can't ride on?

- A seahorse.

#294, cut
Heute → cut
Gestern → cut
Länger her → cut

Cut wird als kət betont. Es wird nicht wie kät betont. Das u in cut wird als ə betont. ə → ət → kət.

- Cut back.
- Cut off.
- Cut in.
- Cut out.
- Cut up.
- Cut down.
- Cut through.
- Cut cost.
- Paper cut.
- Take your cut.
- Haircut.

- What's that cut on your finger?
- A paper cut.
- Streams have cut up the land. You should cut the price if you want to sell it.
- "A river cuts through rock not because of its power, but because of its persistence"
- Would you like a haircut?
- No. I'd like a clear-cut.

#295, sure

- Be sure.
- Make sure.

- For sure.
- Sure thing.
- A sure sign.

- What's a sure way of making friends?
- Render help when they need help is a sure way of making friends.
- Are you sure?
- I'm sure of it. That's a sure way to make friends for sure.
- A sure sign to make sure if a friend is a true friend is to see if he'll jump into the water when you're drowning. Be sure you know how to swim.

#296, watch
- A watch.
- Watch out.
- Watch over.
- Watch for.
- Watch your steps.

- When I fly an airplane, I watch out for birds.
- Relax! They have lifeguards to watch over the swimmers.
- When hiking in the forest, is there anything to watch for?
- Yes. Watch your steps.
- Why are you wearing two watches on both hands?
- Because I have to stand a watch in 30 minutes.
- Why do you have to wear four watches when you stand a watch?
- So that I know the exact time to get off.

#297, color
Color wird als ˈkələr betont. Es wird nicht als ˈkälər betont. Das erste o in color wird als ə betont. Ər → lər → ələr → ˈkələr.

- One color.
- Two colors.
- Bright color.
- True color.
- Background color.
- Color picture.
- Full of colors.
- Colorful.
- Color the picture.
- The change of color.

- What's your favorite color?
- My favorite is blue.
- How do you like people, by the color of the skin or by the content of their mind?
- What a colorful background color you have!
- Would you like to see the change of color?

#298, face

- To face.
- Face up.
- Face down.
- Face to face.
- Happy face.
- The three faces of a triangle.

- Draw a happy face if you're happy.
- How many faces does a triangle have?
- When facing a difficult situation, you can run from it or

face it.
- Do you feel the pain from the mistakes you've made in the past? You can run away from them and keep the pain or face them and be free.
- Face them! It's a painful but wise choice.

#299, wood

- Firewood.
- Wood log.
- Knock on wood.
- Made of wood.
- Solid wood.
- Wood chip.
- Woodchuck.
- Wood carving.
- In the woods.

- What would you like to carve, bamboo or wood?
- Firewood is gathered in the past for fuel and cooking.
- How much wood would a woodchuck chuck if a woodchuck could chuck wood?
- A woodchuck would chuck as much wood as a woodchuck would chuck if a woodchuck could chuck wood.

#300, main

- Main Street.
- Main road.
- Main meal.
- Main menu.
- Main character.

- Main idea.

- The main road of your town is normally called Main Street.
- Go to the main street of your town, and you should see some history.
- The main idea of bringing you appetizers is to bring up your appetite. Be sure to save some room for the main meal.

Die letzten zehn dieser Lektion. Los geht's.

- Do you believe the moon is an alien base?
- Based on my research, I do believe that the moon is the home base of an alien race.
- The basement of your house is a great place to store your old electronic gadgets. Bring them out 200 years later, and they'll become priceless antiques.
- The knowledge base is a good place to look for answers.
- With a large customer base, starting a new business is halfway done.
- If you press your ear against a rock and hear music, what music do you hear?
- Rock music.
- Did you hear the news?
- Yes, I heard the news. The news is no news is good news.
- Where did you hear about that?
- I heard that from the doctor.
- If you want to say something, say it so that they hear you out, and if you'd like to donate $2 million, we'd love to hear from you.
- OK. I heard you.
- What do you learn first, to walk or to ride a horse?
- Would you rather ride a horse or a cow?
- How many horsepower does your car have?
- 200.
- What horse you can't ride on?
- A seahorse.
- What's that cut on your finger?
- A paper cut.
- Streams have cut up the land. You should cut the price if you want to sell it.
- "A river cuts through rock not because of its power, but because of its persistence"
- Would you like a haircut?

- No. I'd like a clear-cut.
- What's a sure way of making friends?
- Render help when they need help is a sure way of making friends.
- Are you sure?
- I'm sure of it. That's a sure way to make friends for sure.
- A sure sign to make sure if a friend is a true friend is to see if he'll jump into the water when you're drowning. Be sure you know how to swim.
- When I fly an airplane, I watch out for birds.
- Relax! They have lifeguards to watch over the swimmers.
- When hiking in the forest, is there anything to watch for?
- Yes. Watch your steps.
- Why are you wearing two watches on both hands?
- Because I have to stand a watch in 30 minutes.
- Why do you have to wear four watches when you stand a watch?
- So that I know the exact time to get off.
- What's your favorite color?
- My favorite is blue.
- How do you like people, by the color of the skin or by the content of their mind?
- What a colorful background color you have!
- Would you like to see the change of color?
- Draw a happy face if you're happy.
- How many faces does a triangle have?
- When facing a difficult situation, you can run from it or face it.
- Do you feel the pain from the mistakes you've made in the past? You can run away from them and keep the pain or face them and be free.
- Face them! It's a painful but wise choice.
- Would you bring the wood inside?

- What would you like, wood or bamboo?
- Firewood is gathered in the past for fuel and cooking.
- How much wood would a woodchuck chuck if a woodchuck could chuck wood?
- A woodchuck would chuck as much wood as a woodchuck would chuck if a woodchuck could chuck wood.
- The main road of your town is normally called Main Street.
- Go to the main street of your town, and you should see some history.
- The main idea of bringing you appetizers is to bring up your appetite. Be sure to save some room for the main meal.

Ziele zu setzen ist der erste Schritt, Unsichtbares in Sichtbares umzuwandeln.
Anthony Robbins

Was auf Englisch zu sagen ist

Rank	Word	Rank	Word
301	enough	326	black
302	plain	327	short
303	girl	328	numeral
304	usual	329	class
305	young	330	wind
306	ready	331	question
307	above	332	happen
308	ever	333	complete
309	red	334	ship
310	list	335	area
311	though	336	half
312	feel	337	rock
313	talk	338	order
314	bird	339	fire
315	soon	340	south
316	body	341	problem
317	dog	342	piece
318	family	343	told
319	direct	344	knew
320	pose	345	pass
321	leave	346	farm
322	song	347	top
323	measure	348	whole
324	state	349	king
325	product	350	size

Rank	Word	Rank	Word
351	heard	376	ten
352	best	377	simple
353	hour	378	several
354	better	379	vowel
355	true	380	toward
356	during	381	war
357	hundred	382	lay
358	am	383	against
359	remember	384	pattern
360	step	385	slow
361	early	386	center
362	hold	387	love
363	west	388	person
364	ground	389	money
365	interest	390	serve
366	reach	391	appear
367	fast	392	road
368	five	393	map
369	sing	394	science
370	listen	395	rule
371	six	396	govern
372	table	397	pull
373	travel	398	cold
374	less	399	notice
375	morning	400	voice

Kapitel 37: 301 – 310 What to Say in English

#301: enough

- Good enough.
- Strong enough.
- Just enough.
- More than enough.
- Fair enough.

- We have enough people to get the job done.
- Is that enough?
- Sweetie, that's more than enough!
- An eight-year-old boy is old enough to do his own laundry.
- An eight-year-old child can get the laundry done easily enough.
- It's so delicious. I can't have enough of it!

#302: plain

- Plain paper.
- Plain water.
- Plain envelope.
- Plainclothes.
- Plain language.
- Plain English.
- Plain area.
- Plain view.
- Plain to see.
- Plain and honest person.

- Get it done and leave. Plain and simple.
- We can mail these plain letters in plain envelopes.
- This book is written in plain English. It's plain and simple to read.
- If you stand on the highest point of East Grand Canyon, the Grand Canyon Plain is in plain view.
- He's a plain and honest person. His intentions are plain to see.

#303, girl

- Pretty girl.
- Beautiful girl.
- Attractive girl.
- Little girl.
- Baby girl.
- Nice girl.
- Good girl.
- Girlfriend.

- What a cute little girl!
- He's proud of his girls.
- Do you have a girlfriend?
- What do you think of the attractive girl over there?
- She's too beautiful. I don't feel secure.
- That's the whole point! If a girl is too beautiful, all boys are staying away from her. She likes boys who are brave enough to talk to her!

#304, usual
Das s in usual wird als zh mit Vibration betont.

- As usual.
- The usual.

- Usual time.
- Usual practice.
- Usual day.
- Usual way.
- Usually.

- Carry out business the usual way.
- Ninety-five percent of people work on their job and carry on their days the usual way.
- Five percent of people work on their goal and get unusual results.

#305, young

- Young man.
- Young lady.
- Young woman.
- Young people.
- Young age.
- Young coconut.
- Young love.
- Young mind.
- Very young.
- Too young.
- Care for the young.

- Let these young girls make their own mistakes and grow.
- The more mistakes a young man makes, the more experience he'll gain, and the more he'll achieve at a young age.
- Let a child be a child. Let a young mind be a young mind.
- Most animals care for their young.

#306, ready

- Get ready.
- Be ready.
- All ready.
- Are you ready?
- Ready for.
- Ready to.

- Get ready for a change.
- Are you ready for the change?
- Yes, I'm so ready for a change in life. In fact, I'm ready to die for the change.
- A ready supply of tools is waiting for you to use for the change.
- You're one of the lucky ones who have ready access to the tools.
- When I got on board, the plane was ready to depart.

#307, above

- Above all.
- As above.
- See above.
- Rise above.
- Same as above.
- Above and beyond
- Above 95% of regular people.
-

- Above the darkness, three bright lights appeared.
- A child eight years or above is capable of doing the laundry for the family.
- Is your grade above average?
- Of every 100 people you meet, 5% of them are above regular people. You can be one of them if you set a

goal, take action, and persist.
- Look at the above sentence, it shows you the door to success.

#308, ever

- Ever before.
- Ever after.
- Ever since.
- Evermore.
- Whatever.
- Whoever.
- Wherever.
- Forever.
- Hardly ever.
- Never ever.

- Ever since I discovered the secret to happiness, I'm happier than ever before.
- Since applying Ken's My Fluent English formula, my English is getting ever more fluent.
- Will Ken ever stop talking about his humble background?
- Whoever has a humble background will try to hide it wherever possible, but Ken is proud of his humble background because he turned his humble background into power and sent him to success.
- Whatever background you have, you can succeed.

#309, red

- Redline.
- Red light.
- Red wine.
- Red pepper.

- Red alert.
- Bright red.
- Dark red.
- Turn red.

- Which of these is your favorite color, red or blue?
- If you ask a shy girl to dinner, her face will turn red.
- Stop in front of red lights.
- Respect others. Stay behind the red line.

#310, list

- Packing list.
- Price list.
- Waiting list.
- Long list.
- Word list.
- Mailing list.
- Shopping list.
- List of names.
- List to the side.

- Is 500 a long list?
- Compare to 500,000, 500 is a short list, and you can learn the list in six months.
- Mentor the success. List the names of successful people and put the list on your wall.
- The boat listed to the one side, but everyone is safe.

Holen wir sie uns!

- We have 10 people to work on the project. It'll be enough.
- Is it fair to let a child do the laundry?
- Yes. It's fair enough for a child eight years or older to do the laundry for the family.
- These potato chips are so delicious. I can't have enough of them!
- Get the job done and leave. Plain and simple.
- These plain letters can be mailed out in plain envelopes.
- This book is written in plain English.
- Standing on the highest point of East Grand Canyon, the Grand Canyon Plain is in plain view.
- He's a plain and honest person. His intentions are plain to see.
- What a cute little girl!
- The dad is so proud of his girl.
- Do you have a girlfriend?
- What do you think of the attractive girl over there?
- She's too beautiful. I don't feel secure.
- That's the whole point! If a girl is too beautiful, all boys are staying away from her and she wants a boyfriend! She likes boys who are brave enough to talk to her! Just talk to her. It works like a chemical.
- Carry out business the usual way.
- Ninety-five percent of people work on their job and carry on their days the usual way.
- Five percent of people work on their goal and get unusual results.
- We grow up by making mistakes. The more mistakes young people make, the more experience they gain and the more they'll achieve at a young age.
- Let a child be a child. Let a young mind be a young mind.
- Are you ready for a change?

- Yes, I'm so ready for a change in life. In fact, I'm ready to die for the change.
- A ready supply of tools is waiting for you to use for the change.
- You're one of the lucky ones who have ready access to the tools.
- Above the darkness, three bright lights appeared.
- A child eight years or above is capable of doing the laundry for the family.
- Is your grade above average?
- Of every 100 people you meet, 5% of them are above regular people. You can be one of them if you set a goal, take action, and persist.
- Look at the above sentence, it shows you the door to success.
- Ever since I discovered the secret to success, I became more successful than ever before.
- Since applying Ken's My Fluent English formula, my English is getting ever more fluent.
- Will Ken ever stop talking about his humble background?
- Whoever has a humble background will try to hide it wherever possible, but Ken is proud of his humble background because he turned his humble background into power and sent him to success.
- Whatever background you have, you can succeed.
- Which of these is your favorite color, red or blue?
- If you ask a shy girl to dinner, her face will turn red.
- Respect others. Stay behind the red line.
- Is 500 a long list?
- Compare to 500,000, 500 is a just short list, and you can learn the list in six months.
- Mentor the success. List the names of successful people and put the list on your wall.
- The boat listed to the one side, but everyone is safe.

Diejenigen, die verrückt genug sind, zu denken, dass sie die Welt verändern können sind üblicherweise die, die es dann auch tun.
Steve Jobs

Kapitel 38: 311 – 320, What to Say in English

#311, though

- Even though.
- Although.
- As though.
- Seriously though.

- Though Ken spoke no English when he came to America, he can speak like a native now.
- He knows four languages, though he normally speaks two.
- Would you like to practice with me?
- I already have other plans, but thank you though!
- Although it was raining, everybody showed up.

#312, feel

Heute → feel
Gestern → felt
Länger her → felt

- To feel.
- Feel good.
- Feel like.
- Feel better.

- Feel well.
- Play by feel.

- If you want to feel the heat, go to Death Valley.
- If you want to experience what it feels like to be stung by bees, go destroy their hives.
- He plays the piano by feel rather than by music.

#313, talk

- A talk.
- To talk.
- Talk to.
- Talk with.
- Talk about.
- Talk back.
- Talk into.
- Talk over.
- Talk show.
- Small talk.

- The kids started to talk two minutes after they played together.
- Start small talks to start making friends.
- Treat others like you want to be treated. Talk to others like you want to be talked to.
- What are you talking about?
- We're talking about how to talk to others.
- It sounds like you're trying to talk her into the party.

#314, bird

- Early bird.
- Hummingbird.
- Bird cage.
- Bird watch.
- The early bird catches the worm.

- Most birds fly.
- Use it or lose it. Chickens are birds, but they don't use their wings and can't fly anymore. Use your English even just to talk to yourself.
- The biggest bird in the world is the ostrich. They can reach nine feet tall.
- The smallest bird in the world is the bee hummingbird. They are the size of a bee.

#315, soon

- As soon.
- See you soon.
- Very soon.
- Soon after.
- Sooner or later.
- The sooner the better.
- As soon as possible.

- Practice every day and sooner or later you'll speak English like a native.
- How soon do you want it done?
- Very soon. The sooner the better.
- OK. Then I'll get it done as soon as possible.
- Excellent! See you soon.

#316, body

- Body language.
- Human body.
- Everybody.
- Somebody.
- Arms and body.
- A body of water.

- Good morning, everybody!
- Will somebody go get the door, please?
- What speaks more, words or body?
- The human body speaks a lot more than words.
- If we're blocked by a body of water, we can drain the water or cross the water.

#317, dog

- Dog leash.
- Dog food.
- Dog tag.
- Dog collar.
- Wild dog.
- Pet dog.
- Pet a dog.

- What a cute little dog!
- What breed is the dog?
- I don't know what breed it is. It's a wild dog.
- Can I pet the dog?
- Yes, you can pet him.

#318, family

Um family zu betonen, sagen Sie fa mə ly. Das i in family had den ə Klang. Es kann ebenso still sein. Sagen Sie nicht fa mi ly. Sagen Sie fa mə ly oder einfach fa m ly.

- My family.
- Extended family.
- Family member.
- He's family.
- His family.
- Take care of things like family.
- Family tree.
- Family name.
- Family room.
- Language family.
- Family business.

- What a lovely family!
- Your teenage kids will start thinking about building their own family.
- Treat him well. He's family.
- His family is getting together.
- We've been working together for 20 years. I'm here to take care of things like family.
- English and German are in the same language family.
- This farm has been a family business for 200 years.

#319, direct

- Direct meaning.
- Direct way.
- Direct flight.
- Direct hit.
- Direction.
- Directly.
- Direct to.

- Direct at.
- Direct object.
- Direct current.
- Direct deposit.
- Direct marketing.

- This is a direct flight from New York to Seattle.
- There's a direct way to say something and an indirect way to say the same thing. A leader likes to say it the direct way. An artist likes to say it the indirect way.
- Pick your direction, face the direct heat, and get there directly.
- The general directed his orders to his colonels.
- The Kepler's telescope is directed at the stars.

#320, pose

Wenn pose als ein Nomen verwendet wird, wird es als pose mit einer s Endung betont. Wenn pose als ein Verb verwendet wird, wird es als poze mit Vibration betont. Poze.

- Picture pose.
- Pose for.
- Pose as.
- Pose a question.
- Pose a threat.

- What is she posing for?
- She's posing for a model contest.
- Nice pose!
- She poses a threat.
- What?
- She's too pretty. She poses a threat to other models.

Auf geht's.

- Though Ken spoke no English when he came to America, he can speak like a native now.
- He knows four languages, though he normally speaks two.
- Would you like to practice with me?
- I already have other plans, but thank you though!
- Although it was raining, everybody showed up.
- If you want to feel the heat, go to Death Valley.
- If you want to experience what it feels like to be stung by bees, go destroy their hives.
- He plays the piano by feel rather than by music.
- The kids started to talk two minutes after they played together.
- Start small talks to start making friends.
- Treat others like you want to be treated. Talk to others like you want to be talked to.
- What are you talking about?
- We're talking about how to talk to others.
- Most birds fly.
- The biggest bird in the world is the ostrich. They can reach nine feet tall.
- The smallest bird in the world is the bee hummingbird. They are the size of a bee.
- Practice every day and sooner or later you'll speak English like a native.
- How soon do you want it done?
- The sooner the better.
- OK. Then I'll get it done as soon as possible.
- Good morning, everybody!
- Will somebody go get the door, please?
- What speaks more, words or body language?
- If we're blocked by a body of water, we can drain the water or cross the water.
- Can I pet the dog?

- Yes, you can pet him.
- What a lovely family!
- Your teenage kids will start thinking about building their own family.
- Treat him well. He's family.
- His family is getting together.
- We've been working together for 20 years. I'm here to take care of things like family.
- English and German are in the same language family.
- This farm has been a family business for 200 years.
- This is a direct flight from New York to Seattle.
- There's a direct way to say something and an indirect way to say the same thing. A leader likes to say it the direct way. An artist likes to say it in the indirect way.
- Pick your direction, face the direct heat, and get there directly.
- The general directed his orders to his colonels.
- The Kepler's telescope is directed at the stars.
- What is she posing for?
- She's posing for a model contest.
- Nice pose!
- She poses a threat.
- What?
- She's too pretty. She poses a threat to other models.

Kapitel 39: 321 – 330, What to Say in English

#321, leave

Heute → leave
Gestern → left
Länger her → left

Das v in leave ist mit Vibration. Lea v. Wenn es einen v Klang am Ende gibt, ist der ea Klang länger. Leaaaaaaaaa v. Im Vergleich zu leaf, ist leaf sehr kurz. Lea f, leaaaaaaaa v, lea f, leaaaaaaa v.

- Leave alone.
- Leave behind.
- Leave out.
- Leave a place.
- Leave a tip.
- Leave a message.
- Leave it like that.
- Leave more choices.
- Leave it to us.

- She's leaving her job of 20 years to work on her passion.
- She left a big tip after getting her favorite meal.
- She's not here. Would you like to leave her a message?
- Though I can change this design, it's better to leave it like that.
- There is still something left over from lunch.
- That decision will leave us more choices.
- Leave it to us. We'll take care of it.

#322, song

- Romantic song.
- Love song.
- Theme song.
- Favorite song.
- Beautiful song.
- Sing a song.
- The song of the wind.
- The song of the birds.

- This is a beautiful song. I'm enjoying it.
- I say we should sing a song while we walk.
- I like the song of the wind.
- I like the song of the birds.

#323, measure
Das s in measure wird als zh mit Vibration betont. Measure wird als meZHer betont.

- Measure up.
- Measure out
- Measure word
- Measure the distance.
- Measure the length.
- Measure the height.
- Measure the number.
- Measure against.
- Measure up to.
- A measure of.
- Safety measure.
- Tape measure.

- Measure once, cut twice.

- Measure twice, cut once.
- Measure the distance between two points.
- Students measure their height every year.
- Jenny measured out the ingredients.
- Measure yourself against an average person around you, where are you at?
- Are you measure up to the standard?
- If you do not measure up to the standard, congratulations, you have a lot of room to grow! As a country boy with no special talent, I was able to jump from the very bottom to the very top. So can you.
- To get to the top, you only need a goal, actions, and a measure of faith.

#324, state

- Solid state.
- Liquid state.
- The United States.
- A state visit.
- State the situations.
- State of the art.
- State of the mind.

- Water can exist in three states: solid state, liquid state, and gas state.
- There are 50 states in the United States of America.
- The hikers stated they saw an avalanche.
- Their vehicle is equipped with state of the art technology.

#325, product

- Products and services.
- Product key.
- Product quality.
- Useful products.
- Dairy product.
- Domestic products.
- The product of two numbers.

- The product of 4 x 2 is 8.
- We offer high-quality products and friendly customer services.
- Success is the product of a goal, actions, and persistence.
- Enter your product key to activate your product and services.
- A harvester is a useful product at harvest season.

#326, black

- Black and white.
- Pitch-black.
- Black tea.
- Black ink.
- Black hole.
- Blackberries.
- Blackout.

- What do you like more, a color painting or a black and white painting?
- The night was pitch-black when we got lost in the mountains.
- Black tea is too strong for my stomach.

- Blackberries are everywhere in Oregon.

#327, short

- Short story.
- Short hair.
- Short walk.
- Short break.
- Short vowels.
- Shortcut.
- Short term.
- Short time.
- Short circuit.
- Short-handed.
- In short.

- Eh is a short vowel. It's always closed by a consonant.
- Most parents here read to their children short stories at bedtime.
- She cut her hair short.
- There's a shortcut to the barbershop. It's just a short walk away.
- I'm going to take a short break and get there now.

#328, numeral

- A numeral number.

- Roman numeral one → I.
- Roman numeral two → II.
- Roman numeral ten → X.

- The clock on the tower is in Roman numerals.

#329, class

- English class.
- Math class.
- Go to class.
- First class.
- Middle class.
- Working class.
- World class.
- Upper class.
- High class.
- Classmate.
- Class of 2020.

- You can learn English in an English class or in daily life.
- They're the class of 2018.
- In America, if you graduate college and find a job, you're automatically middle class. If you don't graduate college but persist to work on something big, you'll be upper class.

#330, wind

- Wind farm.
- Wind power.
- Wind energy.
- Blowing wind.
- Howling wind.
- Strong wind.
- Southeast wind.

- It'll be windy today.
- The northwest wind is blowing right at us. This is a good place build a wind farm.
- Wind energy is all that's needed here.
- Strong winds blowing at tree branches create my favorite song of the wind.

Machen wir uns an die Arbeit.

- She's leaving her job of 20 years to work on her passion.
- She left a big tip after getting her favorite meal.
- She's not here. Would you like to leave her a message?
- Though I can change this design, it's better to leave it like that.
- There is still something left over from lunch.
- That decision will leave us more choices.
- Leave it to us. We'll take care of it.
- This song is beautiful. I'm enjoying it.
- I say we should sing a song while we walk.
- I like the song of the wind.
- I like the song of the birds.
- Measure once, cut twice.
- Measure twice, cut once.
- Measure the distance between two points.
- Students measure their height every year.
- Jenny measured out the ingredients.
- Measure yourself against an average person around you, where are you at?
- Are you measure up to the standard?
- If you do not measure up to the standard, congratulations, you have a lot of room to grow! As a country boy with no special talent, I was able to jump from the very bottom to the very top. So can you.
- To get to the top, you only need a goal, actions, and a measure of faith.
- Water can exist in three states: solid state, liquid state, and gas state.
- There are 50 states in the United States of America.
- The hikers stated they saw an avalanche.
- The product of 4 x 2 is 8.
- We offer high-quality products and friendly customer services.

- Success is the product of a goal, actions, and persistence.
- A harvester is a useful product at harvest season.
- What do you like more, a color painting or a black and white painting?
- The night was pitch-black when we got lost in the mountains.
- Black tea is too strong for my stomach.
- Blackberries are everywhere in Oregon.
- Eh is a short vowel. It's always closed by a consonant.
- Most parents here read to their children short stories at bedtime.
- She cut her hair short.
- There's a shortcut to the barbershop. It's just a short walk away.
- I'm going to take a short break and get there now.
- Roman numeral one → I.
- Roman numeral two → II.
- Roman numeral ten → X.
- The clock on the tower is in Roman numerals.
- You can learn English in an English class or in daily life.
- They're the class of 2018.
- In America, if you graduate college and find a job, you're automatically middle class. If you don't graduate college but persist to work on something big, you'll be upper class.
- It'll be windy today.
- The northwest wind is blowing right at us. This is a good place build a wind farm.
- Wind energy is all that's needed here.
- Strong winds blowing at tree branches create my favorite song of the wind.

> Gewinner sind nicht Menschen, die nie versagen, sondern
> Menschen, die nie aufgeben.
> Anonym

Kapitel 40: 331 – 340, What to Say in English

#331, question

- Ask question.
- Good question.
- In question.
- Out of the question.
- Without question.
- Quick question.
- No question.
- Questioned for answers.

- May I ask a stupid question?
- There's no such thing as a stupid question. The stupid thing is you don't ask when you have a question.
- Everyone needs water and oxygen. There's no question about it.
- You can question for an answer, but just like chicken and eggs, there's no answer to this question.

#332, happen

- Happen to.
- Happen again.
- May happen.
- About to happen.

- What happened?
- How did it happen?
- Happen to be in the same place at the same time.

- What happened? You look frightened.
- Something weird just happened. Five navy airplanes suddenly disappeared in the Bermuda Triangle.
- What happened to them?
- They just suddenly vanished. A rescue plane was sent out to look for them, but it, too, vanished from Earth.
- It happened again many times in later years and no one knows what happened to the planes.

#333, complete

- Complete set.
- Complete recovery.
- Complete works.
- Complete darkness.
- Complete list.
- Complete genius.
- Completely.
- Completed.

- I'm going to take one more course to complete my degree.
- Here is a complete list of the courses. Which one would you like to take?
- A complete genius who just completed this course suggested me to take this one.
- This course is completely full, but one student just canceled it. Would you like to take it right away?
- That would be completely awesome!

#334, ship

- Spaceship.
- Cruise ship.
- Cargo ship.
- Rocketship.
- Travel by ship.
- Ship out.
- Ship overseas.
- Ship by air.
- Shipping cost.

- As of 2018, our fastest spaceship can travel to the nearest star in 40,000 years.
- Six ships ship six sheep when the sheep are asleep.
- Shipping the sheep by ship is much cheaper than shipping the sheep by air. Shipping cost will be greatly reduced.

#335, area

- The surrounding area.
- A quiet area.
- A safe area.
- The area of a square.

- This quiet area is one of the safest areas in America.
- Salem, Oregon, and the surrounding areas were in complete darkness during a total solar eclipse in 2017.
- The area of the square is 16 square miles.

#336, half

Half unterscheidet sich von have. Vergleichen Sie den

Unterschied. Half, have, half, have. Das v ist betont mit Vibration, /v/. Das f ist stimmlos ohne Vibration, /f/. Half, have, half, have. Im Wort half ist die Vokallänge kurz, half. In Wort have ist die Vokallänge länger, have.

- Half hour.
- Half-life.
- One half.
- Half of the circle.
- Half a dollar.
- Half full.

- Half of the class went to see the solar eclipse.
- Half of the sun was blocked by the moon.
- Let me cut the price by half.
- How much is half price?
- Half a dollar.
- What do you see in this half glass of water? Half full or half empty?
- If you see this half glass of water as half full, your goal is half finished at start!

#337, rock

- Piece of rock.
- Moon rock.
- Rock music.
- Rocking chair.
- Rocking cradle.
- Rock and roll.
- Rockstar.
- Rock bottom.
- Rock climber

- Pick up a piece of rock, you pick up a piece of history.

Rocks take millions of years to form.
- Rocks on the Moon are older than rocks on Earth. Where did the Moon come from?
- Put the baby in a cradle and give it a rock; the baby will fall asleep.
- Sit on a rocking chair and look back in life, what have I accomplished?

#338, order

- In order.
- On order.
- Out of order.
- Purchase order.
- Money order.
- Put them in order.
- Put in an order.
- In order to.
- Take order from.
- Give orders to.
- Doctor's orders.
- Order from the captain.
- Place an order.

- Can you put the numbers in order?
- The doctor has just put in an order.
- In order to complete the process, the doctor needs to put in a release order and then I'll put the numbers in order.
- Who does the captain take orders from? Who does he give orders to?
- We need to order a box of papers.
- It's been ordered. Sally ordered them yesterday.

#339, fire

- On fire.
- Wildfire.
- Campfire.
- Gunfire.
- An open fire.
- Fire engine.
- Fire truck.
- Fire drill.
- Fire extinguisher.
- Fire a shot.
- Fire an under-performed employee.
- Fire a rocket.
- Fire up.

- The 8000-year old drawing of a firing rocket in a cave fired up my imaginations of aliens' visitations to Earth in the past.
- To be polite, say let go of an under-performed employee rather than fire a lazy employee.
- Campfires are allowed in campsites. Campers normally cook on an open fire.

#340, south

- North and south.
- In the south.
- Go south.
- Down south.
- Southside.
- Due south.
- South coast.
- South wind.
- South of the equator.

- The South Pole.

- Where do you want to travel to to see the aurora, north or south?
- I'll travel to the North Pole.
- The warm south wind is what's needed in the winter months.

Es ist an der Zeit, dass wir die Wörter lernen.

- May I ask a stupid question?
- There's no such thing as a stupid question. A stupid thing is you don't ask when you have a question.
- Everyone needs water and oxygen. There's no question about it.
- You can question chickens for an answer, but just like chicken and eggs, there's no answer to this question.
- What happened? You look frightened?
- Something weird just happened. Five navy airplanes suddenly disappeared in the Bermuda Triangle.
- What happened to them?
- They just vanished. A rescue plane was sent out to look for them, but it, too, vanished.
- It happened again many times in later years and no one knows what happened to the missing planes.
- I'm going to take one more course to complete my degree.
- Here is a complete list of the courses. Which one would you like to take?
- A complete genius who just completed this course suggested me to take this one.
- This course is completely full, but one student just canceled it. Would you like to take it right away?
- That would be awesome!
- As 2018, our fastest spaceship can travel to the nearest star in 40,000 years.
- Six ships ship six sheep when the sheep are asleep.
- Shipping the sheep by ship is much cheaper than shipping the sheep by air. Shipping cost will be greatly reduced.
- This quiet area is one of the safest areas in America.
- Salem and its surrounding areas were completely darkened during the total solar eclipse in 2017.
- Half of the class went to see the solar eclipse.
- Half of the sun was blocked by the Moon.

- What do you see in this half glass of water? Half full or half empty?
- If you see this half glass of water as half full, you're a positive person. Your goal is half complete at start!
- Pick up a piece of rock, you pick up a piece of history. Rocks take millions of years to form.
- Some rocks on the Moon are older than rocks on Earth. Where did the Moon come from?
- Sit on a rocking chair and look back in life, what have I accomplished?
- In order to complete the process, the doctor needs to put in a release order and then I'll put the numbers in order.
- Who does the captain take orders from? Who does he give orders to?
- We need to order a box of papers.
- It's been ordered. Sally ordered them yesterday.
- The 8000-year old drawing of a firing rocket in a cave fired up my imaginations of aliens' visitations to Earth in the past.
- To be polite, say let go of an underperformed employee rather than fire a lazy employee.
- Campfires are allowed in campsites. Campers normally cook on an open fire.
- Where are you going to see the aurora, north or south?
- North Pole.
- The warm south wind is what's needed in the winter months.

Kapitel 41: 341 – 350, What to Say in English

#341, problem

- No problem.
- Math problem.
- Financial problem.
- Same old problem.
- Solve the problem.

- There are 10 problems in today's math test.
- Our school is facing a financial problem. Donations are welcome.
- Can it get done by the end of the day?
- No problem.

#342, piece

- One piece.
- Piece of cake.
- Piece of advice.
- Piece of art.
- Piece of luggage.
- Piece of evidence.
- Piece of paper.
- Cut into pieces.
- Piece together.

- Take good care of it. This is a piece of art from the 13th century.
- How many pieces of luggage are you checking in?

- Just one.
- Discovered cities underwater is a piece of evidence of ancient civilizations.
- Kids like the game of cutting papers into pieces and then piecing them together.

#343, told

Heute → tell
Gestern → told
Länger her → told

- Told the truth.
- Told a story.
- Told about.
- We told you so.
- Was told to do so.

- It's a story told from generation to generation.
- The underwater cities told a new story of ancient civilizations.
- The divers were told to come back up.

#344, knew

Heute → know
Gestern → knew
Länger her → known

- Knew about.
- Knew how.
- Just knew.

- Did you know about that?
- Yes, I knew about that.
- The divers couldn't tell what it was, but they knew they found a piece of ancient artifact.
- She knew from her heart that being a model was something she wanted to do.

#345, pass

- Pass out.
- Pass by.
- Pass on.
- Pass through.
- Pass up.
- Pass down
- Pass to.
- Pass over.
- Pass the gate.
- Pass the test.
- Boarding pass.

- Does everyone have a pass? You need to show your pass to get in.
- The quickest way to drive to Spokane is through Steven's Pass.
- I just passed by Steven's Pass last year.
- Congratulations! You pass the test.
- Can you pass the salt, please?
- I passed out soon after I went to bed.
- Ancient stories pass on from generation to generation.

#346, farm

- Farmland.
- Farmer.
- Farmworker
- Farm animals.
- Fish farm.
- Energy farm.
- Wind farm.

- An average farmer in this area farms 200 acres of farmland.
- Farmers here farm fish for a living.
- Consumers like wild caught fish rather than farmed fish.
- Farmers can farm fish, animals or farmlands.
- This company farms energy from wind, water, and solar.

#347, top

- Top up.
- Top with.
- Top notch.
- Top secret.
- Top speed.
- Topsoil.
- Top of the hill.
- Top of the class.
- On top.
- To the top.
- Mountaintop.
- Top 500 most useful words.

- I'd like a macaroni pizza topped with peppers, please.

- Learn the top 100 most useful phrases.
- Ken didn't speak English when he came to the United States at age 17, but now he's a top teacher in English fluency.
- The top of the mountain gives you a nice view of the city.
- Can you walk to the top of the hill in high heels?

#348, whole

- Whole world.
- Whole day.
- Whole life.
- Whole body.
- Whole piece.
- Whole bottle.
- Whole thing.
- Whole point.
- Whole number.
- Whole new meaning.
- On the whole.
- As a whole.

- He finished the whole pizza and then finished the whole bottle of water.
- Researchers spent a whole year studying an underwater city in the Bermuda Triangle and told a whole new story of ancient civilizations.
- The whole point of studying underwater cities is to find ancient civilizations.

#349, king

- The king.
- King-size.
- King bed.
- King crab.
- Live like a king.
- The king of chess.
- The king of ski.

- Lions are king of all animals.
- Yo-yo Ma is the king of cello.
- The king is the most important piece of the chess.

#350, size

- Font size.
- Actual size.
- Shoe size.
- Full size.
- Large size
- King-size.
- One size fits all.
- Size 1.
- Size 10.

- What's your shoe size?
- 9.
- What size do you wear?
- 10.
- This cap is the right size for everyone. It's one size fits all.

Es ist wieder soweit, lernen wir diese zehn Wörter.

- There are 10 problems in today's math test.
- Our school is facing a financial problem. Donations are welcome.
- Can it get done by the end of the day?
- No problem.
- Take good care of it. This is a piece of art from the 13th century.
- How many pieces of luggage are you checking in?
- Just one.
- Discovered cities underwater is a piece of evidence of ancient civilizations.
- Kids like the game of cutting papers into pieces and then piecing them together.
- It's a story told from generation to generation.
- The underwater cities told a new story of ancient civilizations.
- The divers were told to come back up.
- Did you know about that?
- Yes, I knew about that.
- The divers couldn't tell what it was, but they knew they found a piece of ancient artifact.
- She knew from her heart that being a model was something she wanted to do.
- Does everyone have a pass? You need to show your pass to get in.
- The quickest way to drive to Spokane is through Steven's Pass.
- I just passed by Steven's Pass last year.
- Congratulations! You pass the test.
- Can you pass the salt, please?
- I passed out soon after I went to bed.
- Ancient stories pass on from generation to generation.
- An average farmer in this area farms 200 acres of farmland.

- Farmers here farm fish for a living.
- Consumers like wild caught fish rather than farmed fish.
- Farmers can farm fish, animals or farmlands.
- This company farms energy from wind, water, and solar.
- I'd like a macaroni pizza topped with peppers, please.
- Learn the top 100 most useful phrases.
- Ken didn't speak English when he came to the United States at age 17, but now he's a top teacher in English fluency.
- The top of the mountain gives you a nice view of the city.
- Can you walk to the top of the hill in high heels?
- He finished the whole pizza and then finished the whole bottle of water.
- Researchers spent a whole year studying an underwater city in the Bermuda Triangle and told a whole new story of ancient civilizations.
- The whole point of studying underwater cities is to find ancient civilizations.
- Lions are king of all animals.
- Yo-yo Ma is the king of the cello.
- The king is the most important piece of the chess.
- What size do you wear?
- Size 10.

Der Sieg des Erfolgs ist halb gewonnen wenn einer die Angewohnheit annimmt, sich Ziele zu setzen und diese zu erreichen.

Og Mandino

Kapitel 42: 351 – 360, What to Say in English

#351, heard

Heute → hear
Gestern → heard
Länger her → heard

- Have heard.
- Be heard.
- An unheard of.
- Never heard of.

- Did you hear that?
- What is it?
- Everyone needs to do a hearing test.
- Yes. I heard it.
- Have you heard of that place?
- Never heard of it.

#352, best

- Best time.
- Best way.

- Best friend.
- Best with.
- Best wish.
- Best practice.
- Best of.
- The best.
- My best.
- All the best.

- The best time of the day for most people is morning. The best time of the day for Ken is 10 P.M.
- The best way to climb Mount Everest is by foot.
- This is a good one, this is a better one, and that is the best one.
- I like my ink pen best.
- This dish is best eaten hot.
- Do the best you can.
- I'll do my best.

#353, hour

- An hour.
- Two hours.
- Morning hours.
- Into the hour.
- The last hour.
- Happy hour.
- Rush hour.
- Per hour.

- I'll get it done in an hour.
- It'll take two hours to get to Portland.
- The best time to see the city is in the morning hours.

- We're into the second hour.
- Two o'clock is the last hour to turn in your papers.

#354, better

- Better time.
- Better way.
- Better with.
- Better off.
- Better than.
- Better late than never.
- Get better.
- Much better.
- Feel better.
- Even better.

- A better time to go around the city is in the morning.
- A better way to climb Mount Everest is by foot.
- This is a good one, this is a better one, and that is the best one.
- I like my ink pen better.
- This dish is better eaten with pepper.
- It's better off this way.
- I'll do an even better job.

#355, true
Um true zu betonen, sagen Sie es rückwärts. Ue, Rue, True.

- True north.
- True friend.
- True love.
- True or false.

- Dream come true.

- A true friend will stand with you when you need help.
- A friend who renders help when you need help is a true friend.
- To see your true self, record yourself all the time.
- The air show was truly amazing.
- True or false. Airplanes are not the invention of the 20th century.
- True. Model airplanes were excavated from 3000-year old tombs.

#356, during

- During the day.
- During the week.
- During the break
- During the summer.
- During the winter.

- Bears hibernate during the winter.
- It was completed during the day.

#357, hundred
Um hundred zu betonen, sagen Sie es rückwärts. Ed, Red, Dred, Undred, Hundred.

- One hundred.
- A 100 dollar bill.
- Two hundred.
- Hundreds of people.
- 1900.

- A hundred people came yesterday.
- Hundreds of people came today.
- A 100 dollar bill is the largest bill I have.
- This happened in the nineteen hundreds.

#358, am

- I am.
- I'm.

- I am a human being.
- I am living on Earth.
- No matter what happens around me, I have the power to choose my responses. If I choose to look at the positive side on everything, I'm a happy person.

#359, remember

- Remember to.
- Remember that.
- Easy to remember.
- As far as I can remember.
- Remember the past.
- They are remembered.

- Remember to turn off the light before you leave.
- Remember to turn in the papers today.
- You can remember the past or forget about the past.
- The first few people who choose to live on Mars will be remembered by everyone on Earth even after 1000 years.

#360, step

- Step in.
- Step out.
- Step down.
- Step up.
- Step one.
- Step two.
- Step back.
- Step forward.
- Last step.
- Doorstep.
- One step at a time.
- Step-by-step.

- "That's one small step for man, one giant leap for mankind."
- Learn to speak English one step at a time.
- Follow the step-by-step instructions in the book to get your results.
- Step one is to repeat over and over again to get it into your subconscious mind.
- The last step is to keep practicing.
- Follow the doorsteps I showed you and take steps to your success.
- When your friends are in trouble, step forward for them.

Nun ist es wieder an der Zeit. Stürzen wir uns auf die Wörter.
- Did you hear that?
- What is it?
- Everyone needs to do a hearing test.
- Yes. I heard it.
- Have you heard of that place?
- Never heard of it.
- The best time of the day for most people is morning. The best time of the day for Ken 10 P.M.
- The best way to climb Mount Everest is by foot.
- This is a good one, this is a better one, and that is the best one.
- I like my ink pen best.
- This dish is best eaten hot.
- Do the best you can.
- I'll do my best.
- I'll get it done in an hour.
- It'll take two hours to get to Portland.
- The best time to see the city is in the morning hours.
- We're into the second hour.
- Two o'clock is the last hour to turn in your papers.
- A better time to go around the city is in the morning.
- A better way to climb Mount Everest is by foot.
- This is a good one, this is a better one, and that is the best one.
- I like my ink pen better.
- This dish is better eaten with pepper.
- It's better off this way.
- I'll do an even better job.
- A true friend will stand with you when you need help.
- A friend who renders help when you need help is a true friend.
- To see your true self, record yourself all the time.
- The air show was truly amazing.
- True or false. Airplanes are not the invention of the

20th century.
- True. Model airplanes were excavated from 3000-year old tombs.
- Bears hibernate during the winter.
- It was completed during the day.
- A hundred people came yesterday.
- Hundreds of people came today.
- A 100 dollar bill is the largest bill I have.
- This happened in the nineteen hundreds.
- I am a human being.
- I am living on Earth.
- No matter what happens around me, I have the power to choose my responses. If I choose to look at the positive side on everything, I'm a happy person.
- Remember to turn off the light before you leave.
- Remember to turn in the papers today.
- You can remember the past or forget about the past.
- The first few people who choose to live on Mars will be remembered by everyone on Earth even after 1000 years.
- "That's one small step for man, one giant leap for mankind."
- Learn to speak English one step at a time.
- Follow the step-by-step instructions in the book to get your results.
- Step one is to repeat over and over again to get it into your subconscious mind.
- The last step is to keep practicing.
- When your friends are in trouble, step forward for them.
- Follow the doorsteps I showed you and take steps to your success.

Kapitel 43: 361 – 370, What to Say in English

#361, early

- Early bird.
- Early life.
- Early morning.
- Very early.
- Too early.
- As early as.
- Better early than late.
- Early start.
- Early flowers.

- It's better to get there early than late.
- He begins his work early in the morning to get an early start.
- She got her work done early.
- Who is she?
- The girl you met earlier.
- These early flowers begin to bloom in March.
- The early bird gets the worm.

#362, hold

Heute → hold
Gestern → held
Länger her → held

- Hold on.
- Hold off.
- Hold up.
- Hold down.

- Hold back.
- Hold out.
- Hold the door.
- Hold the opportunity.
- Hold a meeting.
- Hold the sugar.
- On hold.
- Get hold of.

- Hold on for just a moment. I'll be right with you.
- Grab a hold of something when riding the train.
- Hold the door, please.
- We've just held a meeting on this project. This project is on hold. I'll hold the opportunity for you. I can hold it for two weeks.
- Hold the sugar on the tea, please.
- Keep a hold on the bag. It's important.

#363, west

- Go west.
- To the west.
- In the west.
- West wind.
- West coast.

- Today's weather forecast, sunny, west wind at 19 mph.
- The east coast has beautiful shorelines. The west coast has more beautiful shorelines.
- The west side of the hill is a great place to see the sunset.

#364, ground

- Grounded.
- Ground cover.
- Ground floor.
- Ground zero.
- On the ground.
- Common ground.
- To the ground.
- Above ground.

- Planes were grounded due to strong winds from the west.
- We have lots of ground to cover, but we've already covered a lot of ground.
- They both want to learn to speak English. They found a common ground to start building their friendship.
- Summertime is a good time to enjoy the sun on the ground.
- Kids enjoy playing on the playground in the summer.

#365, interest

Interest kann als /in te rest/ betont werden. Wenn Sie interest bei normaler Geschwindigkeit sagen, sagen Sie /in trest/. Wenn Sie interest bei reduzierter Geschwindigkeit sagen, sagen Sie /in te rest/.

- Interest rate.
- Interest in.
- Common interest.
- Bank interest.
- Credit card interest.
- Showing interest.
- Listen with interest.
- Personal interest.

- A topic of interest.

- Interest rate changes from time to time.
- If we put the money into a savings account, we'll earn some interest.
- Credit card interests are very high. Pay your credit card bills in full to avoid paying interests.
- This is a topic of his personal interest. He's showing intense interest and listening with interest.

#366, reach

- Reach out.
- Reach over.
- Reach for.
- Reach up.
- Reach to.
- Reach your goal.
- Reach someone.
- Reach something.
- Out of reach.
- Within reach.

- Practice this course over and over again and speaking English like a native is within reach.
- Can you reach Jill?
- I called Jill. She's out of reach.
- Reach out to her again.
- Benjamin reached over again to reach for the phone.
- As soon as I reach my goal, I celebrate.

#367, fast

- Fast food.

- Fast car.
- Fast result.
- Fast writer.
- Run fast.
- Drive fast.
- Very fast.
- As fast.
- On fasting.

- He's got a fast car.
- He's driving too fast.
- Well. You're eating too fast.
- I've been fasting for three days. Try it and you'll know how fast you should be eating after you've been fasting for three days.
- No matter if you're a fast writer or a slow writer, you can get fast results on speaking.

#368, five

- Five o'clock.
- Five dollars.
- Five years old.
- Five twenty-five.
- High five.
- Five thousand five hundred and fifty-five.

- What time is it?
- Five o'clock.
- What time is it now?
- 5:05.
- How much is your watch?
- Twenty-five dollars.
- How old is your son?
- Five.

#369, sing

Heute → sing
Gestern → sang
Länger her → sung

- Sing in.
- Sing out.
- Sing up.
- Sing-off.
- Sing a song.
- Sing along.
- Sing well.
- Sing together.

- If they're happy, they sing a song.
- When he's happy, he sings his heart out.
- If you're happy, sing along.

#370, listen

Ähnlich dem Wort often, ist das t in listen stimmlos, also anstatt li sten zu sagen, sagen Sie li sen.

- Listen to.
- Listen for.
- Listen out.
- Listen again.
- Listen carefully.

- Listen to this. It's a strange noise.
- Listen, I can get us out of here if you'll listen to me.
- Listen to your teenage children carefully. What they're telling you is just the tip of an iceberg. You need to listen for the hidden meaning.

Sie wissen was kommt. Lernen Sie nun diese Wörter.
- It's better to get there early than late.
- He begins his work early in the morning to get an early start.
- She got her work done early.
- Who is she.
- The girl you met earlier.
- These early flowers begin to bloom in March.
- The early bird gets the worm.
- Hold on for just a moment. I'll be right with you.
- Grab a hold of something when riding the train.
- Hold the door, please.
- We've just held a meeting on this project. This project is on hold. I'll hold the opportunity for you. I can hold it for two weeks.
- Hold the sugar on the tea, please.
- Keep a hold on the bag. It's important.
- Today's weather forecast, sunny, west wind at 19 mph.
- The east coast has beautiful shorelines. The west coast has more beautiful shorelines.
- The west side of the hill is a great place to see the sunset.
- Planes were grounded due to strong winds from the west.
- We have lots of ground to cover, but we've already covered a lot of ground.
- They both want to learn to speak English. They found a common ground to start building their friendship.
- Summertime is a good time to enjoy the sun on the ground.
- Kids enjoy playing on the playground in the summer.
- Interest rate changes from time to time.
- If we put the money into a savings account, we'll earn some interest.
- Credit card interests are very high. Pay your credit card bills in full to avoid paying interests.

- This is a topic of his personal interest. He's showing intense interest and listening with interest.
- Practice this course over and over again and speaking English like a native is within reach.
- Can you reach Jill?
- I called Jill. She's out of reach.
- Reach out to her again.
- Benjamin reached over again to reach for the phone.
- As soon as I reach my goal, I celebrate.
- He's got a fast car.
- He's driving too fast.
- Well. You're eating too fast.
- I've been fasting for three days. Try it and you'll know how fast you should be eating after you've on a three day fast.
- No matter if you're a fast writer or a slow writer, you can get fast results on speaking.
- What time is it?
- Five o'clock.
- What time is it now?
- 5:05.
- How much is your watch?
- Twenty-five dollars.
- How old is your son?
- Five.
- If you're happy, sing a song.
- When he's happy, he sings his heart out.
- Birds singing is a sign of spring.
- Listen to this. It's a strange noise.
- Listen, I can get us out of here if you'll listen to me.
- Listen to your teenage children carefully. What they're telling you is just the tip of an iceberg. You need to listen for the hidden meaning.

Ich habe es 99 mal versucht und bin gescheitert, aber beim 100sten Versuch wurde es ein Erfolg.
Albert Einstein

Kapitel 44: 371 – 380, What to Say in English

#371, six

- Six o'clock.
- Six years old.
- Six feet tall.
- Six pack.
- Six hundred thousand six hundred and sixty-six.
- Group of six.

- What time is it?
- Six o'clock.
- How much is your watch?
- Twenty-six dollars.
- How old is your girl?
- Six.
- How tall are you?
- Six feet.
- These six are the giants of our school. They're six feet tall.

#372, table

- Dining table.

- Round table.
- Wooden table.
- Put food on the table.
- The negotiating table.
- The multiplication table.

- We need a dining table.
- We already have a dining table.
- Ours is a round dining table. We need a long dining table.
- We're lucky. We can put food on the table.
- The two parties will hold talks on the negotiating table.
- Kids need to remember the multiplication table if they want to be good at math.

#373, travel

- Travel agent.
- Travel abroad.
- Travel expense.
- Travel by foot.
- Travel around the world.
- Air travel.
- Space travel.
- Time travel.

- Do you like to travel?
- Yes. I travel a lot.
- I like to travel around the world to learn about the world.
- It's okay to travel by foot.
- Travel is required for the job.
- Travel costs will be paid by the company.
- If you haven't traveled, you haven't really learned.

#374, less

- Less than.
- Less amount.
- Less and less.
- More or less.
- Much less.
- Less expensive.
- Even less.
- No less.

- Teenage kids spend less time on sleeping and more time on social networking.
- They used to sleep eight hours a day, but nowadays, they sleep less than five.
- Teenagers use computers less. They use their cell phones more.
- They earn a dollar on each sale less 30% commission.

#375, morning

- Good morning.
- In the morning.
- Every morning.
- Early morning.
- Early in the morning.

- Good morning!
- He runs every morning.
- She runs early in the morning.

#376, ten

- Ten points.
- Ten years old.
- Ten o'clock.
- Ten thousand.
- Ten minutes.
- Ten percent.

- A decade is ten years.
- How old is your girl?
- She's ten.
- The meeting is scheduled for ten.
- Good job! You got ten points!
- Here's a ten-dollar bill. You can play ten games if you want.

#377, simple

- Simple task.
- Simple color.
- Simple truth.
- Simple life.
- Simple country boy.
- Very simple.
- Fairly simple.
- Quite simple.

- Repeating a simple task over and over again can make you a master.
- Studying simple words over and over again will help you master them.
- Wear simple clothes if you want to be like everyone else.
- Even a simple country boy like Ken can be successful. So can you! That's a simple truth. Just set a target, get on your feet, and keep working until you

get there. As simple as that.

#378, several

- Several hours.
- Several days.
- Several months.
- Several times.
- Several people.

- How long did you stay in Europe?
- A week.
- I stayed several days more.
- This is a big project. It'll take several months to complete.
- Several people tried that several times.

#379, vowel

- Vowels and consonants.
- Vowel sounds.
- Long vowel.
- Short vowel.

- There are five vowels in the English language.
- The vowels are a, e, i, o, u.
- Each vowel can combine with other vowels to make more vowel sounds.

#380, toward

- Toward the front.

- Toward the back.
- Toward the beginning of next year.
- Toward success.
- Move toward.
- Turn toward.
- Lean toward.
- Run toward.

- Where did Benjamin go?
- He just walked toward the front of the house.
- Be careful. The door will open toward you.
- Work your way all the way toward success.

Legen wir los.
- What time is it?
- Six o'clock.
- How much is your watch?
- Twenty-six dollars.
- How old is your girl?
- Six.
- How tall are you?
- Six feet.
- These six are the giants of our school. They're six feet tall.
- We need a dining table.
- We already have a dining table.
- Ours is a round dining table. We need a long dining table.
- We're lucky. We can put food on the table.
- The two parties will hold talks on the negotiating table.
- Kids need to remember the multiplication table if they want to be good at math.
- Do you like to travel?
- Yes. I travel a lot.
- I like to travel around the world to learn about the world.
- It's okay to travel by foot.
- Travel is required for the job.
- Travel costs will be paid by the company.
- If you haven't traveled, you haven't really learned."
- Teenage kids spend less time on sleeping and more time on social networking.
- They used to sleep eight hours a day, but nowadays, they sleep less than five.
- Teenagers use computers less. They use their cell phones more.
- They earn a dollar on each sale less 30% commission.
- Good morning!

- He runs every morning.
- She runs in the morning and in the evening.
- A decade is ten years.
- How old is your girl?
- She's ten.
- The meeting is scheduled for ten.
- Good job! You got ten points!
- Here's a ten-dollar bill. You can play ten games with it.
- Repeating a simple task over and over again can make you a master.
- Studying simple words over and over again will help you master them.
- Wear simple clothes if you want to be like everyone else.
- Even a simple country boy like Ken can be successful. So can you! That's a simple truth. Just set a target, get on your feet, and keep working until you get there. As simple as that.
- How long did you stay in Europe?
- A week.
- I stayed several days more.
- This is a big project. It'll take several months to complete.
- Several people tried that several times.
- There are five vowels in the English language.
- The vowels are a, e, i, o, u.
- Each vowel can combine with other vowels to make more vowel sounds.
- Where did Benjamin go?
- He just walked toward the front of the house.
- Be careful. The door will open toward you.
- Work your way all the way toward success.

Kapitel 45: 381 – 390, What to Say in English

#381, war

- Tug of war.
- Cold war.
- Civil war.
- World war.
- At war.
- Declare war.
- After the war.
- A war between aliens.
- The war against drought.

- After World War II, Earth's population thrived.
- The two UFOs crashed in Roswell, New Mexico were believed to be a war between aliens.
- There hasn't been any rain in six months. The State of California is fighting a war against drought.

#382, lay

Heute – lay
Gestern – laid
Länger her – laid

- Lay down.
- Layout.
- Lay off.
- Layup.
- Lay back.

- Lay on.
- Lay the table.
- Lay eggs.

- The mom laid down the baby before she warmed the milk.
- They laid the table before dinner.
- He laid out the plan and then began at once to execute the plan.
- Some birds lay up to 10 eggs a year.

#383, against

- Go against.
- Rise against.
- Turn against.
- Compete against.
- Against the law.
- Against all odds.
- The war against drought.
- Pushing against the wall.
- Racing against time.
- Team Crystal against Team Megatron.

- California is racing against time to fight the war against drought.
- What strange exercises they're doing. One is banging against the desk. One is pushing against the wall.
- Team Crystal is racing against time preparing the game against Team Megatron. It'll be quite a match.

#384, pattern

- Pattern recognition.
- Pattern matching.
- Regular pattern.
- Traffic pattern.
- Usual pattern.
- Work pattern.
- Textile pattern.
- Same pattern.

- These houses are built in the same pattern.
- They follow the work pattern to complete the work.
- I have the same textile pattern in my house.

#385, slow

- Slow speed.
- Slow lane.
- Slow process.
- Slow clock.
- Slow season.
- Slow business.
- Slow reader.
- Slow down.
- Slow motion.
- Very slow.
- Too slow.
- Go slow.

- The subway train suddenly slowed down and stopped. Everyone wondered why.
- He's a slow reader but a fast writer.
- Business is slow in the summer but will pick up in the winter.
- Summer is the slow season.

- This clock is three minutes slow.
- Growing up is a slow process.
- If you drive too slow, stay in the slow lane.

#386, center

- Center of the universe.
- Center of the galaxy.
- Center the subject.
- Call center.
- Shopping center.
- City center.
- Town center.
- Service center.
- In the center.

- When taking pictures, never center the subject. The subject should be off center.
- The tallest building in town is the center of the light speed research.
- When a newborn baby comes to Earth, she acts like she's the center of the universe.

#387, love

- Love can be a noun.
- Love can be a verb.
- Love someone.
- Give love to someone.
- Fall in love.
- In love.
- True love.

- Pure love.

- Love is a noun. You can give love to someone.
- Love is a verb. You can take actions to love someone.
- You can hide your love in you. You can also show your love by doing something.
- Hiding your love will keep you in the same place. Showing your love will get you somewhere.

#388, person

- A person.
- In person.
- Contact person.
- Per person.
- Good person
- Nice person.

- She's a person who likes to help others.
- She's a nice person. She'll help you clean up your desk.
- Registration fee is $10 per person.

#389, money

- Earn money.
- Make money.
- Save money.
- Spend money.
- Transfer money
- Get money.

- We normally say we work to make money.
- The correct way is we work to earn money.

- We can earn money by trading hours for dollars.
- We can also earn money by using our brain.

#390, serve

- Serve as.
- Serve in.
- Serve up.
- Serve with.
- Serve a purpose.
- Enough to serve.
- First come first serve.

- He serves as the department manager in the store.
- This restaurant serves this community.
- The restaurant serves hot food in large dishes.
- A dish there serves two people.
- Using large dishes serves the purpose of washing fewer dishes, therefore, saving water.

Sie wissen es ganz genau. Es ist Zeit Wörter zu lernen.
- After World War II, Earth's population thrived.
- The two UFOs crashed in New Mexico were believed to be at war between aliens.
- There hasn't been any rain in six months. The State of California is fighting a war against drought.
- The mom laid down the baby before she warmed the milk.
- They laid the table before dinner.
- He laid out the plan and then began at once to execute the plan.
- Some birds lay up to 10 eggs a year.
- California is racing against time to fight the war against drought.
- What strange exercises they're doing. One is banging against the desk. One is pushing against the wall.
- Team Crystal is racing against time preparing the game against Team Megatron. It'll be quite a match.
- These houses are built in the same pattern.
- They follow the work pattern to complete the work.
- I have the same textile pattern in my house.
- The subway train suddenly slowed down and stopped. Everyone wondered why.
- He's a slow reader but a fast writer.
- Business is slow in the summer but will pick up in the winter.
- Summer is the slow season.
- This clock is three minutes slow.
- Growing up is a slow process.
- If you drive too slow, stay in the slow lane.
- When taking pictures, never center the subject. The subject should be off center.
- The tallest building in town is the center of the light speed research.
- When a newborn baby comes to Earth, she acts like she's the center of the universe.
- Love is a noun. You can give love to someone.

- Love is a verb. You can take actions to love someone.
- You can hide your love in you. You can also show your love by doing something.
- Hiding your love will keep you in the same place. Showing your love will get you somewhere.
- She's a person who likes to help others.
- She's a nice person. She'll help you clean up your desk.
- Registration fee is $10 per person.
- We normally say we work to make money.
- The correct way is we work to earn money.
- We can earn money by trading hours for dollars.
- We can also earn money by using our brain.
- He serves as the department manager in the store.
- This restaurant serves this community.
- The restaurant serves hot food in large dishes.
- A dish there serves two people.
- Using large dishes serves the purpose of washing fewer dishes, therefore, saving water.

Kapitel 46: 391 – 400, What to Say in English

#391, appear

- Appear on.
- Appear in.
- Appear to.
- Appear again.
- Appear suddenly.
- Appear to be.

- Why do stars appear to be blinking?
- That's because of the flow of air.
- You appeared on TV yesterday.
- When you're freezing, it's a wonderful thing to see the sun appear on the horizon.
- The word appear appears nine times on this page and 14 times in this chapter.

#392, road

- Road trip.
- Roadmap.
- Road sign.
- Roadside.
- Toll road.
- Main road.
- Off-road.
- Country road.
- On the road.
- Down the road

- Main Street is the main road of the town.
- This country road will take you to the main road.
- If you'd just stay on this road, it'll take you to the main road.
- Benson's well on the road to becoming a project manager.

#393, map

- Map out.
- Map up.
- Mindmap.
- Roadmap.
- World map.
- City map.
- On the map
- Mapping system.

- This is a world map and this is a roadmap.
- Your navigation system has a world map as well a detailed roadmap. You can zoom in to see the local maps of any city in the world.
- Mapping systems are used to map the Earth, the Moon, Mars, and stars and galaxies.

#394, science

- Science fiction.
- Science world.
- Science invention.
- Computer science.
- Life science.

- Physical science.
- Rocket science.
- Space science.
- Bachelor of science.
- Master of science.

- Science is a requirement in high school.
- Computer science is Ben's favorite subject.
- Which field of science is your favorite, rocket science, space science, or computer science?

#395, rule

- Rule of thumb.
- Rule the water.
- Rule the field.
- Rule the country.
- Rule the sky.
- Rule in.
- Rule out.
- Rule of law.
- Ground-rule.
- General rule
- Grammar rules.
- Safety rules.
- Follow the rule.

- Please follow the rules. Safety rules must be followed when on board the ship.
- Some languages have many grammar rules while some languages have no grammar rules.
- The rule of thumb for writing is KISS.
- What does KISS stand for?
- KISS stands for Keep It Simple, Stupid.
- Sharks rule the water.

- Lions rule the fields.
- Genghis Khan ruled the biggest land in human history.

#396, govern

- Govern a country.
- Govern himself.
- Govern by rules.

- People who have the vision to govern a country are usually the ones who do.
- Self-control is an important factor in governing oneself.
- This country is governed by rules.

#397, pull

Pull wird als pull betont. Das u in pull wird als /ʊ/ betont. /ʊ/, pull. Es wird nicht als pole betont. Dies ist ein anderer Klang. Pull.

- Pull up.
- Pull down.
- Pull in.
- Pull out.
- Pull off.
- Pull back.
- Pull through.
- Pull away.
- Pullover.

- Pull up into the parking lot.
- Pull up the records.
- Pull out the records.
- Throw an object into the air and gravity will pull it

- down.
- If you see a tornado, run. The tornado will pull you in.
- Always pull over for emergency vehicles.
- Pull it to see what happens.
- The pull of the moon creates tides on Earth.

#398, cold

- Cold weather.
- Cold day.
- Cold drink.
- Cold person.
- Hot and cold.
- Very cold.
- Catch a cold.

- It's a cold day today.
- It's going to be a cold day tomorrow.
- He likes cold drinks.
- He's a cold person who he never smiles.

#399, notice

- Noticeboard.
- Notice period.
- Notice it.
- Notice something.
- Take notice.
- Short notice.
- Advance notice.
- Legal notice.
- Give notice.
- Further notice.

- Without notice.

- Sorry for the short notice, but we have a meeting in two hours.
- That's better than a meeting without notice.
- I noticed something when I passed by the cafeteria. People were so quiet today.

#400, voice

- Voicemail.
- Voice recorder.
- Voice recognition.
- Tone of voice.
- Active voice.
- Passive voice.
- Voice your opinion.
- Voiced consonant.

- Record your voice through a voice recorder.
- You can activate voice recognition and use your voice to control your phone.
- Did you hear a voice?
- Yes. It was a faint voice from far away.
- She lost her voice today by singing the whole day yesterday.
- Voice your opinion to let your voice heard.
- D is a voiced consonant while T is a voiceless consonant.

Meine Glückwünsche! Dies ist der letzte Zehner-Satz. Lernen wir sie immer und immer und immer und immer wieder.

- Why do stars appear to be blinking?
- That's because of the flow of air.
- You appeared on TV yesterday.
- When you're freezing, it's a wonderful thing to see the sun appears on the horizon.
- The word appear appears nine times on this page and 14 times in this chapter.
- Main Street is the main road of the town.
- This country road will take you to the main road.
- If you'd just stay on this road, it'll take you to the main road.
- Benson's well on the road to becoming a project manager.
- This is a world map and this is a roadmap.
- Your navigation system has a world map as well a detailed roadmap. You can zoom in to see the local maps of any city in the world.
- Mapping systems are used to map the Earth, the Moon, Mars, and stars and galaxies.
- Science is a requirement in high school.
- Computer science is Ben's favorite subject.
- Which field of science is your favorite, rocket science, space science, or computer science?
- Please follow the rules. Safety rules must be followed when onboard the ship.
- Some languages have many grammar rules while some languages have no grammar rules.
- The rule of thumb for writing is KISS.
- What does KISS stand for?
- KISS stands for Keep It Simple, Stupid.
- Sharks rule the water.
- Lions rule the fields.
- Genghis Khan ruled the biggest land in human history.
- People who have the vision to govern a country are

usually the ones who do.
- Self-control is an important factor in governing oneself.
- This country is governed by rules.
- Pull up into the parking lot.
- Pull up the records.
- Pull out the records.
- Throw an object into the air and gravity will pull it down.
- If you see a tornado, run. The tornado will pull you in.
- Always pull over for emergency vehicles.
- Pull it to see what happens.
- The pull of the moon creates tides on Earth.
- It's a cold day today.
- It's going to be a cold day tomorrow.
- He likes cold drinks.
- He's a cold person who he never smiles.
- Sorry for the short notice, but we have a meeting in two hours.
- That's better than no notice.
- I noticed something when I passed by the cafeteria. People were so quiet today.
- Did you hear a voice?
- Yes. It was a faint voice from far away.
- She lost her voice today by singing the whole day yesterday.
- Voice your opinion to let your voice heard.
- D is a voiced consonant while T is a voiceless consonant.

Alles wird kommen wenn man nur darauf wartet... ein menschliches Wesen mit einer gesetzten Bestimmung wird es erreichen und nichts kann sich einem Willen widersetzen, einem Willen der die Existenz für seine Erfüllung abgesteckt hat.
      Benjamin Disraeli

Specialized Knowledge

Rank	Word	Rank	Word
401	fall	426	drive
402	power	427	stood
403	town	428	contain
404	fine	429	front
405	certain	430	teach
406	fly	431	week
407	unit	432	final
408	lead	433	gave
409	cry	434	green
410	dark	435	oh
411	machine	436	quick
412	note	437	develop
413	wait	438	sleep
414	plan	439	warm
415	figure	440	free
416	star	441	minute
417	box	442	strong
418	noun	443	special
419	field	444	mind
420	rest	445	behind
421	correct	446	clear
422	able	447	tail
423	pound	448	produce
424	done	449	fact
425	beauty	450	street

Rank	Word	Rank	Word
451	inch	476	age
452	lot	477	dry
453	nothing	478	wonder
454	course	479	laugh
455	stay	480	thousand
456	wheel	481	ago
457	full	482	ran
458	force	483	check
459	blue	484	game
460	object	485	shape
461	decide	486	yes
462	surface	487	not
463	deep	488	miss
464	moon	489	brought
465	island	490	heat
466	foot	491	snow
467	yet	492	bed
468	busy	493	bring
469	test	494	sit
470	record	495	perhaps
471	boat	496	fill
472	common	497	east
473	gold	498	weight
474	possible	499	language
475	plane	500	among

Kapitel 47: 401 – 410 Specialized knowledge

#401, fall
Heute → fall
Gestern → fell
Länger her → fallen

- Fall in.
- Fall out.
- Fall by.
- Fall down.
- Fall back.
- Fall off.
- Fall from.
- Fall over.
- Fall into.
- Fall apart.
- Fall within.
- Fall in love.
- Fall asleep.
- The fall of.
- The rise and fall.
- A waterfall.
- Nightfall.

- If that's what you want to do, fall in love with it.
- I'm falling into the habit of learning new things about my passion every day.
- Sales fell 2% last month but gained 4% this month.
- Falling down from a chair may hurt, but a baby learns from it and will not fall again.
- The waterfall from Niagara Falls falls 167 feet down to the bottom.
- The rise and fall of the dinosaurs took 100s of millions

of years.
- We'll begin our journey at nightfall.

#402, power

- Power up.
- Power down.
- Power on.
- Power off.
- Power by.
- Power plant.
- Powerpoint.
- Power supply.
- Solar power.
- Wind power.
- Full power.

- Let's power up the cell phone to see if it'll work now.
- This camera is powered by two batteries.
- Clean energy such as wind power and solar power is getting more and more popular.
- If fully harnessed, solar power has the power to change the world.
- This is a powerful car. At full power, it can go 300 mph.
- He's a powerful man in the company. He leads the company not with his power but with his passion.

#403, town

- Townhall.
- Town center.
- Town square.
- Small town.

- Big town.
- In town.
- Out of town.
- Uptown.
- Downtown.
- Around town.

- The circus is in town this week.
- Professor Hartman is not in school today, but he's in town.
- Learn these 500 words and speak English around town.
- "This is an uptown train. Next stop, Sixth Avenue."

#404, fine

- Fine art.
- Fine tune.
- Fine day.
- Fine. Thanks.
- Fine with me.
- That's fine.
- A fine of $.10 per day.

- How are you?
- Fine. Thanks.
- This is a fine piece of art. Do you mind if I keep it here for two days?
- Fine with me.
- It's a fine day to go swimming today. Should we meet at 12?
- Twelve is fine.
- If you return your book late, you'll be charged a fine of $.10 per day.

#405, certain

- For certain.
- Make certain.
- Be certain.
- Certainly.
- Certain way.
- Certain time.
- Certain amount.
- Certain condition.
- Certain about.

- May I use your pen?
- Certainly.
- Who do you want to learn from, a generalist or a specialist?
- A specialist.
- Are you certain?
- I'm certain about that. A specialist has specialized knowledge.

#406, fly
Heute → fly
Gestern → flew
Länger her → flown

- Fly high.
- Fly by.
- Fly out.
- Fly off.
- Fly back.
- Fly away.
- Fly a kite.
- On the fly.
- Fly 30 mph.
- Fly across the world.

- Butterfly.
- Dragonfly.
- Firefly.

- Butterflies can fly 20 mph.
- Dragonflies can fly 30 mph.
- Dandelions can fly five miles.
- Butterflies can fly 3000 miles.
- Dragonflies can fly halfway across the world.
- On July 4th, countless flags will fly in town.

#407, unit

- Unit price.
- Unit cost.
- Unit one.
- Unit test.
- One unit.
- Per unit.
- Control unit.
- Power unit.

- Unit one of the book is the first unit of the book.
- One unit has been sent out the study the site.
- A unit test is given at the end of each unit.

#408, lead
Heute → lead
Gestern → led
Länger her → led

- Lead time.
- Lead to.
- Leader.

- Lead singer.
- Lead up.
- Lead on.
- Lead in.
- Lead-out.
- Lead the way.
- Take the lead.

- Where is the leader of your unit?
- The leader is on the other side of the mountain. This is the road that leads to the other side.
- Lead the way.
- Newport is leading Bellevue 10-7.

#409, cry

- Cry out.
- Cry on.
- Cry over.
- Cry for help.
- Far cry.
- Warcry.
- Battle cry.
- A baby's cry.
- A bird-cry.

- Babies crying is innate. Babies are born with the ability to cry.
- Babies cry for help, but if you pay too much attention to their cries, they'll cry more often.
- "Watch out!" he cried.
- Why do owls cry out at night?
- Because owls are nocturnal creatures.

#410, dark

- Dark red.
- Dark blue.
- Dark side.
- Dark night.
- In the dark.
- Very dark.

- It's going to be a dark night tonight. Be sure to come back before dark or you'll be stranded in the dark.
- Which of these do you like, dark green, dark blue, or dark red?
- Dark green.

Üben wir diese Wörter jetzt immer und immer und immer wieder!
- If that's what you want to do, fall in love with it.
- I'm falling into the habit of learning new things about my passion every day.
- Sales fell 2% last month but gained 4% this month.
- Falling down from a chair may hurt, but a baby learns from it and will not fall again.
- The waterfall from Niagara Falls falls 167 feet down from the top.
- The rise and fall of the dinosaurs took 100s of millions of years.
- We'll begin our journey at nightfall.
- Let's power up the cell phone to see if it'll work now.
- This camera is powered by two batteries.
- Clean energy such as wind power and solar power is getting more and more popular.
- If fully harnessed, solar power has the power to change the world.
- This is a powerful car. At full power, it can go 300 mph.
- He's a powerful man in the company. He leads the company not with his power but with his passion.
- The circus is in town this week.
- Professor Hartman is not in school today, but he's in town.
- Learn these 500 words and speak English around town.
- "This is an uptown train. Next stop, Sixth Avenue."
- How are you?
- Fine. Thanks.
- This is a fine piece of art. Do you mind if I keep it here for two days?
- Fine with me.
- It's a fine day to go swimming today. Should we meet at 12?
- Twelve is fine.

- If you return your book late, you'll be charged a fine of $.10 per day.
- May I use your pen?
- Certainly.
- Who do you want to learn from, a generalist or a specialist?
- A specialist.
- Are you certain?
- I'm certain about that. A specialist has specialized knowledge.
- Butterflies can fly 20 mph.
- Dragonflies can fly 30 mph.
- Dandelions can fly five miles.
- Butterflies can fly 3000 miles.
- Dragonflies can fly halfway across the world.
- On July 4th, flags will fly in town.
- Unit one of the book is the first unit of the book.
- One unit has been sent out the study the site.
- A unit test is given at the end of each unit.
- Where is the leader of your unit?
- The leader is on the other side of the mountain. This is the road that leads to the other side.
- Lead the way.
- Newport is leading Bellevue 18-3.
- Babies crying is innate. Babies are born with the ability to cry.
- Babies cry for help, but if you pay too much attention to their cries, they'll cry more often.
- "Watch out!" he cried.
- Why do owls cry out at night?
- Because owls are nocturnal creatures.
- It's going to be a dark night tonight. Be sure to come back before dark or you'll be stranded in the dark.

**Es ist egal wie viele Fehler Sie machen oder wie langsam Ihr Fortschritt ist, Sie sind immer noch all jenen weit voraus, die es nicht wenigstens versuchen.
Anthony Robbins**

Kapitel 48: 411 – 420, Specialized knowledge

#411, machine

- Washing machine.
- Drying machine.
- Vending machine
- Fax machine.
- Cash machine.
- Mining machine.
- Rolling machine.
- Heavy machines.

- Construction companies use heavy machines to move stones.
- Machines increase productivity and reduce costs.
- A machine can work 24 hours a day, seven days a week.
- I am a human, not a working machine. I work and take breaks.

#412, note

- Note down.
- Notebook.
- Sticky note.
- Take note.

- Delivery note.
- Credit note.
- Make a note.
- Leave a note.

- Take notes in class to help you study.
- A notebook is a good tool to take notes.
- Make notes in the notebook to help you understand.
- Please leave a note on my desk when I'm not in the office.

#413, wait

- Wait for.
- Wait on.
- Wait up.
- Wait until.
- Wait a moment.
- Wait a while.
- Wait a minute.

- A table for five, please.
- Sure. There's a 10-minute wait. Would you like to wait?
- Sure. I'll wait.
- How long have you been waiting for a table?
- We've been waiting for five minutes.
- I'll be back. I'm going to wait outside.

#414, plan

- Plan A.
- Plan B.

- Plan of the day.
- Plan of the week.
- Plan of the month.
- Plan of the year.
- Plan of life.
- Plan ahead.
- Plan our future.
- Business plan.
- Action plan.
- Master plan.
- Contingency plan.
- Floor plan.
- Site plan.
- Lesson plan.
- Change of plan.

- Do you have a plan?
- I have two. This is Plan A. This Plan B. We'll go for Plan A.
- A change of plan. Plan A is not working according to plan. Let's go for Plan B.
- We have a daily plan for our daily tasks. We have a weekly plan for our weekend getaways. We have a monthly plan to pay the bills. We have a yearly plan for a vacation. What we don't have is a plan for life. We can plan for our life. This is the biggest and the most important plan in our life. What do I want in life? Let's create a plan for life!

#415, figure

- Figure up.
- Figure out.
- Figure One.
- Figure Two.

- Figure skating.
- Figure of speech.
- Public figure.
- Father figure.

- If you earn a six-figure income, you're in the upper middle class.
- Can you figure out what this picture means?
- What's another way of saying this six-figure number?
- What number?
- Five hundred thousand.
- Half million.
- She likes her own figure. She likes to keep her body that way.

#416, star

- Star sign.
- Starfruit.
- Rockstar.
- Pop star.
- Movie star.
- Rising star.
- Shooting star.
- Five-star hotel.

- Being a foreigner, Arnold Schwarzenegger is a successful movie star.
- The Terminator is a movie starring Arnold Schwarzenegger.
- What hotel do you think Arnold would stay, three-star or five-star?
- Five-star.
- Our sun is an average star in the universe.

#417, box

- Box up.
- Box in.
- Box office.
- Lunchbox.
- Cardboard box.
- Fuse box.
- Gift box.

- Kids in Bellevue like to bring their lunchbox to school.
- Here's a box of empty boxes.
- Put the toys in a box. We're going to box them up before we move.
- The 1939 film *Gone with the Wind* topped the box office with $3.4 billion worldwide.

#418, noun

- A noun.
- Proper noun.
- Single noun.
- Plural noun.

- An apple is a noun.
- A tree is a noun.
- Love is a noun. Love is also a verb.

#419, field

- Field day.
- Field trip.
- Field of study.

- Soccer field.
- Magnetic field.
- Football field.
- Cornfield.

- Somerset Elementary has a playground. Newport High has a football field.
- Kids went to a cornfield on their field trip.
- Benson has a degree in computer science. Brian has a degree in the same field.

#420, rest

- Rest assure.
- Rest your feet.
- At rest.
- Take rest.
- The rest.

- Take some rest before we leave.
- It's a good idea to rest between classes.
- Half of the group went to the fields. The rest of the group took care of the rest of the jobs.

Nehmen wir uns nun die zehn Wörter vor.
- Construction companies use heavy machines to move stones.
- Machines increase productivity and reduce costs.
- A machine can work 24 hours a day, seven days a week.
- I am a human, not a working machine. I work and take breaks.
- Take notes in class to help you study.
- A notebook is a good tool to take notes.
- Make notes in the notebook to help you understand.
- Please leave a note on my desk when I'm not in the office.
- A table for five, please.
- Sure. There's a 10-minute wait. Would you like to wait?
- Sure. I'll wait.
- How long have you been waiting for a table?
- We've been waiting for five minutes.
- I'll be back.
- I'm going to wait outside.
- Do you have a plan?
- I have two. This is Plan A. This Plan B. We'll go for Plan A.
- A change of plan. Plan A is not working according to plan. Let's go for Plan B.
- We have a daily plan for our daily tasks. We have a weekly plan for our weekend getaways. We have a monthly plan to pay the bills. We have a yearly plan for a vacation. What we don't have is a plan of life. We can plan for our life. This is the biggest and the most important plan in our life. What do I want in life? Let's create a plan of life!
- If you earn a six-figure income, you're in the upper middle class.
- Can you figure out what this picture means?
- What's another way of saying this six-figure number?

- What number?
- Five hundred thousand.
- Half million.
- She likes her own figure. She likes to keep her body like that.
- Being a foreigner, Arnold Schwarzenegger is a successful movie star.
- The Terminator is a movie starring Arnold Schwarzenegger.
- What hotel do you think Arnold would stay, three-star or five-star?
- Five-star.
- Our sun is an average star in the universe.
- Kids in Bellevue like to bring their lunchbox to school.
- Here's a box of empty boxes.
- Put the toys in a box. We're going to box them up before we move.
- The 1939 film *Gone with the Wind* topped the box office with $3.4 billion worldwide.
- An apple is a noun.
- A tree is a noun.
- Love is a noun. Love is also a verb.
- Somerset Elementary has a playground. Newport High has a football field.
- Kids went to a cornfield on their field trip.
- Benson has a degree in computer science. Brian has a degree in the same field.
- Take some rest before we leave.
- It's a good idea to rest between classes.
- Half of the group went to the fields. The rest of the group took care of the rest of the jobs.

Erfolg ist die Summe von kleinen Erfolgen die tagtäglich wiederholt werden.
Robert Collier

Kapitel 49: 421 – 430, Specialized knowledge

#421, correct

- Correct answer.
- Correct information.
- Correct time.
- Correct day.
- Correct a mistake.

- If we made a mistake, correct it and learn something from it.
- Which is the correct answer? A. Do not do anything because you can be wrong. B. Do many things even some of them can be wrong.
- Correct me if I'm wrong. The correct answer is B.

#422, able

- Able to.
- Be able to.

- She's able to speak English fluently.
- Ken is able to speak English like a native.
- If I do the same things, I'll be able to speak English like a native, too.
- Eric was able to play the piano at the age of three.

#423, pound

- One pound.
- Two pounds.
- Pound sign.
- Pound on the door.
- Pound for pound.

- A pound of water.
- Two pounds of tomatoes.
- You have two choices to get the door open, knock on the door or pound on the door.
- Her heart is still pounding after seeing the python.

#424, done

Das o in done wird als uh betont. Done wird als duhn betont. Uh, uhn, duhn. Es wird NICHT als don betont. Es wird als duhn betont. Vergleichen Sie den Unterschied. Duhn, don, duhn, don. Done wird als duhn betont.

Heute → do
Gestern → did
Länger her → done

- Done deal.
- Done with it.
- Be done.
- Get done.
- Have done.
- Well done.
- Almost done.
- It's done.

- Everything else has been done. Just sign the documents and it's a done deal.
- Can you clean up the hallway?

- It's done! (I'll get it done right away.)
- The Math Adventure games will be done at nine.
- The games are scheduled for three hours; kids can get them done in two.
- Kids who have done this before can quickly find their way in.
- Riding on a tiger is different than riding on a bike. Have you done it before?
- Yes. I've done it once and I'm done with it. I'm never going to ride on a tiger again.

#425, beauty

- Beauty contest.
- Beauty product.
- Beauty salon.
- Beauty shop.
- Beauty and the Beast
- Beauty is in the eye of the beholder.
- Natural beauty.
- The beauty of.

- Are you going to encourage your daughter to the beauty contest?
- No. I'm going to encourage her to the intelligence contest.
- The beauty of working from home is saving time for me and saving the environment for Earth.
- Who do you like as a beauty? A girl who has a beautiful face or a girl who has a beautiful heart?
- A girl who has a beautiful face and a beautiful heart.

#426, drive

Ive, Rive, Drive.
Heute → drive
Gestern → drove
Länger her → driven

- Drive out.
- Drive off.
- Drive away.
- Drive a car.
- A driveway.
- A long drive.
- Go for a drive.
- Hard drive.

- Want to go for a drive.
- Pull out of the driveway then drive north.
- Here are some snacks. It's going to be a long drive.
- It's just a mile away. You can drive it or walk it.
- I'll drive you to the airport.

#427, stood

Heute → stand
Gestern → stood
Länger her → stood

- Stood up.
- Stood by.
- Stood in.
- Stood out.
- Stood for.
- Stood against.

- He stood up for his friends when they were in trouble. That earned him their loyalty.

- He's so passionate about biology that he stood for five hours in the lab yesterday to study.
- Since his graduation, the lab had stood empty for three months.

#428, contain

- To contain.
- Will contain.

- This dish contains sugar and wheat.
- That dish contains soy and milk.
- These large containers can contain iron and steel.
- Three days after it started, the fire department was able to contain the wildfire.

#429, front

- Front end.
- Front door.
- Front page.
- Front cover.
- Front desk.
- Front yard.
- Front row
- Front side.
- In front.
- In front of.

- Leaders lead in the front, not in the back.
- To be a leader, stay in the front.
- She looked at the front cover of the book and then looked at the back cover.
- What's on the front page?
- The nine-year-old who stunt the nation with her

singing.
- It went to the front page of the newspaper?
- It's not on the second page or the back page. It's on the front page.
- The main entrance is on the front side of the building.

#430, teach
Heute → teach
Gestern → taught
Länger her → taught

- Teach a lesson.
- Teach English.
- Teach in high school.
- Teach yourself.
- Teach children

- Tell your children and they will listen and forget. Show your children and they will see and remember. Involve your children and they will experience and learn. How are you going to teach your children?
- To really teach them a lesson, let them make mistakes.
- Ken teaches English by involving students to use what they've learned.

Lernen wir nun wieder diese Wörter.
- If we made a mistake, correct it and learn something from it.
- Which is the correct answer? A. Do not do anything because you can be wrong. B. Do many things even some of them can be wrong.
- Correct me if I'm wrong. The correct answer is B.
- She's able to speak English fluently.
- Ken is able to speak English like a native.
- If I do the same things, I'll be able to speak English like a native, too.
- Eric was able to play the piano at the age of three.
- A pound of water.
- Two pounds of tomatoes.
- You have two choices to get the door open, knock on the door or pound on the door.
- Her heart is still pounding after seeing the python.
- Everything else has been done. Just sign the documents and it's a done deal.
- Can you clean up the hallway?
- It's done! (I'll get it done right away.)
- The Math Adventure games will be done at nine.
- The games are scheduled for three hours; kids can get them done in two.
- Kids who have done this before can quickly find their way in.
- Riding on a tiger is different than riding on a bike. Have you done it before?
- Yes. I've done it once and I'm done with it. I'm never going to ride on a tiger again.
- Are you going to encourage your daughter to the beauty contest?
- No. I'm going to encourage her to the intelligence contest.
- The beauty of working from home is saving time for me and saving the environment for Earth.
- Who do you like as a beauty? A girl who has a

- beautiful face or a girl who has a beautiful heart?
- A girl who has a beautiful face and a beautiful heart.
- Want to go for a drive.
- Pull out of the driveway then drive north.
- Here are some snacks. It's going to be a long drive.
- It's just a mile away. You can drive it or walk it.
- I'll drive you to the airport.
- He stood up for his friends when they were in trouble. That earned him their loyalty.
- He's so passionate about biology that he stood for five hours in the lab yesterday to study.
- Since his graduation, the lab had stood empty for three months.
- This dish contains sugar and wheat.
- That dish contains soy and milk.
- These large containers can contain iron and steel.
- Three days after it started, the fire department was able to contain the wildfire.
- Leaders lead in the front, not in the back.
- To be a leader, stay in the front.
- She looked at the front cover of the book and then looked at the back cover.
- What's on the front page?
- The nine-year-old who stunt the nation with her singing.
- It went to the front page of the newspaper?
- It's not on the second page or the back page. It's on the front page.
- The main entrance is on the front side of the building.
- Tell your children and they will listen and forget. Show your children and they will see and remember. Involve your children and they will experience and learn. How are you going to teach your children?
- To really teach them a lesson, let them make mistakes.
- Ken teaches English by involving students to use what they've learned.

Kapitel 50: 431 – 440, Specialized knowledge

#431, week

- Week One.
- Week Two.
- Weekday.
- Weekend.
- Last week.
- This week.
- Next week.
- One week.
- Two weeks.
- Per week.
- Once a week.
- Every week.
- During the week.

- She wants to take care of her family, so she works three days a week.
- He wants to achieve his goal on time, so he works 10 hours a day, seven days a week.
- Week One of the program will be math.
- Week Two of the program will be science.
- This shop opens on weekends and closes on weekdays.
- Spend 14 hours a week on your passion for 20 years, and you'll be the best in that area.

#432, final

- Final exam.

- Final call.
- Final round.
- Final decision.
- Final report.
- Final payment.
- Final cost.
- It's final.

- The final exam will be at the end of this week.
- The lucky number is 5523388.
- Ticket holder of 5523388 please come up to the stage. Final call.
- This is the final round of the game.
- This is the World Cup final.
- This is your class leader. Whatever he says is final.

#433, gave
Heute → give
Gestern → gave
Länger her → given

- Gave in.
- Gave back.
- Gave up.
- Gave away.
- Gave out.
- Gave off.
- Gave birth.
- Gave it a try.
- Gave 100%.

- They gave him a week to work on it. It was just what he needed.
- His parents gave him what he needed in getting specialized knowledge in his field of specialty.
- He gave it a try to see what happen.

- She gave 100% of her time and effort into her passion.
- What was her name? She didn't give her name. She gave an email address.

#434, green

- Green tea.
- Green beans.
- Green pepper.
- Greenlight.
- Green card.
- Greenland.
- Green energy.

- Greenland is not green. It's covered with ice.
- Iceland is not covered with ice. Iceland is green.
- A hundred percent of Iceland's power energy is green energy.
- Go ahead. You got the green light!

#435, oh

- Oh! I see.
- Oh! That's why.
- Oh! Yes! That's dream come true.

#436, quick

- Quick start.
- Quick look.
- Quick search.

- Quick time.
- Quick fix.
- Quick response.
- Quick learner.
- Quick and easy.
- Be quick,
- Very quick

- Focus your energy on one specific area and your energy will quickly break through.
- If you have a ton of energy, what are you going to do with it?
- You can use the energy on 100 tasks and get general knowledge or focus the energy on one specific area and get a quick breakthrough.
- She's a quick learner.
- Let me take a quick look at your computer. It may just be a quick fix.

#437, develop

- Develop into.
- Develop friendship
- Develop a habit.
- Developing world.
- Developed world.
- Develop specific knowledge.

- The developing world is more likely to focus on all areas of development.
- The developed world is more likely to focus on one specific area of development.
- Doing something consistently will develop a habit.
- Focus on one area to develop specific knowledge.

#438, sleep

Heute → sleep
Gestern → slept
Länger her → slept

- Sleep in.
- Sleep well.
- Sleep early.
- Sleepover.
- Good sleep.
- Deep sleep.
- Go to sleep.
- Sleeping giant.

- I sleep well every day for being a good person.
- I had a good night of sleep last night because I'm a good person.
- The baby is in deep sleep for being a good baby.
- You have a sleeping giant inside you. You just don't know about it. Wait up this sleeping giant, and you can do things as big as you can imagine.

#439, warm

- Warm up.
- Warm day.
- Warm water.
- Warm weather.
- Warm smile.
- Warm welcome.
- Keep warm.
- Very warm

- It's going to be a warm day today.
- I'll take a jacket to keep me warm.

- It was such a warm smile I saw on her face.
- Warm it up. Warm up the food before you eat it.

#440, free

- Free up.
- Free to.
- Free gift.
- Free time.
- Free space.
- Free lunch.
- Free of charge.
- Free to go.
- Free energy.
- Duty-free.
- Break free.
- Set free.
- For free.
- Toll-free.
- Financially free.

- Free up your energy from all areas and focus on one specific area. You can't imagine what the energy will do for you.
- You receive a free gift at birth, freedom of thinking. This gift is free of charge. You can use it at your free time. Use this free gift and you can be financially free.
- Free the birds from the cage and the birds will be free. Free your mind from all areas and your mind will be free.

Wie oft sollte ich üben? Immer und immer wieder.

- She wants to take care of her family, so she works three days a week.
- He wants to achieve his goal on time, so he works 10 hours a day, seven days a week.
- Week One of the program will be math.
- Week Two of the program will be science.
- This shop opens on weekends and closes on weekdays.
- Spend 14 hours a week on your passion for 20 years, and you'll be the best in that area.
- The final exam will be at the end of this week.
- The lucky number is 5523388.
- Ticket holder of 5523388 please come up to the stage. Final call.
- This is the final round of the game.
- This is the World Cup final.
- This is your class leader. Whatever he says is final.
- They gave him a week to work on it. It was just what he needed.
- His parents gave him what he needed in getting specialized knowledge in his field of specialty.
- He gave it a try to see what happen.
- She gave 100% of her time and effort into her passion.
- What was her name? She didn't give her name. She gave an email address.
- Greenland is not green. It's covered with ice.
- Iceland is not covered with ice. Iceland is green.
- A hundred percent of Iceland's power energy is green energy.
- Go ahead. You got the green light!
- Oh! I see.
- Oh! That's why.
- Oh! Yes! That's dream come true.
- Focus your energy on one specific area and your energy will quickly break through.

- If you have a ton of energy, what are you going to do with it?
- You can use the energy on 100 tasks and get general knowledge or focus the energy on one specific area and get a quick breakthrough.
- She's a quick learner.
- Let me take a quick look at your computer. It may just be a quick fix.
- The developing world is more likely to focus on all areas of development.
- The developed world is more likely to focus on one specific area of development.
- Doing something consistently will develop a habit.
- Focus on one area to develop specific knowledge.
- I slept well last night.
- I had a good night of sleep last night.
- The baby is in deep sleep.
- You have a giant sleeping in you. You just don't know about it. Wait up this sleeping giant, and you can do things as big as you can imagine.
- It's going to be a warm day today.
- I'll take a jacket to keep me warm.
- It was such a warm smile I saw on her face.
- Warm it up. Warm up the food before you eat it.
- Free up your energy from all areas and focus on one specific area. You can't imagine what the energy will do for you.
- You receive a free gift at birth, freedom of thinking. This gift is free of charge. You can use it at your free time. Use this free gift and you can be financially free.
- Free the birds from the cage and the birds will be free. Free your mind from all areas and your mind will be free.

Erfolg wird durch die Entwicklung von Stärken erreicht, nicht durch das Eliminieren von Schwächen.
Marilyn vos Savant

Kapitel 51: 441 – 450, Specialized knowledge

#441, minute

- One minute!
- Just a minute!
- In a minute.
- Per minute.
- Last minute.
- Sixty minutes.

- Excuse me.
- Just a minute.
- He's very good at this. It'll just take him a minute.
- It would have taken 60 minutes to complete the job, but he took only 40.
- Launch countdown. One day, two hours, 43 minutes and 20 seconds.

#442, strong

- Strong man.
- Strong player.
- Strong competition.
- Strong current.
- Strong feeling.

- Strong will.
- Strong relationship.
- Strong enough.
- Very strong.
- Too strong.

- He's a strong player and one of the best in the team.
- It takes a strong man to lift three hundred pounds. It takes a big man to say "I was wrong."
- A strong current will block your way. A strong will will get you to your destination. A strong relationship will keep you together.

#443, special

- Special needs.
- Special energy.
- Special thing.
- Special offer.
- Special effect.
- Special feature.
- Special guest.
- Special edition.
- Special day.
- Today's special.
- Nothing special.

- All tools are here. Do you have any special needs?
- Yes. I need some special energy.
- What special energy do you need?
- It's a special thing.
- Today's special is pepperoni pizza.

#444, mind
- Open mind.
- Bear in mind.
- Peace of mind.
- State of mind
- In mind.
- Do you mind?
- Never mind.
- Mind your own business.
- The great minds.
- Set your mind.

- Do you mind if I use your pen?
- Not at all.
- Never mind. I found mine.
- What's on your mind?
- I'm rehearsing the speech in my mind.
- Set your mind on your goal and start at once to get it. It doesn't need a great mind to achieve it. An average mind with a strong will will achieve it.

#445, behind
Es ist okay behind als BeeHind zu betonen, es ist jedoch besser, es als Bhind zu betonen. Erinnern Sie sich noch an die drei Elemente die nötig sind, um wie ein Einheimischer zu sprechen? Diese Betonung verwendet das zweite Element – Intonation. Der zweite Teil wird betont und der "E" Klang in "BE" wird vermindert. Als Ergebnis wird das Wort als Bhind betont.
- Behind me.
- Behind you.
- Behind the scene.
- Behind schedule.
- Look behind.

- Fall behind.
- Far behind.
- From behind.
- Leave behind.

- Leaders lead in the front, not in the back. Lead in front of them, not behind them.
- Who was behind this idea?
- Ted was behind this idea.
- Where are you, Tom?
- I'm right behind you.
- He's got a lot of work to do. He's behind everybody on homework.
- A landslide caused the project two years behind schedule.

#446, clear

- Clear up.
- Clear out.
- Clear away.
- Clear off.
- Clear water.
- Clear air.
- Clear mind.
- Clear skies.
- Crystal clear.

- It's clear that the water has been cleared. It looks so clear.
- A lot of work has been done to clear the water and air in this city.
- Clear your mind and focus only on what you want. A clear mind will keep your energy focused.
- Clear the corn fields. We're going to burn it down.

- The sky has become clear after a day of rain. There will be clear skies in the next five days.

#447, tail

- Tail off.
- Tailgate.
- Long tail.
- Tail light.
- Pony tail.
- Lobster tail
- Chasing its own tail.

- Flip a coin to decide on who goes first. Head or tail?
- You should stop and think it over. You're just like a puppy chasing your own tail.
- Give them some space. Do not tailgate when driving.

#448, produce

Produce hat zwei Klänge. Wenn es ein Verb ist, wird es als pro**duce** betont. Wenn es ein Nomen ist, wird es als **pro**duce betont.

- A produce.
- To produce.
- Fresh produce.
- Produce products.
- Produce good results.

- Fresh produce is delivered daily.
- Where is the produce department?
- The produce department is on the left.
- California's Napa Valley produces excellent grapes.

#449, fact

- A fact.
- The fact.
- In fact.
- A matter of fact.
- Despite the fact that.

- Collect facts about the crash. Our goal is to learn from the facts of why it crashed. As a matter of fact, take all the people you need.
- These are all the facts collected. A meteor caused the crash.

#450, street

- Street fair.
- Street address.
- The street.
- Main street.
- In the street.
- On the street.
- Down the street.
- One way street
- Tenth Street.
- Wall Street.
- Across the street.

- The street fair is being held on Tenth Street.
- It's a one-way street.
- Turn right on Broadway and go straight to Wall Street.
- What's the street address?
- 222.
- The building is right across the street.

Nehmen wir uns die zehn Wörter jetzt vor.

- Excuse me.
- Just a minute.
- He's very good at this. It'll just take him a minute.
- It would have taken 60 minutes to complete the job, but he took only 40.
- Countdown to the launch. One day, two hours, 43 minutes and 20 seconds.
- He's a strong player and one of the best in the team.
- It takes a strong man to lift three hundred pounds. It takes a big man to say "I was wrong."
- A strong current will block your way. A strong will will get you to your destination. A strong relationship will keep you together.
- All tools are here. Do you have any special needs?
- Yes. I need some special energy.
- What special energy do you need?
- It's a special thing.
- Today's special is pepperoni pizza.
- Do you mind if I use your pen?
- Not at all.
- Never mind. I found mine.
- What's on your mind?
- I'm rehearsing the speech in my mind.
- Set your mind on your goal and start at once to get it. It doesn't need a great mind to achieve it. An average mind with a strong will will achieve it.
- Leaders lead in the front, not in the back. Lead in front of them, not behind them.
- Who was behind this idea?
- Ted was behind this idea.
- Where are you, Tom?
- I'm right behind you.
- He's got a lot of work to do. He's behind everybody on homework.

- A landslide caused the project two years behind schedule.
- It's clear that the water has been cleared. It looks so clear.
- A lot of work has been done to clear the water and air in this city.
- Clear your mind and focus only on what you want. A clear mind will keep your energy focused.
- Clear the corn fields. We're going to burn it down.
- The sky has become clear after a day of rain. There will be clear skies in the next five days.
- Flip a coin to decide on who goes first. Head or tail?
- You should stop and think it over. You're just like a puppy chasing your own tail.
- Give them some space. Do not tailgate when driving.
- Fresh produce is delivered daily.
- Where is the produce department?
- The produce department is on the left.
- California's Napa Valley produces excellent grapes.
- Collect facts about the crash. Our goal is to learn from the facts of why it crashed. As a matter of fact, take all the people you need.
- These are all the facts collected. A meteor caused the crash.
- The street fair is being held on Tenth Street.
- It's a one-way street.
- Turn right on Broadway and go straight to Wall Street.
- What's the street address?
- 222.
- The building is right across the street.

Kapitel 52: 451 – 460, Specialized knowledge

#451, inch

- One inch.
- Two inches.
- Square inch.
- Every inch.
- Inch by inch.
- Inch forward.

- A man who is too comfortable won't budge an inch. A man who has nothing to lose will take risks to succeed.
- He inches his car forward on a snowy day.

#452, lot

- Lot of.
- Lot number.
- A lot of.
- A lot more.
- Quite a lot.
- Parking lot.

- A lot of people make a lot of mistakes a lot of times in the parking lot.
- A lot of them learn from their mistakes and move forward.
- A lot of people make few mistakes when they're

young. They'll make more mistakes when they grow up.
- It's much better to make a lot of mistakes when they're young.

#453, nothing
Das th in nothing ist stimmlos, /TH/. Nothing.

- Nothing more.
- Nothing much.
- Nothing to say.
- Nothing to do.
- Nothing at all.
- Nothing else.
- Nothing special.
- For nothing.
- Do nothing.

- What's that?
- Nothing!
- What do you have in common?
- We have nothing in common.
- What went wrong?
- Nothing went wrong. Everything is fine.
- Sorry about that.
- That's nothing.
- The important thing is to get there on time. Nothing else matters.

#454, course

- On course.
- Off course.

- Of course.
- Main course.
- Golf course.
- Training course.
- English course.
- Course of action

- Captain. We're off course.
- How far are we off?
- We're off by 1800 miles.
- What? How can we be off by 1800 miles? What caused us to get off course?
- The reason is unknown.
- Set a new course and make sure we're on course.
- Aye, captain.
- What are you studying?
- I'm studying an English course.
- Can I take a look at your course?
- Of course.

#455, stay

- Stay in.
- Stay out.
- Stay up.
- Stay down.
- Stay here.
- Stay calm.
- Stay with.
- Stay tuned.
- Stay home.
- Stay alive.
- Stay away.
- Stay in touch.
- Stay focused.

- Stay on course.

- Please stay here while I go register.
- Two of us will need to go check it out. Who's staying?
- Thank you for staying with me throughout the journey.
- Stay with your family. Stay calm. It'll be over soon.

#456, wheel

- Car wheel.
- Steering wheel.
- Behind the wheel.
- Wheel in.
- Wheel out.
- Wheel around.

- My car is old a car with four wheels. Every part of the car makes noise except the radio.
- A lot of drivers are nice people on the street, but when they're behind the wheel, they lose their temper.
- Thomas wheeled around to see what was happening. He saw a group of soldiers wheeled out a round-shaped vehicle that looked like a UFO.

#457, full
Wie in pull, wird das u in full als /ʊ/. /ʊ/ ll, f /ʊ/ ll betont.

- Full name.
- Full moon.
- Full time.
- Full house.
- Full circle

- Full life.
- Full speed.
- Full stop.
- Full of.
- In full.

- They enjoyed the view of the city under the full moon.
- She lived a full life. Her life was full of fun.
- Please fill out your full name. You'll get a full tank of gas.
- OK. I'm fully prepared.
- Do you have full confidence in yourself?
- Absolutely! I'm full of confidence. We'll go full speed ahead.

#458, force

- Force open.
- Force by.
- Physical force.
- Mental force.
- Police force
- Task force.
- By force.
- In force.
- Air force.
- Labor force.
- Driving force.

- If you're hungry, you'll force yourself to find food.
- Some scientists believe there were four alien forces fighting in the past to gain control of Earth.
- They're believed to take control by force.
- Starting from the age of seven, Ken was forced to

work in the fields. He was forced to cook for the entire family. He was forced to carry water home. He was forced to join the labor force for the family. The good thing is because of this experience, he forced himself to turn this experience into a driving force which sent him to success. Can you turn anything into a driving force to help you practice your English?

#459, blue

- Blue sky.
- Blue moon.
- Blue jeans.
- Light blue.
- Dark blue.
- Out of the blue.
- Sky blue.

- What's your favorite color?
- Blue.
- What are you going to wear to the party?
- Blue jeans.
- In the beginning, the sky was light blue; it slowly turned to dark blue.
- Once in a blue moon, use a semicolon instead of a period.

#460, object
(Object hat zwei Klänge. Wenn es ein Verb ist, wird es als ob**ject** betont. Wenn es ein Nomen ist, wird es als **ob**ject betont.)

- An object.

- Unidentified flying object.
- Large object.
- Hidden object.
- To object.

- Thomas wheeled around to see what was happening. He saw a group of soldiers wheeled out a round-shaped object.
- The object was about six feet wide.
- It was an object that he had never seen before.
- He went closer to see if it was an unidentified flying object.
- The object was indeed an unidentified flying object. He could never ob**ject** to that.
- If you ob**ject** to UFOs, wake up! Search "UFO drawing energy from the sun" and you'll find NASA videos showing Earth-size UFOs refueling at the sun.

Immer und immer und immer wieder.

- A man who is too comfortable won't budge an inch. A man who has nothing to lose will take risks to succeed.
- He inches his car forward on a snowy day.
- A lot of people make a lot of mistakes a lot of times in the parking lot.
- A lot of them learn from their mistakes and move forward.
- A lot of people make few mistakes when they're young. They'll make more mistakes when they grow up.
- It's much better to make a lot of mistakes when they're young.
- What's that?
- Nothing.
- What do you have in common?
- We have nothing in common.
- Sorry about that.
- That's nothing.
- The important thing is to get there on time. Nothing else matters.
- Captain. We're off course.
- How far are we off?
- We're off by 1800 miles.
- How can we be off by 1800 miles? What caused us to get off course?
- The reason is unknown.
- Set a new course and make sure we're on course.
- Aye, captain.
- What are you studying?
- I'm studying an English course.
- Can I take a look at your course?
- Of course.
- Please stay here while I go register.

- Two of us will need to go check it out. Who's staying?
- Thank you for staying with me throughout the journey.
- Stay with your family. Stay calm. It'll be over soon.
- My car is old a car with four wheels. Every part of the car makes noise except the radio.
- A lot of drivers are nice people on the street, but when they're behind the wheel, they lose their temper.
- Thomas wheeled around to see what was happening. He saw a group of soldiers wheeled out a round-shaped vehicle that looked like a UFO.
- They enjoyed the view of the city under the full moon.
- She lived a full life. Her life was full of fun.
- Please fill out your full name. You'll get a full tank of gas.
- OK. I'm fully prepared.
- Do you have full confidence in yourself?
- Absolutely! I'm full of confidence. We'll go full speed ahead.
- If you're hungry, you'll force yourself to find food.
- Some scientists believe there were four alien forces fighting in the past to gain control of Earth.
- They're believed to take control by force.
- Ken was forced to work in the fields starting at the age of seven. He was forced to cook for the entire family. He was forced to bring water home. The good thing is because of this experience, he forced himself to achieve something an average person does not do.
- What's your favorite color?
- Blue.
- What color is your car?
- Blue.
- What color are you going to wear?
- Blue.
- Thomas wheeled around to see what was happening. He saw a group of soldiers wheeled out a round-shaped object.
- The object was about six feet wide.

- It was an object that he had never seen before.
- He went closer to see if it was an unidentified flying object.
- The object was indeed an unidentified flying object. He could never ob**ject** to that.
- If you ob**ject** to UFOs, wake up! Search "UFO drawing energy from the sun" and you'll find NASA videos showing Earth-size UFOs refueling at the sun.

Kapitel 53: 461 – 470, Specialized knowledge

#461, decide

- Decide to.
- Decide on.
- Decide upon.
- Decide against.

- Have you decided on what to do?
- What have you decided to do?
- Have you decided which offer to take?
- I have decided to learn to speak English like a native.

#462, surface

- Surface area.
- Surface tension.
- Surfaced from water.
- Surface of the earth.
- Surface of the moon.
- Flat surface.
- Smooth surface.
- Work surface.
- Inner surface.
- On the surface.
- Scratch the surface.

- The earth's surface contains 71% water and 29% land.
- Seventy-one percent of Earth's surface is covered by water.

- The moon's surface is heavily cratered by asteroids.
- Mushrooms quickly surface after spring rains.
- Take a break. Return to the surface after diving for a while.
- If you don't believe in UFOs, congratulations! You're below the surface of this topic and can live a normal life.
- If you believe UFOs and believe they're as big as cities on Earth, wake up! You haven't scratched the surface of UFOs yet. Many UFOs recorded in videos by NASA's SOHO spacecraft are as big as 10 times the size of the earth. Aliens don't live on the surface of these UFOs. They live 10s of miles below the surface of these UFOs.

#463, deep

- Deep valley.
- Deep dive.
- Deep down.
- Deepwater.
- Deep sea.
- Deep spring.
- Deep sleep.
- Deep breath.
- Deep thought.
- Deep into the valley.

- Deep in the valley, mushrooms have surfaced in the deep spring.
- Divers took a deep breath and dove deep into the ocean to search for the underground city.
- In deep waters, the temperature remains cold.
- He stayed in a deep thought for a while.

#464, moon
- The moon.
- Moon cake.
- Moon walk.
- Moon eclipse.
- New moon.
- Full moon.
- Blue moon.
- Over the moon.
- Surface of the moon.

- Earth has one moon.
- Venus has no moon.
- Jupiter has 67 moons.
- A solar eclipse occurs when the moon passes between the sun and the earth casting a shadow on Earth.
- Once in a blue moon, use a semicolon instead of a period.
- If you believe the moon is a natural **ob**ject, congratulations! Sit under the full moon, enjoy a moon cake, and live a normal life.
- If you believe the moon is an alien spacecraft, congratulations! You have scratched the surface of the moon.

#465, island
- An island.
- On the island.
- Main island.
- Thousand island.
- Long Island.
- Desert island.

- Traffic island.
- Treasure island.
- Floating island.
- Safety island.

- An island can be a quiet place to stay for a vacation.
- New York's Long Island has a population of over seven million people.
- An island is a land surrounded by water.
- A safety island can be a nice place to wait for the green light.

#466, foot

Eins → foot
Zwei oder mehr → feet

- One foot.
- Two feet.
- On foot.
- By foot.
- Set foot.
- Left foot.
- Right foot.
- Footprint.
- Square foot.
- Go on foot.

- It's okay to hop on one foot.
- It's better to walk on two feet.
- We'll get there by foot.
- To get results, stand on your feet and get going.
- Watch out! A ten-foot pool is too deep for a little kid.
- Footprints of early human have been found around the world.
- Some bamboos grow two feet per day.

#467, yet

- As yet.
- Just yet.
- Not yet.
- Yet again.

- The water was deep, yet he managed to surface from 75 feet.
- The kids have been playing all afternoon, yet they still have lots of energy.
- Are you ready?
- Not yet. I need to massage my feet.
- Did you tell anyone about the news?
- I haven't told anyone yet.

#468, busy

Das s in busy wird als z mit Vibration betont. Busy wird als buZy betont. Es wird nicht wie buSy betont. Es wird als buzy betont.

- Busy day.
- Busy street.
- Busy market.
- Busy time of the day.
- Busy themselves.
- Busy signal.
- Get busy.
- Very busy.
- Too busy.
- Not busy.
- Keep busy.

- Ants busy themselves in the summer and rest in the winter.
- Ants busy themselves by collecting food for the

winter.
- Which location do you choose to open a business, a quiet town or a busy street?
- Pike Market is a busy market in Seattle. Every day is a busy day there.

#469, test

- English test.
- Math test.
- Blood test.
- Driving test.
- Flight test.
- Pass the test.
- Test the students.
- Test their strength.
- Test tube.
- Test drive.

- Students are given an evaluation test before they join the class.
- The test tests students on their language, math, and sciences levels.
- Students must pass all three tests to join the class.
- A blood test is given before a CT scan.
- These ropes are tested for their strength.

#470, record

Record hat zwei Betonungen. **Re**cord und re**cord**. Wenn es ein Nomen ist, wird es als **re**cord betont. Wenn es ein Verb ist, wird es als re**cord** betont.

- Track record.
- Off the record.
- Break a record.

- World record.
- Dental record.
- Re**cord** your voice.

- The achievement rewrote the world record.
- This is a list of the Olympic records.
- The highest temperature recorded in the world is 134°F recorded in 1913 in California.
- To improve your English, re**cord** your voice, listen to your record, and compare your English with that of native speakers to see where you need improvement.

Schnappen wir uns diese Wörter.

- Have you decided on what to do?
- What have you decided to do?
- Have you decided on which offer to take?
- The earth's surface contains 71% water and 29% land.
- Seventy-one percent of Earth's surface is covered by water.
- The moon's surface is heavily cratered by asteroids.
- Mushrooms quickly surface after spring rains.
- Take a break. Return to the surface after diving for a while.
- Deep in the valley, mushrooms have surfaced in the deep spring.
- Divers took a deep breath and dove deep into the ocean to search for the underground city.
- In deep waters, the temperature remains cold.
- Earth has one moon.
- Venus has no moon.
- Jupiter has 67 moons.
- A solar eclipse occurs when the moon passes between the sun and the earth casting a shadow on Earth.
- New York's Long Island has a population of over seven million people.
- An island is a land surrounded by water.
- An island can be a quiet place to stay for a vacation.
- It's okay to hop on one foot.
- It's better to walk on two feet.
- We'll get there by foot.
- To get results, stand on your feet and get going.
- Watch out! A ten-foot pool is too deep for a little kid.
- Footprints of early human have been found around the world.
- Some bamboos grow two feet per day.

- The water was deep, yet he managed to surface from 75 feet.
- The kids have been playing all afternoon, yet they still have lots of energy.
- Are you ready?
- Not yet. I need to massage my feet.
- Did you tell anyone about the news?
- I haven't told anyone yet.
- Ants busy themselves in the summer and rest in the winter.
- Ants busy themselves by collecting food for the winter.
- Which location do you choose to open a business, a quiet town or a busy street?
- Pike Market is a busy market in Seattle. Every day is a busy day there.
- Students are given an evaluation test before they join the class.
- The test tests students on their language, math, and sciences levels.
- Students must pass all three tests to join the class.
- A blood test is given before a CT scan.
- These ropes are tested for their strength.
- The achievement rewrote the world record.
- This is a list of the Olympic records.
- The highest temperature recorded in the world is 134°F recorded in 1913 in California.
- To improve your English, re**cord** your voice, listen to your record, and compare your English with that of native speakers to see where you need improvement.

> Handeln ist der wichtigste Schlüssel zu jeder Art von Erfolg.
> **Anthony Robbins**

Kapitel 54: 471 – 480, Specialized knowledge

#471, boat

- Lifeboat.
- Wooden boat.
- Fishing boat.
- By boat.
- On the boat.
- Boat down the river.

- Farmers boat their sugar canes down the river.
- All visitors here travel by boat.
- Small boats are equipped with life vests.
- Large boats are equipped with lifeboats.

#472, common

Common wird als K ah mon betont. Das erste o in common wird als AH betont. Common.

- Commonplace.
- Common people.
- Common taste.
- Common names.
- Common sense.
- Common law.
- Common ground

- In common.

- People here use common names.
- Common people have common names, have common sense, follow common laws, and work on common jobs.
- Common people, myself included, are programmed to live a common life.
- The riverbank is a commonplace to enjoy the sunrise.
- What do Earth and Mars have in common?
- They are both planets.
- What do native speakers and non-native speakers have in common?
- They both breathe, eat, and sleep.

#473, gold

- Gold coin.
- Gold bar.
- Gold medal.
- Gold Rush.
- Gold digger.
- Gold plate.
- Gold mine
- Gold and silver.

- Gold and silver were used as currencies in the past.
- Gold coins and gold bars were the most valuable currencies.
- To strive for the gold medal, focus your energy on that specific area.
- In the period of the California Gold Rush, people from around the world rushed to California to dig for gold.
- The Golden Gate Bridge is a landmark of San Francisco.

#474, possible

- As soon as possible.
- As much as possible.
- Whenever possible.

- It's possible for anyone, myself included, to make many mistakes in life.
- It's possible for anyone, myself included, to make the right choices in life.
- It's possible for anyone, myself included, to achieve anything one desires in life.
- What I need is to set the goal toward what I desire, focus all possible energies into that specific area, and take actions right away until I get there.
- Is it possible for me to speak English like a native?
- Absolutely!

#475, plane

- Airplane.
- Model plane.
- Horizontal plane.
- By plane.
- Paper plane.

- Where are you going?
- Nowhere.
- How are you going to get there?
- By plane.
- What plane is going to take you to "nowhere?"
- The "nowhere plane."
- In 1903, the Wright brothers invented the world's first flying airplane.
- Model airplanes were excavated from 2000-year old and 4000-year old ancient tombs.

- Scientists built and tested bigger models of these thousand-year-old planes. These planes flew.

#476, age

- Young age.
- Middle age.
- Ice age.
- Same age.
- Average age
- School-age.
- Golden age.
- Modern age.

- He was able to read at the age of three.
- Some kids can read and write at a very young age with no prior schooling.
- School-age kids also learn to make friends at school.
- The modern age is a golden age for science.

#477, dry

- Dry up.
- Dry out.
- Dry place.
- Dry wine.
- Dry clean.
- Dry your clothes.
- Dry your happy tears.
- Dry season.
- Dried river.

- We'll meet here tomorrow at one, rain or dry.
- In wet days, this side of the tree is a dry place to stay

dry.
- This wine has no sugar at all, it's the driest wine we have.
- Enjoy some dry wine while staying dry.
- The sun is an excellent dryer for your wet clothes.
- The river is dried. Dry your happy tears. Let's cross the dried river.

#478, wonder

Wonder wird als wonder betont. Das o in wonder wird als ə betont. Es wird nicht als wander betont. Es wird als wənder betont.

- I wonder.
- No wonder.
- The Seven Wonders of the World.
- Wonderful place.
- Place of wonder.

- Have you been to any of the Seven Wonders of the World?
- Nope, but I wonder why I haven't been to any of them.
- The Grand Canyon is a wonderful place to visit. No wonder why so many people go there.
- Some stones of the Great Pyramids of Giza weigh thousands of tons. I wonder how these stones were placed up there 4000 years ago.
- OK. Stop wondering. Go find out why.

#479, laugh

- Laugh at.
- Laugh out.
- Laugh it off.
- Funny laugh.

- Silly laugh.
- Laugh as hard as you can.
- Laugh your way to good health.

- Norman Cousins said laughter is the best medicine for healing.
- Watch funny movies, read funny jokes, laugh as hard as you can, and laugh your way to good health.
- He gave a funny laugh. I gave a silly laugh. We all laughed.

#480, thousand

- Thousand Island.
- Thousand-mile.
- One thousand.
- Two thousand.
- Five hundred thousand.
- A 4000-year old building.
- A 3000-ton rock.
- A thousand-mile journey.
- Tens of thousands of people.

- How did ancient people place 3000-ton rocks on the top of the Great Pyramids of Gaza 4000 years ago?
- Tens of thousands of people go there to visit every day.
- Out of the five hundred thousand words in the English vocabulary, let's focus on these 500 and get you going.
- "A journey of a thousand miles begins with the first step."

Es ist an der Zeit, wieder diese Wörter zu lernen.

- Farmers boat their sugar canes down the river.
- All visitors here travel by boat.
- Small boats are equipped with life vests.
- Large boats are equipped with lifeboats.
- People here use common names.
- Common people have common names, have common sense, follow common laws, and work on common jobs.
- Common people, myself included, are programmed to live a common life.
- The riverbank is a commonplace to enjoy the sunrise.
- What do Earth and Mars have in common?
- They are both planets.
- What do native speakers and non-native speakers have in common?
- They both breathe, eat, and sleep.
- Gold and silver were used as currencies in the past.
- Gold coins and gold bars were the most valuable currencies.
- To strive for the gold medal, focus your energy on that specific area.
- In the period of the California Gold Rush, people from around the world rushed to California to dig for gold.
- The Golden Gate Bridge is a landmark of San Francisco.
- It's possible for anyone, myself included, to make many mistakes in life.
- It's possible for anyone, myself included, to make the right choices in life.
- It's possible for anyone, myself included, to achieve anything one desires in life.
- What I need is to set the goal toward what I desire, focus all possible energies into that specific area, and take actions right away until I get there.
- Is it possible for me to speak English like a native?

- Absolutely!
- Where are you going?
- Nowhere.
- How are you going to get there?
- By plane.
- What plane is going to take you to "nowhere?"
- The "nowhere plane."
- In 1903, the Wright brothers invented the world's first flying airplane.
- Model airplanes were excavated from 2000-year old and 4000-year old ancient tombs.
- Scientists built and tested bigger models of these thousand-year-old planes. These planes flew.
- He was able to read at the age of three.
- Some kids can read and write at a very young age with no prior schooling.
- School-age kids also learn to make friends at school.
- The modern age is a golden age for science.
- We'll meet here tomorrow at one, rain or dry.
- In wet days, this side of the tree is a dry place to stay dry.
- This wine has no sugar at all, it's the driest wine we have.
- Enjoy some dry wine while staying dry.
- The sun is an excellent dryer for your wet clothes.
- The river is dried. Dry your happy tears. Let's cross the dried river.
- Have you been to any of the Seven Wonders of the World?
- Nope, but I wonder why I haven't been to any of them.
- The Grand Canyon is a wonderful place to visit. No wonder why so many people go there.
- Some stones of the Great Pyramids of Giza weigh thousands of tons. I wonder how these stones were placed up there 4000 years ago.
- OK. Stop wondering. Go find out why.

- Norman Cousins said laughter is the best medicine for healing.
- Watch funny movies, read funny jokes, laugh as hard as you can, and laugh your way to good health.
- He gave a funny laugh. I gave a silly laugh. We all laughed.
- How did ancient people place 3000-ton rocks on the top of the Great Pyramids of Gaza 4000 years ago?
- Tens of thousands of people go there to visit every day.
- "A journey of a thousand miles begins with the first step."
- Out of the five hundred thousand words in the English vocabulary, let's focus on these 500 and get you going.

Einige Menschen träumen von Erfolg während andere aufwachen und daran arbeiten.
napoleon hill

Kapitel 55: 481 – 490, Specialized knowledge

#481, ago

- A moment ago.
- Ten minutes ago.
- A while ago.
- Years ago.
- Long time ago.
- Long long ago.

- Thousands of years ago, there were snake-like creatures with legs and feet flying in the sky. Ancient people thought they were gods.
- Three years ago, my son and I planted 30 trees in our yard.
- Ten minutes ago, my son came to talk to me about how to get his iPad back.
- A moment ago, I said to him, "to get your iPad back, play me a new song on the recorder every day."

#482, ran

Heute – run
Gestern – ran
Länger her – run

- Ran across.

- Ran away.
- Ran through.
- Ran around.
- Ran into.
- Ran out.
- Ran over.
- Ran the race.
- Ran a business.

- He ran a corner store last year.
- Is the turtle going to run a race against the hare again?
- The project ran over budget.
- As the project ran over budget, the business ran into a financial crisis.
- The cat ran out of the house through the back door.
- He ran around the house searching for the missing cat.
- The cat ran across the street and ran away.

#483, check

- Check-in.
- Check out.
- Checkbox.
- Check up.
- Check down.
- Check again
- Spell check.
- Double check.
- Security check.
- Paycheck.
- Bank check.
- Cashier's check.

- Check out this YouTube video. It's so funny.
- Please go in through the check-in line.
- After you've checked the checkboxes, double check your answers.
- Check out through the check-out line.
- Can I write you a check?
- Yes. You can pay by check.

#484, game

- Game on.
- Game off.
- Game room.
- Game over.
- Video game.
- Football game.
- Olympic Games.
- Board game.
- Computer game.
- Play game.

- Other than playing video games, kids also like to game on their iPads.
- Some boys play computer games all day long.
- The kids are going to play a football game today.
- The Olympic Games started 2800 years ago in Olympia, Greece. That's where the name Olympic Games came from.

#485, shape

- In shape.
- Shape up.
- Good shape.
- Keep in shape.
- Be in shape.
- Shape your child's life.
- Shape the lives of others.

- What you do shape the lives of your children.
- Who shaped our history? Humans or others.
- He got injured yesterday, but he showed up today in good shape.
- He's the designer of the building, and he's proud of the shape of the building.

#486, yes

- Yes?
- Yes!
- Yes or no?
- Yes, of course!
- Oh yes!

- Yes, it is.
- Yes, I do.
- You want to go there, yes?
- Yes, of course!
- Do you want to go there?
- Oh yes!
- Do you need help?
- Yes.

#487, not

- Not yet.
- Not bad.
- Not really.
- Not much.
- Not at all.
- Do not.
- Why not.
- Will not.
- Does not.

- It's not going to be a hot day today. It'll go up to 75.
- Do you like hot peppers?
- Not at all. They're too spicy for me.
- Are you going prepare for the entrance exam?
- Not yet.
- Why not?
- I do not need to study to pass the exam.

#488, miss

- Miss the bus.
- Miss the appointment.
- Miss the exit.
- Miss the call.
- Miss the point.
- Miss out.
- Miss Perry.

- Miss Perry was one of my high school teachers.
- Miss Scott missed the bus.
- Some students missed bringing a few things.
- Students are allowed to miss five classes per semester.
- If you miss a job interview appointment, forget it,

move on to the next one.
- You missed my point. If you missed a job interview, you're considered as untrustworthy. Forget it.
- We missed the exit. We can take the next one which is 70 miles away.

#489, brought

Heute → bring
Gestern → brought
Länger her → brought

- Brought in.
- Brought on.
- Brought out.
- Brought up.
- Brought down.
- Brought forward.

- She brought up the idea of a potluck party.
- I brought some apples.
- Jerry brought some cherries.
- It's a hot day today. We should drink some iced water to bring down the temperature.

#490, heat

- Heat up.
- Heat pump.
- Heat sink.
- Heat transfer.
- To heat.

- The sun has heated up the room.
- Heat up the food.

- Heat it up.
- Where does the heat come from?
- From the pepper.
- When do you turn on the heat?
- We turn the heat on in November.

Herzlichen Glückwunsch!

- Thousands of years ago, there were snake-like creatures with legs and feet flying in the sky. Ancient people thought they were gods.
- Three years ago, my son and I planted 30 trees in our yard.
- Ten minutes ago, my son came to talk to me about how to get his iPad back.
- A moment ago, I said, "to get your iPad back, play me a new song on the recorder every day."
- He ran a corner store last year.
- Is the turtle going to run a race against the hare again?
- The project ran over budget.
- As the project ran over budget, the business ran into a financial crisis.
- The cat ran out of the house through the back door.
- He ran around the house searching for the missing cat.
- The cat ran across the street and ran away.
- Check out this YouTube video. It's so funny.
- Please go in through the check-in line.
- After you've checked the checkboxes, double check your answers.
- Check out through the check-out line.
- Can I write you a check?
- Yes. You can pay by check.
- Other than playing video games, kids also like to game on their iPads.
- Some boys play computer games all day long.
- The kids are going to play a football game today.
- The Olympic Games started 2800 years ago in Olympia, Greece. That's where the name Olympic Games came from.
- What you do will shape your child's life.
- Who shaped our history? Humans or aliens.

- He got injured yesterday, but he showed up today in good shape.
- He's the designer of the building, and he's proud of the shape of the building.
- Yes, it is.
- Yes, I do.
- You want to go there, yes?
- Do you want to go there?
- Yes.
- Do you need help?
- Yes.
- It's not going to be a hot day today. It'll go up to 75.
- Do you like hot peppers?
- Not at all. They're too spicy for me.
- Are you going prepare for the entrance exam?
- Not yet.
- Why not?
- I do not need to study to pass the exam.
- Miss Perry was one of my high school teachers.
- Miss Scott missed the bus.
- Some students missed bringing a few things.
- Students are allowed to miss five classes per semester.
- If you miss a job interview appointment, forget it, move on to the next one.
- You missed my point. If you missed a job interview, you're considered as untrustworthy. Forget it.
- We missed the exit. We can take the next one which is 70 miles away.
- She brought up the idea of a potluck party.
- I brought some apples.
- Jerry brought some cherries.
- It's a hot day today. We should drink some iced water to bring down the heat.
- The sun has heated up the room.
- Heat up the food.

- Heat it up.
- Where does the heat come from?
- From the pepper.
- When do you turn on the heat?
- We turn the heat on in November.

Die erfolgreichsten Menschen haben mit Nichts begonnen. Sie haben nicht auf die Gelegenheit gewartet sondern die Möglichkeit für sich selbst geschaffen. Arbeiten Sie hart und glauben Sie daran, dass Sie erfolgreich sein werden.

Anonym

Kapitel 56: 491 – 500, Specialized knowledge

#491, snow

- Snow flake.
- Snow day.
- Snow peas.
- Snow cone.
- Snow leopard.
- Snow shovel.

- There's a snowstorm coming our way. It'll snow for two days.
- Schools will be closed for the snow, and kids will enjoy playing in the snow.

#492, bed

- Twin-size bed.
- Queen-size bed.
- King-size bed.
- Before bed.
- Go to bed.

- Riverbed.

- The boy thought about the new game before bed.
- Mom made the bed for him.
- The boy jumped out of bed when he heard the game.
- There has been no rain for five months. The river bed has dried out.

#493, bring
Heute → bring
Gestern → brought
Länger her → brought

- Bring in.
- Bring on.
- Bring up.
- Bring down.
- Bring forward.
- Bring over.

- It's a hot day today. We need to drink some iced water to bring down the heat
- Do you have any?
- Yes. I'll bring it out.
- She's going to bring up the topic during the meeting.
- Can you bring it in?
- Can you bring it over?
- Can you bring me a glass of water?

#494, sit

Heute → sit
Gestern → sat

Länger her → sat

- Sit up.
- Sit down.
- Sit back.
- Sit around.
- Sit on.
- Sit still.

- Sit down, please. We will do ten sit-ups.
- Please sit down while we sit back and wait.
- We'll sit around while we wait for the result. You're welcome to sit on the chair to take a nap or sit on the floor if you want to meditate.
- The box has been sitting here for two days and no one touched it.

#495, perhaps

- Perhaps so.
- Perhaps not.

- Perhaps I should take a break.
- That's perhaps a good idea.

#496, fill

- Fill up.
- Fill in.
- Fill with.
- Fill out.

- Can you fill out the form?
- What needs to be filled out?
- Just fill in the highlighted areas.
- The library is filled with children.
- Fill up the tank.
- Fill up with 87.

#497, east

- East coast.
- East wind.
- Eastside.
- Go east.
- Due east.
- To the east.
- In the east.

- The entrance to the east is in the east.
- The entrance to go east is on the east side of the building.
- It's going to be a warm day with an east wind at 10 mph.
- Perhaps it's a good idea to watch sunrise on the East Coast and sunset on the West Coast.

#498, weight

- Weight loss.
- Weightlifting.
- Weight training.
- Lose weight.
- Gross weight.
- Net weight.
- Gain weight.

- Put on weight.
- Average weight.
- Body weight.

- This rock is 100 pounds in weight.
- Charlie has been doing weight training for six years.
- Be careful. This box is got some weight in it.
- It'll be okay. He can easily move something 300 pounds in weight.
- The weight of the moon moves the oceans of Earth.

#499, language

- Native language.
- Foreign language.
- Body language.
- Learn a language.
- Written language.
- Computer language.
- Everyday language.

- What language do you speak?
- Do you speak another language?
- Who speaks another language?
- A computer language is a foreign language to most people.
- What was your foreign language in high school?
- Use everyday language to keep it simple.

#500, among

- Among them.

- Among you.
- Among us.
- Among others.
- Among these.
- Among those.
- Among people.

- The very actions of setting a goal and persistently working on it put him among the winners!
- A 13-year old boy was among the successful people for one reason – he achieved his goal.
- The word "among" is among the most useful words in the English language.
- Professors are among the group of people who don't make much money, but they are among the group of people who achieve academic success.

Glückwunsch! Das ist der letzte Satz der 500!

- There's a snowstorm coming our way. It'll snow for two days.
- Schools will be closed for the snow, and kids will enjoy playing in the snow.
- The boy thought about the new game before bed.
- Mom made the bed for him.
- The boy jumped out of bed when he heard the game.
- There has been no rain for five months. The river bed has dried out.
- It's a hot day today. We need to drink some iced water to bring down the heat
- Do you have any?
- Yes. I'll bring it out.
- She's going to bring up the topic during the meeting.
- Can you bring it in?
- Can you bring it over?
- Can you bring me a glass of water?
- Sit down, please. We will do ten sit-ups.
- Please sit down while we sit back and wait.
- We'll sit around while we wait for the result. You're welcome to sit on the chair to take a nap or sit on the floor if you want to meditate.
- The box has been sitting here for two days and no one touched it.
- Perhaps I should take a break.
- That's perhaps a good idea.
- Can you fill out the form?
- What needs to be filled out?
- Just fill in the highlighted areas.
- The library is filled with children.
- Fill up the tank.
- Fill up with 87.
- The entrance to the east is in the east.
- The entrance to go east is on the east side of the

- building.
- It's going to be a warm day with an east wind at 10 mph.
- Perhaps it's a good idea to watch the sunrise on the East Coast and the sunset on the West Coast.
- This rock is 100 pounds in weight.
- Charlie has been doing weight training for six years.
- Be careful. This box is got some weight in it.
- It'll be okay. He can easily move something 300 pounds in weight.
- The weight of the moon moves the oceans on Earth.
- What language do you speak?
- Do you speak another language?
- Who speaks another language?
- A computer language is a foreign language to most people.
- What was your foreign language in high school?
- Use everyday language to keep it simple.
- The very actions of setting a goal and persistently working on it put him among the winners!
- A 13-year old boy was among the successful people for one reason – he achieved his goal.
- The word "among" is among the most useful words in the English language.
- Professors are among the group of people who don't make much money, but they are among the group of people who achieve academic success.

Ja! Wir haben es geschafft!

Lassen Sie uns feiern!

Nachdem wir gefeiert haben, werden wir von vorne anfangen! Wir werden direkt an den Anfang zurückkehren und ganz von vorne beginnen.

Ja, von vorne anfangen! Denken Sie daran, sie werden wie ein Einheimischer sprechen! Üben Sie weiter!

Mein Name ist Ken Xiao. Ich bin der Autor dieses Buches und die Audio Version davon ist meine eigene Stimme. Ich bin ein Landjunge. Ich sprach kein Wort Englisch als ich im Alter von 17 Jahren in die Vereinigten Staaten kam. Wenn ich wie ein Einheimischer sprechen kann, dann können Sie das auch. Kehren Sie zum ersten Kapitel zurück und üben Sie weiter.

www.amazon.de

Printed by Amazon Italia Logistica S.r.l.
Torrazza Piemonte (TO), Italy

44623507R00288